SELF-CONCEPT, ACHIEVEMENT AND MULTICULTURAL EDUCATION

In this collection of essays, the editors bring together radical but scholarly papers from the disciplines of social psychology, sociology and education, organised around the theme of education in a multicultural society. The majority of the papers concern Britain, but American and Canadian case studies are also included.

A proper multicultural education is one of the means by which the identity of all children may be fostered. Evidence is presented showing that, although young coloured children have to battle with the racist stereotypes of black people inherent in British culture and language, nevertheless as they grow older they acquire a self-concept which is quite as adequate as that of white children. A number of papers in this book are concerned with the problems of labelling and teacher expectations, and a national survey of child development is reported, indicating that the negative views of teachers can be an important factor in the scholastic underachievement of ethnic minority children. Such labelling, and the sentencing of black children to subnormal schooling, is seen as part of the general problem of the racial stereotypes.

4 Week Loan

This book is due for return on or before the last date shown below

B27686

SELF-CONCEPT, ACHIEVEMENT AND MULTICULTURAL EDUCATION

Edited by

Gajendra K. Verma
University of Bradford, UK

and

Christopher Bagley
University of Calgary, Canada

First published 1982 by
THE MACMILLAN PRESS LTD
London and Basingstoke
Companies and representatives
throughout the world

ISBN 0 333 30944 8

Printed in Hong Kong

Contents

Notes on the Contributors

Gajendra K. Verma is Senior Lecturer in Psychology of Education at the University of Bradford Postgraduate School of Studies in Research in Education. He is also Director of a two-year research project (1980–82), funded by Nuffield Foundation, concerned with occupational adaptation of ethnic minority adolescents in their early working life.

Christopher Bagley is Professor of Social Welfare at the University of Calgary, Canada.

Robert B. Burns is Lecturer in Psychology of Education at the University of Bradford Postgraduate School of Studies in Research in Education.

Loretta Young is a Senior Social Worker with Dr Barnardo's Children's Society.

A. G. Davey is Reader in Applied Social Studies at the University of Newcastle upon Tyne.

Geoffrey Driver is Research Fellow, Applied Anthropology Group, in the Centre for Applied Social Studies at the University of Leeds.

Sally Tomlinson is a Lecturer in the Department of Educational Research at the University of Lancaster.

Kanka Mallick is Senior Lecturer in Psychology of Education at the West London Institute of Higher Education.

Joti Bhatnagar is Professor of Education at the University of Concordia, Canada.

Elizabeth M. Thomas-Hope is a Lecturer in Geography at the University of Liverpool.

Introduction: Issues in Multicultural Education

GAJENDRA K. VERMA and CHRISTOPHER BAGLEY

This collection of papers in the field of multicultural education is a sequel to our two previous edited collections, *Race and Education Across Cultures* (1975) and *Race, Education and Identity* (1979). Our aim in these volumes is to bring together collections of papers, some of which have been given at conferences, but few of which have been published in any form. We aim to publish papers which are both radical and scholarly in orientation, and which indicate strategies for rethinking, action or change in the field of race relations and education.

Our own approach is that of radical social psychology, in which our value commitment to the values of pluralism, multiculturalism and anti-racism are invested in empirical and statistical studies of education in multiethnic settings. These approaches are illustrated too in our recent work in comparative and multicultural education, and the radical study of prejudice and racism (Bagley, 1979; Bagley and Verma, 1979; Bagley *et al.*, 1979c; Verma, *et al.*, 1980).

We have argued that Britain is, through the ideologies of its cultural institutions and the attitudes and behaviour of many of its citizens, a fundamentally racist society, which denies many of the rights and legitimate aspirations of ethnic minorities. In this kind of climate, the movement towards multicultural education (which fosters the development and identity of all ethnic groups on the basis of a culturally appropriate education for each ethnic group, combined with education for intercultural understanding and equality, not only of opportunity but also of achievement) is painfully slow. As Lea (1980) has argued, race relations policy in Britain, far from aiding such relations, has made the lot of black people significantly worse.

Triandis (1975, 1976) has argued that the crisis in social psychology can be resolved by a greater emphasis on the values and cross-cultural research frameworks offered by pluralist analysis. Pluralism involves different cultural and ethnic groups in the same society not merely existing side by side, but understanding sympathetically each other's folkways, lifestyles, literature, customs and aspirations. Triandis argues in this context that:

> Integration which is mere contact between two groups is held to be potentially counterproductive as a remedy for the inequality seen between blacks and whites, an inequality consequent to persisting exploitation by the majority of the minority group. A three-pronged strategy to achieve *additive multiculturalism*, an essential step forward to a pluralist society, is advocated. The development of interdependence, appreciation, and the skills to interact intimately with persons from other cultures are the requirements laid down (Triandis, 1976, p. 179).

The research by Triandis and his colleagues which we have published in our previous edited volumes (Landis *et al.*, 1975; Landis and McGrew, 1979) offers important research strategies in this direction.

LANGUAGE AND MULTICULTURAL EDUCATION

For centuries the English authorities suppressed and persecuted speakers of Gaelic and Celtish in the colonised parts of Britain, and penalised those who spoke their native language in school. Similarly, in the Caribbean Hindi-speaking children were caned at school. The result has been a tragic alienation of cultural identity. Now only a minority of Welsh people can speak their ancient language, and knowledge of Hindi in the East Indians of Trinidad and Guyana has been all but lost. This language imperialism survives in Britain today, with the assimilationist insistence that children of immigrant parents must, above all things, learn English as early as possible. Their native language, if it is tolerated, is seen as an irrelevant curiosity or an embarrassment. The ethnocentric assumption that 'native' language – the language of nativity – has to be English, can no longer be justified in the multicultural society that Britain has become. The native languages of Britain are English, Welsh, Gaelic, Cantonese, Greek, Bengali, Gujerati, Punjabi, Hindi, Urdu, Hakka, Jamaican Creole, Yuroba, Efik, Italian, Spanish, Polish, Hungarian, Turkish, and many more (Pullum, 1980).

For each child his or her native language is a precious birthright. It is tragic that many immigrant parents under the pressures of assimilation-ist educators have spoken only English to their young children. While this may ensure that children will speak English by the time they enter infant school, it is a form of alienation which robs the child of birthright, and cuts him off from contact with grandparents and a great many intimacies of culture. It is a denial of identity.

We believe ardently that parents should speak to the child in their native language until he or she enters infant school. Then the lingua franca, English, can be learned. There is no good evidence that such practice is in the long run educationally harmful, and there is excellent precedent for such practice in the education of children of North Wales. Here a child from a Welsh-speaking family may well not have heard any English at all until he enters school; but most likely the child in a mixed community will learn English in a mixed playgroup, while continuing to speak his or her native language at home. Consider an example. Nairobi is the chief city of Kenya, and all of the country's 44 languages can be heard in the capital. The young child will not learn the lingua franca, Swahili, from his parents, for that is a language spoken locally in Mombasa, but not in Nairobi. The child's home language is most likely to be Kisii, Kamba, Luo, Kikuyu, Luhya, Masai, Meru, Embu, Turkana, Somali, Duruma, Giriama, Tesos or perhaps Kalenji. In mixed playgroups the preschooler will learn three or four of these languages besides his own, and by the time of school will be learning Swahili. At school, English will be learned too. The facility for language-learning in young children is very great: in J. Z. Young's phrase, the limits of programming the brain are almost boundless. Children have to be made monolingual, or dull, or conforming, or ethnocentric by a rigid and restricting socialisation. Education can be of this nature, but it ought not to be in a multicultural society.

Language is a means to achieve identity, and a means to recover self-esteem. For black children, recovery of Creole by the time they reach secondary school is also part of identity achievement. It is also, analogous to the 'shadow talk' of slavery, a language of resistance. Not speaking English has important symbolic qualities of defiance in, for instance, the Punjabi-speaking West Indian youth of Southall in London. Here West Indian youth are a minority within a minority, and their route to identity is within the subculture of resistance in which they join with Punjabi youth.

A child's first language in a multicultural society should be his traditional cultural language. English, the lingua franca, should be introduced when formal schooling begins; but the onset of schooling should not imply the subordination of the child's native language – that too should be fostered in educational systems and incorporated into the syllabus, formal and informal, of the multicultural school. The importance of 'mother-tongue teaching' in this respect is illustrated by the work with South Asian children in Bradford, England, reported by Rees and Fitzpatrick (1980).

SELF-ESTEEM AND BLACK IDENTITY

As we attempt to show in Chapter 3 in this volume, by Young and Bagley, self-esteem is a complex idea and cannot be considered without reference to the concept of identity. Self-esteem must be subsumed within the concept of identity, and reflexively the self is composed of an organised set of identities (Burke, 1980). Black identity has special components which reflect the particular experience of being black and surviving in a white-dominated society; psychometric instruments standardised on white communities may be inappropriate in the context of black sociology (Saunders, 1973; Verma, 1979). Also, there are political, social and scientific issues in tests and testing as explored in Chapter 11 in this volume, by Verma and Mallick.

It is most important that the idea of black self-esteem should not pass into the pseudo-scientific literature in the way that IQ has done. There is a danger, however, that now that the notion of IQ has been shown to be of little worth (except as an instrument for use in clinical settings to reflect changes in environment – cf. Bagley and Young, 1979), that scientific racists may attempt to use self-esteem as a deterministic substitute. They allege that because self-esteem is 'lower' than that of whites, black motivation is equally low, and this causes school failure. Here are the seeds of yet another self-fulfilling prophecy. In the hands of teachers this condescending notion can lead to assumptions about the lack of educability of black children, which rapidly lead to damaging stereotypes, which can ultimately determine black children's performance: the prophecy has been fulfilled.

The research question we should ask is, as Mungo (1980) has argued: how can we help prevent the 'mountain of information on deprivation and disadvantage from destroying the black child's self image'? And how can disadvantage, in Booker T. Washington's dictum, become a challenge for the black child to overcome?

Erikson's idea of identity development can be particularly fruitful in this kind of research, for it provides a model of how different parts of self experience, both past and present, can be synthesised into an ongoing, meaningful identity. Black people in Britain have different identity tasks than whites (cf. Coleman *et al.*, 1977). First, the experience of immigration creates particular problems for adults for as Cottle (1979) has argued, losing the physical setting of one's childhood and adolescence means that one has to re-create an identity which largely excludes the physical possibility of experiencing the institutions and culture which gave meaning to one's childhood. The immigrant, and his or her children, require powerful ego strengths in this task. The chapter by Thomas-Hope in this volume (Chapter 14) suggests that black immigrants from the West Indies to America have had an easier task in this respect than similar migrants to Britain. Not only is Britain more racist in its frustrations of the aspirations of a highly motivated group of migrants (Bagley, 1976); but also in New York, children of West Indian migrants are absorbed directly into the prosperous black middle classes which their parents have aspired to enter.

Black children in Britain have a more difficult struggle than those in New York, and it is remarkable and indeed heartening how successful in both academic and ego identity terms many black children are (cf. Stone, 1980). Though black children have to struggle with the colonially imposed legacy of the devaluation of blackness, as Chapter 12 by Young and Bagley in the present volume shows, they can develop positive views of themselves as they grow older – the research by Davey in Chapter 4 of the present volume supports that view. Our most recent research with children aged 10–16 (reported in this volume) has failed to show any differences in levels of self-esteem between white, West Indian, Asian and Cypriot children in the schools we have sampled. An important reason for this may be, as Louden (1978) has argued, that with the growth in numbers of minority communities, the setting of their 'locus of control' changes favourably. In ethnic communities, and in schools in which black or Asian groups are a majority or substantial minority, the demeaning slights of racism can be more successfully guarded against.

BEHAVIOUR DISORDERS, OR RESISTANCE TO ALIENATION?

In his brilliant critique of medical ideologies in the 'treatment' of behavioural disorders in children, Box (1980) points out that in America a vocal and influential school of medical opinion has attributed racial problems (blacks getting out of hand in school and ghetto) to various kinds of brain disease and disorder, which have to be treated by powerful tranquillising drugs. 'Hyperactivity', a particular problem for urban teachers, is particularly susceptible to this medical intervention.

In Britain such diagnosis and 'treatment' seems particularly likely for children incarcerated in special schools and homes with education (Perinpanayagam, 1980).[1] It is noteworthy that black children are seriously over-represented in such schools, and in the London area comprise on average a half of all children in such schools and homes. Referral is usually not on grounds of educational failure, but is based on a combination of perceived behavioural deviance (in which subjective labelling may play a large part), and the perception by the authorities of home circumstances (Cawson, 1979).

The data from the National Child Development Survey on ethnic minorities which are reported in the present volume show clearly how such labelling takes place. Even at the age of 7, black children are seen by teachers (in contrast to parental reports) as displaying marked amounts of behaviour disorder – particularly that involving aggression towards adults, including teachers! Concomitantly, in that survey black children were seen as markedly under-achieving in the classroom, and 19 per cent were thought to need exclusion from normal schooling.

Deviant children can be excluded from school in a number of ways – into ESN schools; into special schools for delinquent children; by suspension from school; or by being placed in special 'disruptive units'. A survey in London indicates that a disproportionately high percentage of pupils in such units are black. In our view black pupils are put into such units not because they are failing educationally, but because they are reacting in an aggressive but positive way against an alienating and culturally deficient school system – we argue this point more fully in a report of so-called behaviour disorders in a large sample of 10-year-olds in a London Borough (Bagley, 1975b).

The National Association for Multi-racial Education has pointed to the many disadvantages of these segregated units: students are often referred arbitrarily, without consultation with them or their parents; reasons for referral are often vaguely stated, but once labelled as 'disruptive' a student seldom returns to mainstream schools; in these units only a limited curriculum is offered, giving little opportunity to follow examination courses; in many units the emphasis is on treatment and control rather than on education, and behaviour-modification techniques (crude reward and punishment for 'good' behaviour) are used; local communities have expressed concern at the large number of black children being forced to attend such units, but educational authorities are singularly unsympathetic to such protests; units may be used as a first resort for schools in difficulty, when extra resources, a reappraisal of the curriculum and a more responsive and flexible structure are appropriate alternatives.

The segregation and exclusion of black children in this way represents a singular failure on the part of the British educational system, and major reform is needed here. Such reforms involve not only major resource inputs into schools, but curriculum changes and changes in teachers' attitudes as well (see Chapter 9 in this volume). Nothing less than the removal of schools from the system of institutional racism will serve.

PREJUDICE IN TEACHERS?

Dennis McCarthy wrote in 1971 that:

> From my own experience of seven years in a multi-racial school it seems to me that attitudes are of paramount importance. If the attitudes of the teaching and non-teaching staff are balanced ones, then good personal relationships will develop between teachers and pupils and teachers and parents. Out of this will grow understanding, confidence and trust. But to develop these attitudes there must be an appreciation of what the school is in this changed situation. The very nature of a multi-racial school changes the emphasis of the work of its adult members – much of it is social. If this fact is ignored frustration and resentment will follow (pp. 50–1).

McCarthy's suggestions were true of 1971 and remain true today. There can hardly be a school in Britain today which does not contain some ethnic minority pupils, and all pupils must be prepared for life in a multicultural society, in which the identities and aspirations of all ethnic groups must be respected and balanced in a manner compatible with principles of social justice. But what if some teachers are racially prejudiced, in either an active or a passive manner? How can they fulfil these roles as multicultural educators when their own motives and attitudes contain strong residues of racism? (see Chapter 9 in this volume). We have argued in another context that Britain retains a strong cultural tradition of racism (Bagley and Verma, 1979). We have categorised a large amount of data on racial attitudes in a number of national and local surveys of prejudice in Britain in the following way:

about 20 per cent of the population are hard-line racialists, wanting little contact with minorities, and desiring the suppression of their rights, and ultimately their repatriation.[2] The majority, some 60 per cent, hold a broadly assimilationist position, offering minorities some acceptance at the expense of giving up their alien languages, religions, dress and customs in the face of superior British culture, but often at the price of acceptance into subordinate roles without close contact with the majority group; finally, about 20 per cent of the population accept a broadly pluralist position, accepting minority cultures as valuable contributions to a multicultural society. (It is a pleasant irony that members of this last group, despite their pluralist regard for the culture autonomy of minority groups, are those most likely of the British population to be in a mixed marriage – more than 20 per cent of blacks and Asians in Britain are in such marriages – Bagley, 1979a.)

The principles of multicultural education are compatible only with the last, pluralist position. Yet it is clear that the attitudes of many teachers can be classified in those of the first two groups. First of all, British studies of dogmatism, ethnocentrism, authoritarianism and conservatism which have used teachers as subjects have shown that a substantial minority have scores on these various tests which indicate a strong psychological basis for prejudiced attitudes (Cohen, 1971; Hartley and Holt, 1971; Burns, 1976). Our own work with teachers using the Wilson–Patterson conservatism scale indicates that about a quarter of any group of randomly sampled teachers will display markedly conservative attitudes, and about a tenth will manifest a marked degree of racial prejudice. Even if we are able to conclude that teachers, as an educated, professional group display only half the amount of prejudice manifested in the general population, such incidences do give considerable ground for concern.

It is clear that the dogmatism and authoritarianism of teachers is often reflected in classroom organisation (HMSO, 1979), not least in the continued defence and practice of the barbarities of corporal punishment. Perhaps, as the general secretary of the National Association of Schoolmasters said in 1974, moves to formally abolish corporal punishment would lead teachers to 'greater use of illegal and irregular punishments' such as the ingenious physics master who had devised an apparatus for passing electric shocks through pupils' arms (Casey, 1974). What is clear is that support for corporal punishment is linked to racialist attitudes, as the internal correlations of the Wilson–Patterson conservatism scale make clear (G. Wilson, 1973).

Evidence of teacher prejudice takes various forms. First, evidence has accumulated to show that in their ordinary classroom dealings, teachers often operate on the basis of stereotypes, unproved assumptions, and self-fulfilling prophecies (Pidgeon, 1970). American research on labelling (Rosenthal, 1973) suggests that such stereotypes are particularly prevalent in the teaching of minority pupils. British evidence too shows that teachers hold many negative stereotypes of black and Asian pupils. This is the pattern which has emerged in the analysis of data on the problems of vocational adaptation of Asian teenagers, reported in this volume by Verma (Chapter 6). Haynes (1971) also showed that teacher attitudes (e.g. agreeing that Indian children are less intelligent, lazy, less methodical, lack concentration, etc.) were likely to have an outcome in underachieving Indian children. Even if teachers were passively reflecting the situation of a group of severely disadvantaged pupils, their naive passivity would give considerable cause for concern. Most likely, as Barker-Lunn (1970) found in her study of streaming in primary schools, negative teacher attitudes are of primary and causal significance in children's underachievement. This is certainly the conclusion we have come to in the analysis of data on West Indian children in the National Child Development Survey, reported in the present volume (Chapter 8). This national survey suggests, in our opinion, that by the time the black children were aged 7, teachers' highly negative views had led not only to a marked degree of underachievement, but of exclusion or recommendations for exclusion in ESN schools in a substantial number of black children.

Informal evidence suggests that a minority of teachers do express markedly racist views in various school contexts. Thus Milner (1975) reported that: 'I may have been unfortunate in my experiences, but I have been too frequently horrified by staff room conversations to feel that this minority is unimportant'. The first writer to chronicle the racist folkways of the teachers in some multiracial schools was Maxwell (1969) who gives numerous horrifying examples of the racist stereotypes and actions of teachers, and the frequent intrusion of these stereotypes into classroom teaching. A survey supported by the BNB Research Fund showed that people from the Third World are perceived by white children as members of an undeveloped world who are primitives and battling unsuccessfully against their environment. Although these perceptions and images are created through biased literature and textbooks, the process of transmission from book to child is mediated through the presence of the white racist teacher who interprets the material to the child. The aspect of the survey concerned with classroom research confirmed this (Verma, 1980). Such accounts are not isolated ones, and complaints about the passive or active racism of some teachers continue to appear in the educational press.[3]

More systematic surveys of prejudice in teachers support these impressions – Stanton (1970) in a survey of 400 teachers suggested that over 20 per cent were racially prejudiced. Brittan (1976) carried out the largest survey in this field, of 510 teachers: again, a substantial minority displayed what seem to us to be prejudiced attitudes, and less than half took a pluralist or broadly tolerant attitude towards minority cultures to the extent of accepting curriculum reorganisations which included teaching about minority groups' cultures and religions.

The addiction to the assimilationist position has led many teachers to ignore the reality of the cultural aspirations of minority groups. The message to minority children, in the words of B. Jackson (1979) is that 'you do not exist'. Similarly, many teachers have been unwilling to consider race-related material (for example, the 'race packs' devised by Stenhouse and his colleagues at the University of East Anglia, which we describe in Chapter 1 in the present volume) as part of the curriculum, and still less have they been able or willing to consider general curriculum reform on non-racist lines (Schools Council, 1973). Nevertheless, teachers frequently resort to race-related models to explain, or predict, the performance of minority pupils. Thus Dove (1974) reported from her survey of London schools that: 'Learning failure was fairly often explained in terms of the child's racial group and teachers quite frequently and unintentionally showed their expectations of immigrant pupils' potential. . . .'

What of teachers in the 1980s? They will be less able to ignore the issue of race so far as the formal curriculum is concerned, although they may continue to use racially biased models in allocating pupils to streams and to examinations, and interacting with pupils in ways which confirm stereotyped predictions. The Commission for Racial Equality failed to persuade the courts, in March 1980, that a teacher who called a 16-year-old West Indian boy 'Sambo' and 'Nignog' and many other disparaging remarks was actually discriminating against the boy;[4] and the grosser forms of racial hostility by teachers towards pupils remain unchecked and perhaps uncheckable by the normal means of professional control (Jeffcoate, 1979). There is a gross timidity on the part of professional organisations themselves; the suppression by the Schools Council of their report, 'Multi-racial education: curriculum and content five to thirteen' in 1978 is a case in point.[5]

We cannot express much confidence in teacher organisations in the struggle (for it amounts to that) for multicultural education. The position of some teacher organisations may indeed be singularly unhelpful: the National Association of Head Teachers, for example, in its submission to the Rampton Committee of Inquiry into the Education of Children from Ethnic Minority groups suggested that, 'If there is a difficulty of cultural identity among second generation West Indians, there is also much to counter-balance that deficiency including their natural sense of rhythm, colour and athletic prowess.' Yet there is not a single scrap of evidence to show that sporting or rhythmic abilities have any ethno-genetic basis. It is no more likely that blacks are innately rhythmical and athletic than Jews (as was believed in Britain earlier this century) are natural pugilists. The outcome was self-confirming – for many Jewish lads the only means of upward mobility was through prowess in the ring. Similarly, West Indian boys and girls may be pushed into sporting roles and excluded from more academic aspects of school life (Jones, 1977).

The National Association of Head Teachers in its depressing memorandum of evidence advocates further that the ethnicity of West Indian pupils should be ignored, and all pupils treated on the same basis, ignoring the evidence that this 'colour-blind' approach can have disastrous consequences. Perhaps not surprisingly this Association voted at its annual conference, in May 1980, to continue the practice of corporal punishment by a vote of 500 to three.

Only the National Association of Teachers in Further and Higher Education, in its comprehensive evidence to the Rampton Committee (NATFHE, 1980) has pointed to the fact that,

> One of the most difficult things for the education service to face is that some teachers and lecturers may reflect some of the racialist attitudes and beliefs that are found in the wider community. They too may be prejudiced and may discriminate . . . teacher attitudes play an important part in reinforcing racial consciousness and prejudice. Worse, despite all the data indicating that a 'colour-blind' approach is utterly inappropriate, teachers continue to adopt it . . . it is no longer appropriate to pretend that teachers are colour blind, that children are children, and schools places of racial harmony. Teachers are substantially responsible for the school curriculum, and yet it remains essentially ethnocentric (pp. 2–3).

The solution must be in improvements not only in the basic training of teachers, but in more and better post-qualification training courses for teachers linked to active and frequent in-service training led by specially recruited advisers based in curriculum, support units and centres of multicultural education in each local authority. These vital programmes are expensive, and require the fullest support of government.

MULTICULTURAL SCHOOLS IN A PLURAL SOCIETY

In the face of an educational system which reflects institutional racism, with teachers who may be passive or active supporters of racist ideologies and practices; an educational system which not only fails black students in both academic and cultural terms, but condemns many of them to exclusion as well; how shall black parents react? One solution, practised by black, and particularly by Asian families who can afford to do so, is to have their children educated privately in English preparatory and public schools. While such schools make no pretence at offering anything other than a traditional Anglo-Saxon education, their small classes and concern for individual pupils do offer ethnic minority children a much greater chance of educational success.

Black parents often claim that English education is inferior to education in the Caribbean. Indeed, the visitor to a school in Trinidad or Jamaica is greatly impressed by the smartness of the pupils, the prestige and status which they afford teachers, and the commitment to hard work which every pupil seems to possess. The urban alienation of British city schools is remarkably absent, and despite lack of resources, outcomes in terms of pupil success are often high. It seems a fair proposition that if Caribbean schools had the material resources and pupil–teacher ratios which London schools have, then the intellectual achievements of their students would be very high indeed. Although in formal terms the academic achievements of some rural Jamaican schools is low (Bagley, 1979b), nevertheless with British levels of resource input combined with the high levels of student motivation which exist, high levels of academic success are possible. The same is true of the Indian schools in which we have worked (Verma *et al.*, 1980).

Supplementary schools in Britain are an attempt by West Indian parents to supplement and indeed supplant alienating and poor-quality English schools. Black people have little doubt that English schools are the cause of their children's underachievement (NLP, 1977), and in London especially thousands of black children attend supplementary schools on Saturdays, or in summer school projects. There is evidence that these schools can be rather successful both in terms of scholastic gain, and enhancement of self-confidence (Ntuk-Idem, 1978; Stone, 1980). However, it is also clear that the most alienated group of black children, who are deeply angered by the racist folkways of British education, are indeed too alienated to enter even supplementary schools. As with many compensatory education programmes, it is the relatively advantaged and those with the best motivation who take the most advantage of such provision.

The pluralist position which we emphasised earlier is that the state should respect and foster the autonomy of various ethnic groups of society. This can to some extent be fulfilled through state support for religious schools: thus, as allowed by the 1944 Education Act, state subsidies are given to Anglican, Roman Catholic, Jewish and Methodist schools. There is no reason why similar kinds of state support should not be offered to Islamic and Hindu schools (cf. Kanitkar, 1979), and the development of such religious schools for ethnic minorities in Britain is a likely development for the future. (Verma and Mallick, 1981.)

More problematic is the strategy for black parents who do not have a religious orientation which is different from the mainstream culture, but nevertheless desire an education for their children which has a distinctive cultural and value basis. But there are precedents here, in the American, Japanese, Libyan, Spanish and other schools in London. While West Indian schools could be established on this basis, a major problem is that of finance, for they could not at present attract any state subsidy. The irony is that the racist forces which prevent black people achieving professional qualifications, or jobs commensurate with their qualifications, also restrict their options for private education, or for culturally appropriate schools. In the Netherlands, by contrast, state finance is available for such enterprises, for it is recognised that when the cultural aspirations of ethnic minority groups are fulfilled they make a more positive contribution to the states as a whole. Such a pluralist policy does work in the Netherlands (Bagley, 1973a) and there is no reason why it should not work in Britain.

The alternative to pluralism in an ethnically mixed society is racialism, or the domination of minority groups by the majority group. As in the societies which we have described cross-culturally, so in Britain the only alternative to racialism (including the domination of the minority religious group in Ulster by the majority group) is plural multiculturalism, in which the state both guarantees and balances the aspirations of all ethnic and religious groups. Lijphart's (1978) world survey indicates that this is by no means an impossible task.

NOTES

1. *The Times* (London), 28 May 1980.
2. A good example of this position is the teacher from Reading, a member of the National Front, who openly described himself as 'a nigger-hater and Wog-detester – especially when they are trying to pass as British' (P. Jackson, 1970).
3. See *The Times Educational Supplement* (London), 23 November and 2 November 1973; *The Times* (London), 30 August 1974; *Times Educational Supplement*, (London), 17 May 1974 and 29 September 1972; *New Statesman*, (London), 3 August 1979. See, too, C. Searle, 'Censorship in education', *Race Today* (London), February 1975, p. 40.
4. *The Times* (London), 12 March 1980.
5. *New Society* (London), 16 February 1978.

Part I
Self-Concept, Attitude
Development and Change

1 Self-Concept and Long-Term Effects of Teaching about Race Relations in British Schools

CHRISTOPHER BAGLEY and GAJENDRA K. VERMA

RECENT RESEARCH ON CHANGE IN INTERETHNIC ATTITUDES

Writing about the influence of the schooling on values, Urie Bronfen-brenner (1974) declared that:

> The potentialities of the classroom group . . . [are] one of the most promising and least exploited areas for effecting behavioural change. Although modifications of classroom composition in terms of social class and race can have salutary effects, they by no means represent the most powerful resources at our disposal. Indeed, their potential is realized only to the extent that they facilitate development of the motivating processes (modeling, reinforcement, group commitment, involvement in superordinate goals, etc.) we have outlined. Such development need not be left to chance.

Education itself, without structuring of inputs, can have lasting influence on values. Hyman and Wright (1979) in a review of data from 38 national surveys in America, showed that exposure to education had an enduring effect on the values of whites in areas such as support for civil liberties, and equality of opportunity for minorities. Indeed, it would be surprising if education did not have lasting effects on values. A crucial question to be answered in the present chapter is this, a question

3

asked some 50 years ago by Remmers (1931): 'Propaganda in the schools – do the effects last?' Remmers asked this question in relation to a curriculum project with American high-school students aimed at influencing attitudes in areas such as race relations and various types of civic, responsible and non-discriminatory behaviour. He concluded that:

> This type of material can produce favourable attitude change quite quickly, and . . . once changed, attitudes tend to persist as changed. The present evidence indicates that they are at least no more quickly 'forgotten' than in the conventional subject matter learned in the classroom.

More recent evidence, such as that produced by Miller (1969) has suggested, however, that brief inputs of race relations material, in the hands of teachers without adequate preparation, and in the face of very hostile attitudes at the outset on the part of students themselves, may be counterproductive. However, on balance the evidence is favourable – 32 studies had been carried out in this field up to 1974, and 23 of these had shown favourable change (Verma and Bagley, 1975b). There are problems in making such evaluation (Jenkins *et al.*, 1979), and problems in the ways in which material ought to be presented (whether in a didactic manner, or in an impartial way), as Stenhouse (1975) and Jeffcoate (1979) have argued. Jeffcoate argues, rightly in our view, ' . . . that the totality of what children are up against in a racist society demands from the school a total response. More is required than occasional or isolated multiracial inputs' (p. 4). Such a view does not preclude the use of individual curriculum projects such as 'the race packs' (Stenhouse, 1975); it assumes that such curriculum innovation should not take place without support and reform in other areas of curriculum and school organisation. There is little point, for example, in introducing curriculum materials aimed at changing racial attitudes in a school in which the majority of black pupils are assigned to the lowest streams (Lomax, 1977).

Recent efforts at influencing attitudes in children and adolescents have employed a variety of techniques, including controlled interracial mixing at summer camp (successful – see Eaton and Clore, 1975) and directed study of material about different ethnic groups (unsuccessful – see Lessing and Clarke, 1976). A number of studies have concentrated on preschoolers in which a variety of methods, including role-taking and the use of video displays, all seem to be successful in producing positive attitude change (Colton, 1972; Hohn, 1973; Ayres, 1973). Behavioural techniques using rewards for required behaviour and attitudes, as well as teaching machines, also seem to be successful with preschoolers (Williams and Morland, 1976). What is not known, however, is whether such attitude change has any lasting effect without a full follow-through with curriculum change and behavioural support: for, in the words of the classic study of the development and change of racial attitudes in children, 'They learn what they live' (Trager and Yarrow, 1952). What is most important, as Trager and Yarrow show, is that teachers themselves should be unprejudiced, and committed to non-racist curriculum and school organisation. That is a goal not yet achieved in British education, and indeed a particular problem is the lack of unprejudiced teachers who can use special curriculum materials in British schools.

The use of factual material can be successful in inducing attitude change in the race relations field with older students, while in adults in the American armed forces, programmed instruction plus black leaders of discussion groups can also produce favourable change (Landis *et al.*, 1976); but the use of special materials and seminar groups for teaching race relations policy seems to be less than successful in adults outside institutions of higher education, especially in Britain. Indeed, levels of stereotyping and prejudice in middle-level managers who are responsible in Britain for the interface of race relations is alarmingly high, and the use of such materials in training programmes is often unsuccessful (Cross, 1977).

In a country such as Britain where institutional racism is widespread, multiple messages reach the individual about the normality of racism. In America there are numerous and excessive negative representations of blacks in television programmes and commercials (Pierce *et al.*, 1977). A similar situation exists in Britain, as our review of the effects of mass media on prejudiced attitudes indicates (Bagley and Verma, 1979). Because of the widespread institutional support for racism, writers such as Jeffcoate (1974) have argued (for example, in the context of a Schools Council project on Education for a Multi-Racial Society in pupils aged 5–13) that teachers should be the first target of any programme. Jeffcoate (1976 and 1979) has carefully and eloquently elaborated his designs for curriculum planning to multiracial education, using a humanistic focus. His ideas are impressive, and deserve careful study and implementation.

Other approaches, such as including race-related issues in the introduction of politics in the classroom (Crick and Porter, 1978); increasing multicultural perspectives through the use of anthropological materials (Bulmer, 1977); and enabling pupils to understand the multicultural nature of British cities through the Geography and Young School-Leavers Project pioneered by the Schools Council (Stenhouse, 1980) also deserve careful consideration and evaluation in British Schools.

THE PRESENT STUDY

The problem which we have attempted to confront in our own research (Verma and Bagley, 1973, 1979a) is that of evaluating the different approaches pioneered by Lawrence Stenhouse and his associates (Stenhouse, 1975) in teaching about race relations. After a pilot study using a 'race pack' of prepared materials had shown that positive attitude change in pupils did result (Bagley and Verma, 1972), work proceeded on a large-scale experiment in English secondary schools using three different approaches – a 'neutral chairman' with a seemingly impartial teacher introducing the special race pack to pupils over one term; a 'didactic' chairman, offering partisan and reasoned support for the material in the race pack over the same period; and the use of drama, with pupils taking a variety of roles in dramatised race-relations situations.

Thirty-nine schools were studied; 21 of these were multiracial, containing West Indian or Asian pupils in varying proportions. The Asian pupils came from India, Pakistan, Bangladesh or East Africa. In addition, other ethnic groups – mainly Africans and Cypriots – were represented in these schools in smaller numbers.

Three different teaching strategies were employed: 13 schools followed Strategy A; 16 followed Strategy B; and 10 followed Strategy C. All the 1400 pupils in the study were aged 14–15. The strategies were as follows:

STRATEGY A: THE HUMANITIES CURRICULUM PROJECT STRATEGY
(Humanities Curriculum Project, 1970; Stenhouse, 1971, 1975)

The broad aim was 'to develop an understanding in the area of race relations of social situations and human acts and of the controversial value issues which they raise'. The assumption was that this would be conducive to better race relations. The major feature of this strategy was that the teacher adopted the role of a neutral chairman in the classroom. A specially prepared pack of race relations materials, prepared by the teachers themselves, was used in conjunction with the teaching.

STRATEGY B: COMBATING PREJUDICE STRATEGY

The aim was 'to educate for the elimination of racial tensions and ill-feeling within our society – which is and will be multiracial – by undermining prejudice, by developing respect for varied traditions, and by encouraging mutual understanding, reasonableness and justice'. The teacher saw himself as an 'example of a person critical of prejudiced attitudes and opinions held by himself and by society at large and trying to achieve some degree of mutual understanding and respect between identifiably different human groups'. Thus Strategy B was intended to be a strategy more 'positive' in approach than Strategy A. The major characteristic of this strategy was that the teacher would give his/her own view, and would introduce material in order to promote racial tolerance. The same pack of race relations materials was used in this strategy.

STRATEGY C: USE-OF-DRAMA STRATEGY

This was concerned with teaching about race relations through drama. The schools worked mainly through situational improvised drama, pupils taking a variety of dramatic roles in dramatised race-relations situations. The race pack was used as supplementary material in this third strategy.

The instrument we used to measure attitude change, the Bagley–Verma scale, has established reliability and validity, and is associated with interethnic behaviour in adolescents (Bagley and Verma, 1975, 1978). The scale has four sub-scales, measuring General Racism, Anti-Black, Anti-Asian and Anti-White attitudes respectively.

Students involved in the three strategies in the 39 schools, together with untaught control subjects from the same schools (some 1400 students in all) completed these scales, together with a number of psychosocial instruments measuring personality and attitudes to school and society, before teaching commenced, and again three months after the teaching had finished. We found that pupils involved in Strategy A (neutral chairman) and in Strategy B (didactic chairman) showed a significant improvement in attitudes in the race-relations sphere after teaching, in comparison with untaught controls. Strategy B was the most successful, but in Strategy C (use of drama) although there was some favourable change in attitudes, such change was not statistically significant. In making these comparisons ethnic minority pupils were not included, and only the General Racism, Anti-Black and Anti-Asian scales were used (Verma and Bagley, 1979a).

In some ways the failure of the Use-of-Drama Strategy to improve attitudes in a significant direction is surprising, for there is other evidence that use of psychodrama and role-playing can be rather successful as a technique for changing interethnic attitudes (Greenwald, 1969; Moore and Baltes, 1975). Presenting both sides of the case on a controversial issue can also be successful in relation to other approaches (Hovland *et al.*, 1972). It is therefore particularly interesting to note that, in the present study, presenting the race-related materials in a didactic rather than in a neutral way produced the most clearly defined change, which also had the most long-lasting effects (Table 1.4).

Although it is clear that some types of teaching about race relations can have a positive influence on attitudes, two further questions have to be answered: since some students show only a moderate attitude change, and since some indeed show negative change, what social and psychological factors are associated with different types of attitude change? And to what extent do positive attitude changes endure in the longer term (in this case, after only 18 months)?

FACTORS PREDICTING ATTITUDE CHANGE

We have tried to answer the first question by correlational and cluster analysis of a large number of variables from the psychosocial questionnaires administered before teaching about race relations began. The majority of these variables have no significant correlation with attitude change, measured in various ways. However, a number of variables (see Bagley *et al.*, 1979 for a fuller description of the psychosocial measures employed) do have some significant correlation with amount of attitude change.

The subjects of our investigation of psychosocial factors involved in attitude change were the experimental group who had participated in Strategy B, which involved direct attempts at combating prejudice. This produced the largest measured changes in attitudes of all the three strategies, and pupils involved in this strategy showed clear changes in the direction of tolerant attitudes, in comparison with untaught controls. This effect held, too, when the regression to the mean effect was taken into account.

Because Strategy B initially contained the largest number of subjects (426 of those who were involved in the teaching were available at follow-up 6 months later) and because it had produced most variance in the attitude change variables, we decided to examine in more detail the social psychological factors which were associated with attitude change, both negative and positive. We excluded from the analysis subjects with an initial score on the General Racism Scale of less than 5, since the possibility of favourable change in this group was limited. Because of this, and technical problems including missing psychological data in some cases, the final numbers in the analysis were 227. The mean score of this group on the General Racism scale was 18.51 (SD 9.2) before teaching commenced, compared with 16.49 (SD 9.5) in all 426 subjects. The social psychological measures were all completed before the experimental teaching began.

Various kinds of measurement of change were made. We measured absolute change, negative or positive, on the General Racism (GR), Anti-Black (AB) and Anti-Asian (AA) scales, comparing the scores before and after teaching. Change on the General Racism scale was also converted to a log scale, in order to control marked swings. 'Bad' changes, being a negative swing of 5 points or more on the GR scale, were scored as a nominal variable, as were 'good' swings, being a change in a positive direction of 5 points or more on the GR scale. Ten per cent of subjects showed a negative change on the GR scale of 5 or more, compared with 16 per cent of subjects showing a positive change of 5 or more on the GR scale. Clearly, although this teaching strategy overall has positive effects, the attitudes of some individuals do worsen, and it is important to find out why this is so.

The correlations between the change variables and various instruments from the test battery are outlined in Table 1.1, and give us some indication of some of the factors which may be responsible. Although correlations are fairly low, the Tension sub-scales of Cattell's High School Personality Questionnaire (HSPQ), the Coopersmith Self-Esteem scale (the self-evaluation and sociability sub-scales – see Bagley and Evan-Wong (1975) for definitions); alienation from school; an authoritarian view of society; reading ability; being male; and having a high score on the HSPQ Tough-mindedness sub-scale are significant predictors of attitude change of various kinds.

What these results effectively mean is that there is a tendency for those with poorer self-esteem, and who are tense and fretful and alienated from school life, to show little change after the teaching programme. Conversely, those whose attitudes change in a clear, positive direction

TABLE 1.1 Significant correlations of attitude change in 227 adolescents

	General Racism (absolute change)	Anti-Black (absolute change)	Anti-Asian (absolute change)	General Racism (scaled change)	Marked positive change	Marked negative change
Cattell's HSPQ sub-scale: Relaxed, composed versus Tense, fretful	0.21**	0.23**	0.20**	0.19**	−0.22*	0.21**
Coopersmith Self-Esteem scale: Self-evaluation	0.15*	0.19**	0.14*	0.14*	(−0.11)	0.21**
Coopersmith Self-Esteem scale: Sociability	0.16*	0.16*	0.17*	0.13*	(−0.08)	0.22**
Alienation from school life (Verma scale)	−0.18**	−0.16*	−0.18**	−0.17*	0.15*	−0.22**
Alienation from school authority (Sumner scale)	−0.18**	−0.21**	−0.14*	−0.15*	0.21**	(−0.12*)
Himmelweit Authoritarianism scale: Authoritarian view of society	−0.07	−0.15*	(−0.12)	(−0.08)	(0.11)	−0.25**
Sex: Male	(0.03)	(−0.01)	(−0.02)	(−0.02)	(−0.02)	0.19**
Cattell's HSPQ sub-scale: Tough-minded versus tender-minded	(−0.06)	(−0.01)	(−0.08)	(−0.06)	(0.01)	−0.23**
Brimer reading scale	(0.02)	(0.07)	(0.03)	(0.04)	(0.04)	−0.35**

NOTE: Correlations in parentheses are not significant.
* = Significant at the 5 per cent level.
** = Significant at the 1 per cent level or beyond.

tend to have higher self-esteem, and to be less alienated from school. Those who change in a clear negative direction tend in particular to have poorer self-esteem, to be male, poor readers, and somewhat tough-minded and authoritarian.

A clarification of these correlations emerges from a cluster analysis of the data. Ward's hierarchical clustering method (Ward, 1963) produced four clusters, two of which featured attitude change variables. The two other clusters represented individuals with particular configurations of personality not accompanied by any particular type of attitude change, and will not concern us here. The first cluster in the analysis defines 62 individuals. Comparison of the incidence of variables across the four categories delineated variables which were associated with each cluster to a statistically significant degree (using the chi-squared test, with a 5 per cent significance level). The first cluster is seen (Table 1.2) to include individuals whose attitudes have changed in a positive direction on all three scales measuring racialism, measured both in terms of absolute

TABLE 1.2   First cluster associated with attitude change (62 subjects)

General Racism scale: absolute change**
Anti-Black scale: absolute change**
Anti-Asian scale: absolute change**
General Racism scale: scaled change**
Ego-Strength scale of the HSPQ**
Guilt-Proneness scale of the HSPQ (negative association)*
Tension sub-scale of the HSPQ (negative association)*
Self-Esteem (Self-Evaluation component of the Coopersmith scale)**
Self-Esteem (Sociability component of the Coopersmith scale)*
Intelligence sub-scale of the HSPQ*
Excitability sub-scale of the HSPQ (negative association)*
Tough-mindedness sub-scale of the HSPQ (negative association)*
Authoritarianism (Himmelweit scale): authoritarian view of society (negative
    association)*
Brimer reading score scale*

---

  * Significant at the 5 per cent level.
  ** Significant at the 1 per cent level or beyond.

change and, in the case of the GR scale, as scaled change. This group also contains a significant number of individuals whose attitudes have made a marked change in a positive direction. These individuals tend to have good ego-strength (as measured by the HSPQ sub-scale – a correlation which did not emerge in the simple correlation analysis); they are generally free of guilt and tension, and they have high levels of self-esteem. They are intelligent, good readers, not excitable or tough-minded, and they do not display authoritarian attitudes.

In contrast, the second cluster defining individuals with attitude change following the teaching programme concerns negative change (Table 1.3). These individuals who frequently have a marked attitude shift in a negative direction initially held high scores on the GR scale (both in absolute terms, and in relation to their classroom peers), so that their attitude swings have resulted in very hostile ethnic attitudes indeed. These individuals tend to be male, to be alienated from school and school life, to be poor readers, and to hold an authoritarian view of society. This group are also likely to be in classrooms which contain ethnic minorities – Asians, Africans and West Indians who are the targets in the GR, AA and AB scales.

TABLE 1.3   Second cluster associated with attitude change (49 subjects)

General Racism scale: marked change in a negative direction**
Alienation from school life (Verma scale)**
Alienation from school authority (Sumner scale)**
Authoritarianism (Himmelweit scale): authoritarian view of society*
Brimer reading scale (negative association)**
Tough-mindedness sub-scale of the HSPQ**
Male**
Contact with ethnic minorities in the classroom*

* Significant at the 5 per cent level.
** Significant at the 1 per cent level or beyond.

LONGER-TERM EFFECTS OF CHANGE

Our second question was whether this teaching about race relations has a moderately longer-term effect, or whether any gains found after 6 months fade with the passing of time as, perhaps, other aspects of socialisation and influence disposing attitudes in a negative direction take over. We have approached this problem through an analysis of responses of students and controls still available in the 39 target schools 18 months after the commencement of the original curriculum project. By this time the students were aged between 15 and 16 years, and a number had already left school (these in fact were those with poorer achievement, and a greater degree of alienation from school). In addition, because of the usual problem of sample attrition, many pupils present at the beginning of testing were no longer available because of change of residence or school, or absences from the classroom, so that only some 470 subjects were available at the time of final testing.

In Table 1.4 it will be seen that the trend in five out of the six groups is for attitudes to improve over time. Attitudes in all of the control groups improved slightly, and only with Strategy B (involving the directive use of the study materials on race relations – Stenhouse, 1975) was overall change still statistically significant. We can conclude that, in the longer term, teaching about race relations to adolescents does not seem to have overall adverse effects, and where a directive or didactic approach is used a statistically significant change is retained after 18 months. It should be borne in mind, however, that by the time this group of subjects was investigated many of the most hostile in the field of race relations (including the majority of those whose attitudes failed to change, or changed in a negative direction) had left school.

We still have no answer to the problems of racism in this most alienated group of adolescents who come from the most deprived sectors of the white working class. It is these adolescents, as we know from our present fieldwork, who are most likely to be recruited to groups like the National Front and to be actively engaged in the physical persecution of ethnic minorities by means of beating, robbery and destruction, and burning of property and houses.

SELF-CONCEPT AND ATTITUDE CHANGE

We have argued elsewhere, using data from a variety of studies including pre-test variables in the 39 schools study, that self-esteem and self-concept are of crucial importance in understanding an individual's attitudes to the world around him, and the people in it (Bagley *et al.*, 1979); further evidence for this basic proposition is presented in Chapter 2 in this volume, by Burns. It appears that children, adolescents and adults have a pervading need to know that they are of worth, that what they do and what they are has some value and is of some meaning to the people with whom they have to interact. Self-esteem is maintained in a variety of ways, and one of these is the devaluation of others when there is some cultural justification for doing so. When a culture provides a set of stereotypes about the inferior nature of certain groups, individuals for whom society provides rather demeaning self-images will to a greater extent than others draw on those cultural symbols in expressing racist attitudes. If certain ethnic groups can be demeaned, the status of the prejudiced individual is thereby enhanced both subjectively and in terms of peer groups support. Highly prejudiced individuals are

TABLE 1.4   Change in scores on the General Racism scale (Bagley—Verma scale) before, and 18 months after, curriculum innovation in the race relations field

Strategy	N	Before teaching		After teaching		Significance of change – 'difference of difference'
		Mean	SD	Mean	SD	
A: Neutral chairman						
Experimental group	161	15.94	10.01	15.21	10.17	Not significant
Control group	38	19.15	10.28	17.18	10.05	
B: Didactic chairman						
Experimental group	120	15.78	9.57	12.57	9.25	Five per cent level
Control group	30	14.39	9.73	13.51	10.06	
C: Drama						
Experimental group	89	12.62	8.93	13.65	9.71	Not significant
Control group	36	17.07	10.06	15.25	9.44	

NOTE: Calculation of significant differences allows for regression to the mean, and for difference in change between experimentals and controls both before *and* after teaching. The lower the score, the less the racism manifested (see Linn and Slinde, 1977, on statistical problems involved in this type of research).

likely to have a more negative self-esteem than others; moreover, their prejudice is ego-defensive in nature (Bagley *et al.*, 1979).

The programme of teaching about race relations has been successful in so far as the prejudiced attitudes of individuals with moderate or good levels of self-esteem have been concerned. It seems likely that these attitudes were not an integral part of identity structure for these individuals, and they were able to change attitudes in a more enlightened direction in the light of exposure to the 'race pack' when used by enthusiastic and manifestly non-prejudiced teachers. However, such materials have had little success in changing the attitudes of individuals with poor self-esteem. Ziller (1976) argues that self-concept is central in attitude change. Self-concept is the most important concept in a hierarchically arranged model of self-concept, roles, behaviours, values and attitudes. No fundamental attitude change can take place, he argues, without an accompanying change in values, behavioural orientations, the roles the individual has to perform, actually or potentially, and the self-concept the individual has of himself. In this hierarchy self-concept change is the most important and the most fundamental. Our findings tend to bear out Ziller's basic model. Attitude change in our students takes place in those whose self-system (cf. Epstein, 1973) already incorporates the possibility of more tolerant attitudes and behaviour. It is clear that rather different techniques are necessary if the often racist attitudes and behaviour of the highly alienated white minority in British urban schools are to be tackled. Personal counselling can help, for many of these youngsters live on the exploited margins of white society – in the 'white ghettos' of council estates. Such counselling has to be accompanied by material and social support for families if it is to have any permanent effect on self-concept and related attitudes, as an experimental study has shown (Bagley *et al.*, 1979). Alternatively, role change within a school (e.g. promotion from one set or stream to another, or being made a prefect or even head boy) can produce a seemingly favourable change in attitudes and behaviour in prejudiced individuals (Jeffcoate, 1979).

Ultimately, racism in schools will diminish when the structural factors in British society – poverty, poor housing, unemployment, alienated work – change dramatically. Curriculum change in schools can be helpful, but it is by no means the whole answer. Nor indeed does the answer for racism of school students lie wholly within the schools. The exploitation and deprivation of ordinary people inherent in Britain's class system must ultimately bear a heavy burden of responsibility for racism in society.

2 The Relative Influences of Ethnicity, Social Class and Religion of Stimulus Person on Social Distance

ROBERT B. BURNS

Of the three major components of attitudes as generally conceptualised, the behavioural component is the most difficult to predict using conventional attitude questionnaire techniques. There are two main causes of this. Firstly, attitude questionnaire items are usually rather general whereas behaviour occurs in specific contexts and towards specific stimuli. Secondly, although attitude measurement has the prediction of behaviour as a major aim, statements on such scales rarely ask about behavioural intentions but tend to concentrate on theoretically antecedent cognitive and affective components. For instance, subjects are often asked in studies of ethnic attitudes to indicate how far they agree with statements concerning the living habits, intellectual capabilities, etc., of others but are hardly ever asked how they would behave towards some specific other in some specific situation. For studies of ethnic attitudes Bagley (1973c) claims that there is no better a candidate as a measuring instrument than the Social Distance scale which actually poses questions concerning the individual's behavioural intentions.

SOME PREVIOUS WORK

It was Park's (1921) original suggestion of the notion of social distance that stimulated Bogardus (1925) to develop a scale for measuring such a phenomenon and comparing attitudes towards ethnic groups. The value of the concept of social distance is that it allows social relationships to be conceptualised as a continuum ranging from a close degree of social intimacy, through discrimination in certain situations, to exclusion from all forms of relationships and situations.

In Bogardus' original scale the subject is requested to indicate the degrees of social intimacy he would willingly sanction between himself and members of various ethnic and national groups. If the individual is extremely prejudiced he may insist that members of that group should not be allowed even to visit his country; if he is only slightly prejudiced, he may accept group members as neighbours but not accept them to close kinship by marriage. The social distance expressed becomes the index of the subject's level of prejudice. The degrees of intimacy are listed as statements assumed to be representing equidistant points along a continuum of increasing social distance. The statements listed in scale order were:

1. Would admit to close kin by marriage.
2. Would admit to my club as personal friend.
3. Would admit to my street as neighbour.
4. Would admit to employment in my occupation.
5. Would admit to citizenship in my country.
6. Would admit as a visitor only to my country.
7. Would exclude from my country.

Using this scale, Bogardus (1928) found that white Americans displayed very little social distance towards the English, Canadians and northern Europeans, more towards the southern Europeans, and maintained the greatest amount towards Orientals and Negroes. He repeated his test in 1946 and 1956 in America and discerned considerable stability in attitude towards various ethnic groups alongside several understandable changes related to shifts in international relations and to the increasing assimilation of European immigrants into the American culture.

This notion that social distance exists between individuals has stimulated other social–psychological research from time to time. For example, Lewin (1936) compared social distance between individuals in Germany and in the USA, demonstrating that average social distance was larger in the former country. Hartley (1948) showed that an individual who is intolerant to one group is most likely to be intolerant to other groups. Even artificial group names rated on the Social Distance scale produced scores which correlated $+0.78$ to $+0.85$ with the scores from other extant groups in Hartley's study. Distance is employed in much of Peak's work (Peak *et al.*, 1960), while Fiedler (1958) utilises the concept of assumed similarity as a form of social distance. Most research on prejudice and ethnic attitudes is a specialised case of research into social distance. Renewed psychological interest has been generated by the social distance studies conducted by Triandis and Triandis (1960, 1962) and Triandis *et al.* (1965).

Triandis and Triandis (1962) offer an operational definition of social distance when they state that it is the distance that is indicated by the person to exist between himself and another person by means of the endorsement of certain statements. However, a number of criticisms have been levelled at the Bogardus technique as it stands.

(a) It is a very doubtful assumption that the statements represent equidistant points along a continuum. For example, both the psychological and social implications of the difference between relationship in marriage and in a club are likely to be far greater than those existing between club relations and neighbourly relations. Such unequal attitude differences render it incorrect to assign equally progressing arithmetical units to successive statements.

(b) There is no guarantee that the scale is unidimensional; the reactions of a subject may not stem solely from negative attitudes towards an ethnic group. Social distance could equally well be derived from social relationships especially those relating to social class and super-ordinate/sub-ordinate characteristics. Social distance could also be a reflection of a relative lack of common experiences, values or interests. In other words, there is a multifactorial basis to social distance which appears to be a complex of cumulative and possibly conflicting reactions derived from both psychological and non-psychological sources (Banton, 1967).

(c) As a result of the lack of unidimensionality the statements do not form a cumulative scale as supposed. It is quite possible for a subject to indicate that he would be willing to marry a person of a specified group but at the same time be unwilling to have such a member as a workmate because of job competition. Or again, he might be willing to accept a coloured person as a close friend yet reject him as a neighbour for fear of declining property values (M. Hill, 1953).

(d) The use of a list of ethnic groups confounds the various bases on which the judgement is made which in turn leads to the improbability of the scale being unidimensional and cumulative. For example, one never knows the extent to which the rejection of

Irishmen is the outcome of religion, social class, nationality, accent, or even alcohol consumption or again the extent to which rejection of Pakistanis is due to one, some, or all the following – colour, accent, dress, social class, living habits, religion, etc.

(e) Finally, the scoring of the scale is purely a summation of ordinal data which does not lend itself to parametric statistical procedures.

To obviate many of these criticisms Triandis and his co-workers (1965) have developed and refined the technique. They removed the restrictive ordinal scale by applying Thurstone's Equal Appearing Interval scaling technique (Thurstone and Chave, 1929) to a set of social distance statements. Then, a list was generated of all possible combinations of nationalities, religions, occupations, and races to be rated. This factorial design permitted the estimation of the percentage of the variance in social distance scores controlled by each variable, using a factorial analysis of variance. This approach enables a research worker (a) to assess how much importance a subject or group of subjects pay to each of the characteristics and their combinations, and (b) to compare the relative importance of the variance characteristics in contributing to social distance exhibited by different criterion groups of subjects.

In their first study, Triandis and Triandis (1960) showed that for white American students rating stimulus persons who had characteristics consisting of combinations of one of two levels of race (Negro/white), occupation (high/low prestige), religion (same as/different from the subject), and nationality (Portuguese/Swedish), about 77 per cent of the between-group variance in the social distance scores was accounted for by race, about 17 per cent by occupation, 5 per cent by religion, and 1 per cent by nationality. In addition, separate analyses of variance showed marked differences in emphasis on the various characteristics for subjects from various backgrounds. Upper-class subjects emphasised religion more than did lower-class subjects; middle-class subjects emphasised occupation while lower-class subjects emphasised race. Subjects whose parents came from northern or western Europe emphasised race more than those whose forebears came from southeastern Europe. The latter emphasised occupation and religion. Jewish subjects displayed less social distance than Christians, while most social distance was shown by those from a northern and western European background. Subjects who scored high on the California Fascism scale tended to manifest more social distance than those who scored low on that scale. From these results, Triandis and Triandis formulated two hypotheses:

(a) different cultures have different norms about social distance;
(b) within a culture the more insecure and anxious a person is the higher the amount of social distance he will feel towards people who are not like himself.

To test these hypotheses another similar study was conducted (Triandis and Triandis, 1962) comparing the social distance expressed by Greek and American students. The results indicated that about 56 per cent of the distance expressed by Greeks could be attributed to the religious factor, 24 per cent to the racial factor, 5 per cent to occupation, and 0 per cent to nationality. Of the distance expressed by the American students, 86 per cent could be ascribed to race, 8 per cent to religion, 3 per cent to occupation, and 0.5 per cent to nationality. Hence the average American student was focusing on race (as in the earlier study) while the average Greek student focused on religion. Again insecure individuals in each culture – as measured by a set of statements derived from the Dogmatism scale (Rokeach, 1960), F Scale (Adorno *et al.*, 1950) and the Manifest Anxiety scale (Taylor, 1953) – registered on average more social distance to minority groups. In both cultures the father was the chief disciplinarian of high social distance subjects and was the fount of more physical punishment, inconsistent punishment and unclear explanations of parental norms for the highs compared to the lows on social distance.

A replication of the 1962 study with German and Japanese students (Triandis *et al.*, 1965) lent further support to the two hypotheses. The German subjects provided the following set of variance weightings: race 6 per cent, occupation 70 per cent, religion 12 per cent and nationality 2 per cent. The Japanese results were: race 38 per cent, occupation 50 per cent, religion 0 per cent and nationality 3 per cent. The American students again emphasised race. Subjects who scored high on social distance in both America and Germany manifested low tolerance of ambiguity as measured by Budner's (1962) scale. It must be noted that all these various cross-cultural studies necessitated the separate standardisation of the scale in each culture.

There is little doubt that different cultures utilise different characteristics of persons in determining social distance. Americans focus on race, Greeks on religion, Germans on occupational status and the Japanese sample on both race and occupational status. But while cultural norms and the effect of socialisation processes dictate the relative importance of the various characteristics in different cultures there is at the same time a cross-cultural replication of the relationship between personality measures and the amounts of social distance expressed. It appears that insecure and anxious persons find those who are different a threat and only feel comfortable in known and set contexts. They need to follow the rigid 'party line' of society's norms to defend their narrow perspectives. This need to have control over the environment confines and limits perception with subsequent inability to tolerate ambiguity, inability to suspend judgement, and the consequent prejudging of others, using the authority of cultural norms relating to the evaluation of group attributes rather than suspending judgement and evaluating the individual *qua* individual.

K. Little (1947) and Banton (1958) have offered hypotheses to explain the existence of social distance towards coloured persons in Britain. Little advanced the 'colour-class' hypothesis which suggests that prejudice is a manifestation of the English person's overwhelming concern for the class structure with all in their rightful place. Coloured people are avoided and looked down on because of the inferior social connotation of a coloured skin. To identify coloured people with the lowest social class, Little believed, was partly due to the socio-historical legacy of a colonial past, supported at a psychological level by the needs of insecure and inadequate persons to have someone below as a means of assuaging their own inferiority. To introduce a coloured person into one's home is tantamount in middle-class circles to inviting the refuse collector to dinner. One loses one's own status by that sort of association! As Goldman and Taylor (1966) suggest, 'Colour has the same inferior connotation as English spoken ungrammatically' (p. 165).

Banton maintains that Little's theory is inadequate as it does not explain why British people also exclude coloured persons in situations where they have no fear of being identified with them. In his 'Stranger' hypothesis, Banton (1958) suggests that coloured persons are avoided because they are thought to be unfamiliar with British norms and way of life. Hence social relationships with them would be uncomfortable, fraught with anxiety and insecurity-provoking situations, especially for those who need a structured environment to cope with the daily tasks of living. Hence social distance and ethnic attitudes reflect both an unwillingness to be exposed to an object and an unwillingness to be identified with an object. Banton termed the coloured person the 'archetypal stranger' who is located at the farthest end of a range of aliens which to the British encompasses most if not all non-British. This tendency to xenophobia has developed historically as a norm cultured by the moat that has protected our island home. Xenophobia also acts as the need satisfaction of the inadequate individual. So again psychological forces interact with social norms and aid mutual maintenance. Banton has indicated that British and foreign appear to be the two chief categories which influence an Englishman's comprehension of the world. To be a non-member of the group is to be a stranger. This hypothesis has also been supported by Richmond (1955) who claims the antipathy British people exhibit towards immigrants is no more than the cultural norm to avoid too intimate a social contact with strangers.

Both these hypotheses place as much emphasis on the social norms and needs of the perceiver, and how these affect his perception and interpretation of the stimulus, as on the qualities of the stimulus. Fusing both hypotheses it is possible to view social distance as a means of protecting the self and maintaining psychological security in ways congruent with unwritten cultural norms by creating an inferior outgroup at one and the same time alien and of low social class.

Social distance may also stem from differences in religious beliefs which, since they involve basic values and philosophies of life, can be the target of prejudice from those holding other but irreconcilable religious beliefs. The dress of Muslim women, Pakistani marriage laws, Roman Catholic attitudes to divorce and family planning are all examples of religious belief being deeply entrenched in culture. As with colour and social class these differences provide another source of threat to the insecure, and another target at which hostility can be 'justifiably' directed.

No study using Triandis' approach appears to have been conducted in the British milieu apart from the one to be reported here which investigates the effects of differing levels of subjects' characteristics (sex, social class, self-concept) on social distance ratings of stimulus persons bearing combinations of various attributes (ethnic group, occupation, religion). It was considered relevant to investigate self-concept levels in relation to social distance, especially as a number of theorists (e.g. Rosenberg, 1965) believe that insecurity, and the feeling of threat from others, stems theoretically from low feelings of personal worth. A person who evaluates himself largely in negative terms is a threatened individual. Many therapists too have noted that what a person believes about himself is a major factor in his social comprehension of others and that self-acceptance is a prerequisite for the acceptance of others (Raimy, 1948; Rogers, 1951). The consistent cross-cultural findings of a specific personality basis to the amount of social distance expressed suggests a general psychological mechanism which functions fairly independently of culture. The self-concept or the attitudes a person holds towards himself appears to be a suitable candidate for this role. The factorial design in Triandis' modification of Bogardus' technique enables the applicability of both Little's and Banton's hypotheses to be evaluated in relation to the British context. To this end 'Stranger' was included as one of the levels of ethnic group and two levels of occupation formed another effect.

METHOD

(a) THE SUBJECTS

Two hundred second-year students (indigenous white British) studying full-time at a College of Education in the North of England participated in the study. None of the subjects was known to be suffering from any abnormal personality syndrome. There were 54 men (27 per cent) and 146 women (73 per cent) in the sample. The average age of the whole group was 20 years 1 month. The social class composition of the subjects based on the occupation of the father (Hall-Jones scale, 1950), classified 117 female students and 44 male students as middle-class (80.5 per cent of the subjects), and 29 female students and 10 male students as working-class in origin (19.5 per cent of the subjects). Each student was asked to make up a code composed of letters and numbers, males prefixing their code with an 'M' and females with an 'F'. This code, known only to the individual student, was placed on both scales so that the writer could collate data derived from different instruments completed by the same student.

(b) THE SCALES

(i) The social distance scale
Ten statements, indicating various degrees of social distance, were generated. To obviate the statistical limitations of ordinal data, the statements were submitted to scaling by means of the Method of Paired Comparisons (Thurstone and Chave, 1929). Seventy second-year students, not involved in the main study, acted as judges.

The statements and their scale values as computed are given in Table 2.1. A factorial design of stimulus persons was produced, using six ethnic groups, or what might be popularly termed 'race', two categories of religion, and two levels of social class defined by occupation, in every

TABLE 2.1

Statement	Scale value
I would be willing for such a person to visit my country	1.00
I would be willing for such a person to live in my country	1.50
I would be willing for such a person to live in my neighbourhood	2.10
I would be willing for such a person to join my club	2.20
I would play in the same team as such a person	2.40
I would be willing for such a person to live next door to me	2.70
I would sit next to such a person	2.80
I would invite such a person home	2.90
I would have such a person as my best friend	3.00
I would have such a person as a close relative	3.80

possible permutation. This constituted a $6 \times 2 \times 2$ factorial design, enabling the relative influence of these various levels of the three effects on the acceptability of others to be evaluated by means of the analysis of variance technique.

The six ethnic groups chosen were: British, Australian, Pakistani, West Indian, Indian and Stranger.

These particular groups were selected to represent white Anglo-saxons, viz. British and Australian, the coloured commonwealth, viz. West Indian, Pakistani and Indian, and finally unknown aliens who could conceivably be white or coloured, viz. Stranger.

The two categories of religion selected were: (a) same religion as yourself, (b) different religion from yourself.

The two levels of social class by occupation were: (a) doctor (middle class), (b) bus conductor (working class). Every possible combination of complex stimulus persons was generated, e.g. Australian doctor, same religion as yourself; Pakistani bus conductor, different religion from yourself; Indian doctor, same religion as yourself. The full list contained the 24 stimulus persons in random order (drawn out of a hat by a colleague).

Actual religions were not specified since while it was known to which ethnic group the subjects all belonged, and hence would be judging the stimuli from the point of view of a white indigenous Briton, they would, at the same time, encompass a variety of subtle religious shades of Christianity. Also, the specification of religions would have created some null categories in the design, e.g. Australian doctor, Hindu. This would have destroyed the credibility of the complex stimuli. Hence, by using 'same religion' and 'different religion' it was hoped that the subject would still reveal the weighting attributed to the religious characteristic of another person in his evaluation of him. Thus the evaluation would be performed from the reference point of the subject.

The two occupations were chosen to represent two levels in the social stratification system, a middle-class, educated, professional sub-culture, and a lower-class, routine, semi-skilled sub-culture. The particular occupations were also selected as realistic ones in which all the chosen ethnic groups might be encountered. Commonwealth doctors and commonwealth bus conductors are mentioned reasonably frequently in contemporary Britain. Thus it was hoped that the complex stimulus persons would be acceptable to the subjects, being credible and recognisable as representatives of extant groups.

The score for the social distance for each stimulus was computed by summing the scale scores of all the statements agreed with. That is, there was a possible range from 0.00, where no statement was agreed with, to a maximum of 24.4, where all statements were agreed with. A high score thus represents expressed willingness to accept others into a closer social relationship than a low score does.

A test−retest reliability over a 2-month period, based on a separate group of 78 subjects, using Spearman's Rank Order correlation coefficient on the differences between the mean rank of each stimulus on each occasion of testing was 0.95.

(ii) Acceptance of Self scale
The subjects' attitudes to themselves were measured by the Acceptance of Self sub-scale from Berger's (1952) Acceptance of Self and Others scale. Based on the Likert technique, the Acceptance of Self sub-scale is composed of 36 items, 28 of which are worded in a positive direction and 8 in a negative way. The positive and negative items are in random order to obviate the development of a response set. Berger's construction of the sub-scale is discussed in Shaw and Wright (1968) who state that 'This is the most carefully developed scale to measure attitude towards self that we found in the literature' (p. 433).

In a pilot study with 78 students a year earlier the test−retest reliability of the Acceptance of Self scale was 0.76 and an item analysis produced critical ratios for each statement significant at the 1 per cent level in every case. This American scale with alterations of spelling, appears suitable for use with students in Britain.

(c) FORM OF ANALYSIS

Nine analyses of variance were performed on the social distance scores, viz. for total group, men, women, men middle class, men working class, women middle class, women working class, high self-acceptance criterion group comprising the top third of Acceptance of Self scores, and a low Acceptance of Self criterion group comprising the bottom third of Acceptance of Self scores (see Winer, 1962, p. 290). It is, in essence, a straightforward four-way analysis of variance with the effects (A = ethnic group, B = occupation, C = religion, and I = subjects) being perfectly crossed. Effects A, B and C are all considered fixed, while I is random. The appropriate F ratios are formed in each case by the denominator being the corresponding interaction of the numerator with individuals, since all interactions with the subject factor are estimates of experimental error. Scheffé's Multiple Comparisons were computed between the means of the six levels of ethnic group for the total group and sub-groups.

(d) HYPOTHESES

From the research already noted it can be hypothesised that differences in the characteristics of the perceiver in terms of his sex, social class, and self-concept will affect the weighting he gives to various characteristics of the perceived. More specifically it can be postulated (a) that subjects with low acceptance of self scores will display more social distance than those with high acceptance of self scores; (b) that ethnicity will carry most weight in assigning social distance; (c) that there will be no significant difference between the mean ratings for 'Stranger' and those for the coloured stimulus persons; (d) that the mean ratings for 'doctor' stimuli will be significantly different from those for the 'bus conductor' stimuli.

RESULTS

Analysis showed that men had significantly higher scores than women on the Acceptance of Self scale ($p = 0.05$). This indicated the 54 male students (mean 138.81; SD 17.99) hold more positive attitudes to themselves than the 146 female students (mean 132.32; SD 16.55). The value of 't' was 2.29. Table 2.2 lists the means and standard deviations of stimulus persons for men, women and total groups in the Social

Distance scale. While the theoretical means range from 0 to 24.4, the recorded means range from 14.80 to 23.98 (men), 16.43 to 24.10 (women), and 15.99 to 24.07 (total). A high score implies a more favourable attitude.

The rank orders of the stimuli persons for men, women and total group based on mean score are extremely similar as indicated in Table 2.3 (rho for men/women = + 0.945). It is noticeable that there is a general trend for the highest ranks in each group to be held by British and Australian stimuli, while the West Indian, Indian and Pakistani stimuli form the tail of the orders. The highest-ranked coloured stimulus person for the total group is 'West Indian doctor, same religion' in eighth place. This same stimulus is also the highest-placed coloured one for women too, ranking seventh, as well as for men, in eleventh position.

The lowest rankings attained by British or Australian stimuli are ninth for the total group, tenth for men (both Australian bus conductor different religion), and ninth for women (British bus conductor, different religion). In all ranks the doctor status was ranked higher than the bus conductor for the same ethnic group.

From the analysis of variance of the social distance scores of the total group and the eight sub-groups it was possible to compute the percentage of between-group variance accounted for by each main effect and by interactions. The percentage of between-group variance contributed by each effect can be used as an index of that effect's weighting in the scores. These percentages are tabulated in Table 2.4.

In all cases ethnicity controls most of the between-group variance ranging from 60 per cent for the middle-class female sub-group to 80 per cent for the Low Acceptance of Self sub-group. Occupation accounts for between 10 and 34 per cent of the variance in the social distance scores, while the contribution of the religious factor is insignificant. In the sub-groups it is noticeable that men focus more on ethnicity than the women do, while women focus more on occupation than the men do. Respondents of working-class origins appear to use the ethnic criteria as a basis for behavioural intentions towards others more than do respondents of middle-class origins, while the latter place greater stress on occupation than the former. Those who possess positive self attitudes lay less stress on ethnicity and more on occupation than do those who hold unfavourable attitudes to themselves.

The mean differences between the proportions recorded for each main effect for the different sub-groups were tested to discover whether these differences represented true differences between pairs of sub-groups in the relative contribution of each effect to the total between-group

TABLE 2.2 Social Distance scale. Means and standard deviations of stimulus persons for men, women and total group

	Stimulus persons	Total m	σ	Men m	σ	Women m	σ	Mean difference men–women
A	Australian doctor, same religion	24.07	1.64	23.98	2.03	24.10	1.48	n.s.
B	British doctor, same religion	23.79	2.03	23.65	1.86	23.83	2.10	n.s.
C	British doctor, different religion	23.69	2.13	23.92	1.68	23.61	2.35	n.s.
D	Australian doctor, different religion	22.88	3.23	23.15	3.97	22.78	2.84	n.s.
E	British bus conductor, same religion	22.25	4.29	22.60	4.45	22.12	4.20	n.s.
F	Australian bus conductor, same religion	22.08	4.58	21.71	5.76	22.22	3.93	n.s.
G	British bus conductor, different religion	20.97	5.14	22.36	4.66	20.46	5.43	0.05
H	West Indian doctor, same religion	20.95	5.05	20.33	6.83	21.16	4.11	n.s.
I	Australian bus conductor, different religion	20.88	5.01	21.23	5.78	20.75	4.64	n.s.
J	A Stranger, doctor, same religion	20.74	5.42	21.58	5.47	20.43	5.39	n.s.
K	A Stranger, doctor, different religion	19.96	5.44	21.46	5.53	19.40	5.39	0.05
L	Indian doctor, same religion	19.84	6.49	18.89	7.46	20.19	6.01	n.s.
M	Pakistani doctor, different religion	19.65	6.34	18.89	8.16	19.95	5.47	n.s.
N	West Indian doctor, different religion	19.53	5.24	18.75	7.36	19.82	4.16	n.s.
O	Indian doctor, different religion	19.09	6.03	17.75	7.67	19.59	5.21	n.s.
P	Pakistani doctor, same religion	18.79	6.91	17.86	7.70	19.14	6.52	n.s.
Q	West Indian bus conductor, same religion	18.02	6.14	17.93	8.01	18.05	5.31	n.s.
R	A Stranger, bus conductor, same religion	17.90	6.50	18.33	7.42	17.74	6.02	n.s.
S	A Stranger, bus conductor, different religion	17.46	6.61	18.01	7.87	17.26	5.97	n.s.

		m	σ	m	σ	m	σ	
T	West Indian bus conductor, different religion	17.28	6.51	17.49	8.26	17.21	5.66	n.s.
U	Indian bus conductor, same religion	16.79	7.10	15.62	8.81	17.22	6.22	n.s.
V	Pakistani bus conductor, same religion	16.49	7.09	15.60	8.97	16.82	6.10	n.s.
W	Indian bus conductor, different religion	16.10	7.10	15.18	8.90	16.44	6.15	n.s.
X	Pakistani bus conductor, different religion	15.99	7.05	14.80	8.97	16.43	6.13	n.s.

m = mean; σ = standard deviation; n.s. = not significant.

TABLE 2.3   Social Distance scale. Ranks of stimulus persons by mean score (highest rank to highest mean score indicating most acceptance)

		Ranks		
	Stimulus persons	Total	Men	Women
A	Australian doctor, same religion	1	1	1
B	British doctor, same religion	2	3	2
C	British doctor, different religion	3	2	3
D	Australian doctor, different religion	4	4	4
E	British bus conductor, same religion	5	5	6
F	Australian bus conductor, same religion	6	7	5
G	British bus conductor, different religion	7	6	9
H	West Indian doctor, same religion	8	11	7
I	Australian bus conductor, different religion	9	10	8
J	A Stranger, doctor, same religion	10	8	10
K	A Stranger, doctor, different religion	11	9	15
L	Indian doctor, same religion	12	12.5	11
M	Pakistani doctor, different religion	13	12.5	12
N	West Indian doctor, different religion	14	14	13
O	Indian doctor, different religion	15	19	14
P	Pakistani doctor, same religion	16	18	16
Q	West Indian bus conductor, same religion	17	17	17
R	A Stranger, bus conductor, same religion	18	15	18
S	A Stranger, bus conductor, different religion	19	16	19
T	West Indian bus conductor, different religion	20	20	21
U	Indian bus conductor, same religion	21	21	20
V	Pakistani bus conductor, same religion	22	22	22
W	Indian bus conductor, different religion	23	23	23
X	Pakistani bus conductor, different religion	24	24	24

variance. Only two significant differences were revealed and these were between the High Self-Acceptance sub-group and the Low Self-Acceptance sub-group in respect of both ethnicity and occupation ($p < 0.05$). Thus Low Self-Acceptance sub-group places significantly more weight on ethnicity and significantly less on occupation than does the High Self-Acceptance sub-group in expressing social distance towards others.

The relative contribution of each variable to the between-group variance of scores for each group of subjects was submitted to a chi-squared goodness-of-fit test the null hypothesis of the equal contribution of the three variables to the social distance scores. The null

TABLE 2.4 Percentage of between-group variance contributed by the three effects

Group	Percentage of between-group variance			
	Ethnic group	Occupation	Religion	Interactions
Total	68.35	27.55	1.97	2.13
Women	63.98	30.75	2.74	2.53
Men	74.79	18.74	0.58	5.89
Women middle class	59.91	32.94	2.96	4.19
Women working class	75.75	20.79	1.81	1.65
Men middle class	73.40	19.56	0.33	6.71
Men working class	78.48	10.16	4.56	6.80
High acceptance of self	61.09	34.55	2.61	1.75
Low acceptance of self	80.71	15.17	2.88	1.24

hypothesis was rejected with $p < 0.01$ for every set of percentages. This finding, taken in conjunction with the discovery of only two significant mean differences for percentages of between-group variance between various sub-groups indicates that while all sub-groups deviate significantly from the theoretical distribution of equal contribution, they do so in similar fashion.

Table 2.5 summarises the significant F ratios for the nine analyses of variance. In every case the main effects of ethnicity and occupation attained acceptable levels of significance. The six levels of ethnicity were submitted to Scheffé tests for all sub-groups to identify where specific significant differences between means lay. The significant F ratios for the main effect of occupation indicate that the consistently higher means for the 'doctor' stimulus are significantly different from the lower means for the 'bus conductor' stimulus.

The significant interactions between both ethnicity and occupation and ethnicity and religion all revealed, when graphed, that mean scores for both doctor and bus conductor stimuli were lower for 'coloured' stimuli than for 'white' stimuli but that the decrease was greatest for the bus conductor stimuli. A similar relationship was apparent in the ethnicity/religion interactions where different religion showed a relatively greater decrease in mean score than did same religion when moving from 'white' to 'coloured' person stimuli.

TABLE 2.5   Summary of significance levels in nine analyses of variance

Subjects	Main Effects			Interactions			
	A	*B*	*C*	*AB*	*AC*	*BC*	*ABC*
Total group	0.01	0.01	0.01	0.01	0.01	n.s.	n.s.
Men	0.01	0.01	n.s.	0.01	0.01	n.s.	n.s.
Women	0.01	0.01	0.01	0.01	0.01	n.s.	n.s.
Men middle class	0.01	0.01	n.s.	0.01	0.01	n.s.	n.s.
Men working class	0.05	0.05	n.s.	n.s.	n.s.	n.s.	n.s.
Women middle class	0.01	0.01	0.01	0.01	0.01	n.s.	n.s.
Women working class	0.01	0.01	0.05	n.s.	0.01	n.s.	n.s.
High acceptance of self	0.01	0.01	n.s.	n.s.	n.s.	n.s.	n.s.
Low acceptance of self	0.01	0.01	n.s.	0.05	n.s.	n.s.	n.s.

A = levels of ethnic group; B = levels of occupation; C = levels of religion; n.s. = not significant.

DISCUSSION

The subjects in the present study record a sequence and weighting of factors similar to those obtained by Triandis and his colleagues in 1960 and 1965 with American students, but they are quite dissimilar from those obtained from German and Japanese students who both emphasise occupation, and from Greek students who laid most stress on the religious attribute. Triandis' 1962 American sample also focused strongly on the ethnic attribute but in contrast demonstrated a greater weight for religion than for occupation in allocating social distance. The minimal effect of religious characteristics in the present study occurs perhaps because they are not immediately perceivable as ethnic and social class attributes are. In any case for a student group, it is conceivable that religion is an unimportant factor.

   The study by Triandis and Triandis (1960) revealed that American women placed more weight on race than men; this trend is reversed in the present study with ethnic group membership being more heavily emphasised by men, though women of working-class origin followed the American pattern. This reversal on the weighting for race between the two cultures for men and women probably has a subtle cultural origin. The greater stress in American society on race issues may have more impact on girls who are around the house more, learning the cherished norms and values of their parents to a greater extent than boys. It may be, too, that the American sample contained a preponderance of women with a working-class background. This would lead to an emphasis on race since, in general, length of education is negatively related to prejudice (Martin and Westie, 1959) whilst housing shortage and job conflict with minority groups is met with in such an environment. This social class factor in the acceptance of others is supported and illuminated in this 1960 American study by finding that working-class subjects as a whole did emphasise race more than the middle-class, while the middle class placed more emphasis on social class and religious affiliations than the working class did. These trends, while discernible in the present study, are not statistically significant.

The contrast between middle-class and working-class women in the present study follows the American pattern fairly faithfully, but the contrast between middle-class and working-class men was not too distinct, with both focusing strongly on ethnic group. Occupation is also emphasised by middle-class men but religion bears some influence for working-class men. The women students of working-class origin in the present study obviously have not had a shorter formal education than those of middle-class home background. The former emphasise ethnic membership perhaps because they have identified with, and learned the attitudes and values of, their parents towards ethnic stimuli.

It would appear that Banton's 'Stranger' hypothesis (1958) is generally supported by the results from the Social Distance scale. The subjects of this research tended to place, in terms of mean score recorded for levels of ethnic group, the stimulus 'Stranger' in an intermediate position between the more acceptable two 'white' stimuli and the three less acceptable 'coloured' stimuli. However, for three groups (women, women middle class, and men working class), 'Stranger' was placed behind 'West Indian'. This tendency for 'Stranger' to be evaluated in terms of social distance immediately preceding the 'coloured' ethnic stimuli, and on several occasions within that set of stimuli, is defined with greater clarity by the critical differences between the ethnic stimuli, based on the Scheffé procedure which reveals that for only two groups, viz. the total group, and Low Acceptance of Self group, does 'Stranger' possess significant mean differences with any of the 'coloured' stimuli. As a corollary, this implies that for the other seven groups, only chance mean differences exist between the three 'coloured' stimuli and 'Stranger', with the mean of the latter being especially close on many occasions to the mean of 'West Indian', a positioning revealed in the rank orders. No significant mean differences between 'Stranger' and 'West Indian' exist. Thus it is apparent that 'Stranger' and 'West Indian' are being evaluated similarly in terms of social distance. This occurs perhaps because the 'West Indian' was, during the childhood of the subjects, the main immigrant in the conurbation in which the research was conducted and in which many of the subjects had lived for most of their lives. For this sample, 'West Indian' has become synonymous with the connotations of 'Stranger'. It would be interesting to discover whether, in areas where other ethnic groups form the incursors, they will eventually become synonymously evaluated as 'Stranger' in the same way.

There is no doubt that 'Stranger' is clearly differentiated by all subjects, except working-class men, from the 'white' stimuli. 'Stranger' had 6 significant mean differences and 21 non-significant mean differences with 'coloured' stimuli, but 12 significant mean differences and 6 non-significant mean differences with 'white' stimuli. This set of relationships between significance/non-significance and the white/coloured person stimuli in respect of 'Stranger' is highly significant with chi-squared $= 10.32$ (1 d.f.; $p<0.01$).

This highly significant relationship emphasises the close similarity between the level of acceptance of 'Stranger' and the other 'coloured' person stimuli, especially West Indian and of the difference in preferred social distance expressed to 'Stranger' as compared to the two 'white' person stimuli. It also lends support to Banton's hypothesis in this research. 'Stranger' is unmistakably part of an out-group populated essentially by coloured immigrant groups in the British context, with coloured people generally allocated to the end position on the continuum of strangeness. In terms of stereotyping, these results on the Social Distance scale suggest that the rational way most subjects anticipate interaction with a stranger is similar to that with coloured persons. White and foreign, manifest themselves as the two major categories for evaluating humanity even in this student group.

The results also reveal, in no uncertain fashion, the expected British concern with the necessary differentiation of class levels in this preference for closer social distance with a middle-class stimulus than with a working-class stimulus. Just as members of coloured ethnic groups are held at arms' length, so are persons with working-class occupations; but it must be borne in mind that the greater social distance at which such working-class persons are acceptable may be influenced by beliefs that have substance in reality. For example, lack of common interests and common talking points must affect acceptability.

Both the 'Stranger' and 'colour–class' hypotheses are very similar in one respect. This is perhaps why support can be shown for both in the results. They both view negative ethnic attitudes as the means of raising self-esteem, restoring confidence, and security for those who possess low self-esteem, by evaluating one's in-group, either British or middle class, as superior.

The data from the Social Distance scale confirm the general belief of the Rogerian school (Sheerer, 1949; Stock, 1949; Rogers, 1951) that a person who is unsure about his own merit, who has low esteem for himself, tends to display less acceptance for others than a person who evaluates himself more positively. In this respect the significant differences in the weightings the Low Acceptance of Self and High Acceptance of Self criterion groups give to ethnicity and occupation in their respective evaluations of others is an understandable and expected finding bearing on the suggested positive relationship between acceptance of self and acceptance of others. In this study a person who is secure and confident because of his positive self-appraisal, appears able to accept and have more positive attitudes towards others, and lay less stress on ethnic characteristics in evaluative procedures than those with a lower level of self acceptance. To these latter persons, those who are different would seem to pose a real threat. Perceived characteristics, especially ethnic ones, are emphasised and used as the basis of judgement in a rationalisation that 'different equals strange equals threat'. Fear of losing status and security of group membership results in a powerful attempt to identify as one with the group, directing hostility and rejection at out-groups seen in various combinations as coloured, of an inferior social class, as strangers, in visible and obvious ways different from self, and from known and secure ways of behaving. In all their different cloaks of many hues, members of other ethnic groups are threatening and strange.

It can be hypothesised that there is such a strong relationship between level of self-concept and the degree of ethnocentrism displayed by a subject because both are founded on the same child-training experiences so that those experiential processes conducive to the learning of a negative attitude to self could well be liable to produce ethnocentric attitudes through the projection and displacement of anxiety, frustration and inferiority. Other developments deriving from child training experiences documented by Frenkel-Brunswik (1948) and Rokeach (1948) that support and give succour to the negative attitudes to others, are concrete and rigidly categorised thinking, and the inability to tolerate ambiguity and suspend judgement until more information is available.

CONCLUSIONS

Cross-cultural studies have only explored the responses of a few national groups towards a small number of stimulus persons so far, but the evidence confirms the views of Triandis and Triandis (1962), that there are three basic sources of variance determining acceptance of others:

(a) the culture of the perceiver;
(b) the characteristics of the perceived, and
(c) the characteristics of the perceiver.

The first source lies behind the general uniformity of the data within each culture. This can be seen in the present research in the extremely similar rank orderings of the six ethnic stimuli on the Social Distance scale. In all societies there appear to be norms and values to regulate what are the 'right' or 'appropriate' behaviours for members in their encounters with various types of others.

The other two sources of variance suggest that within this framework of norms in any particular society, different kinds of personalities register different degrees of social distance towards others who possess various characteristics. This is done mainly by controlling which attributes of perceived persons are emphasised in individual perception and which are ignored. Self-concept level, social class level, and sex of the subject appear to play a significant role in determining the emphases placed on various attributes of others in Britain when judging the acceptability of these others.

Thus differences are found in this study in both absolute amounts of social distance and in the relative emphasis placed on the attributes of ethnic group membership, social class and religion of others by groups of subjects who themselves are grouped by categorising levels of self-attitude, sex and social class. But bluntly, this British student sample, and the sub-groups within it, focus, consistently and emphatically, on others essentially in terms of the ethnic characteristics of these others. The distinguishing feature of the ethnic characteristics that is singled out in the evaluative procedure can certainly be designated as 'colour'. The evidence to support this lies in that pattern of significant mean differences, in which the six separate ethnic groups fused into two blocks in the form of a dichotomy between 'white' and 'coloured'.

The present modified Social Distance scale is revealed to be extremely sensitive to significant determinants of social distance that have their sources in both the subject and the perceived stimulus. Such a scale is also very flexible in that it is a technique rather than a fixed set of items. Numerous sets of statements could be devised and many different groups, bearing innumerable attributes, could be rated in this factorial design, depending on the interests and hypotheses of the research worker. However, the development of diverse sets of items reduces the possibility of the comparability and replicability of studies.

Part II
Identity and Self-esteem
in a Multicultural Society

3 Self-Esteem, Self-Concept and the Development of Black Identity: A Theoretical Overview

LORETTA YOUNG and CHRISTOPHER BAGLEY

INTRODUCTION

In this chapter we outline some of the important theories of how children come to acquire a sense of their identity, and ideas of themselves as individuals having attributes and qualities of various kinds. We will try and link various theories of development in this field, including theories of Mead, Maslow, Erikson, Lewin and others. We try and relate the difficult ideas of self-esteem, self-concept and identity to one another, in the context of the development of black identity and self-concept. We conclude that the idea of self-esteem should be subsumed under and incorporated within the notion of global self-concept, which is equivalent to Erikson's idea of identity. Adequate self-esteem is a necessary but not a sufficient condition of adequate identity. What is important is the way in which global identity integrates both past and present experiences, particularly in adolescence, in ways which enable the individual to maximise his potential. Obviously social structure is an important potentiator of identity, and in a racist society such as Britain (Bagley and Verma, 1979) black identity takes particular forms as young people cope, by various means, with the society in which they live.

THEORIES OF THE SELF

Nash (1976) has pointed out that there are basically three traditions of 'self' theory. We shall begin by discussing the second tradition of self theory as it is the simplest and most obvious of the three. This involves the interactionist conception of the self and is contained in the work of James, Mead and their associates. Meadian theory suggests that the self is the product of the process during which the individual comes to accept as his own the ideas about himself that he perceives others to hold of him. Thus, this process, 'taking the role of the other', shows how the child develops self-concepts, i.e. ideas about himself similar to those his significant others have of him.

Mead conceptualised the self as a process that consists of two distinct but simultaneous aspects: the 'I' and the 'Me'. The 'Me' comes about through taking the attitudes of others towards oneself. It is the objectified aspect of the self, which is presented to others, and which we 'see' when we take their attitude towards our self. The 'Me' is what the individual 'sees' when he interacts with another person; just as he sees himself when he looks in the mirror. An individual has several 'Mes' at any one time – there is the physical me, the me in a particular interaction (being, for instance, patient, understanding and warm), the me as a parent, the me as a child, the me as a graduate student and so on.

The 'I' is logically involved in the self, however, since an objective self (formed through taking the attitude of others) presupposes a subjective aspect of the self that reacts to the 'me', and that also responds to the 'me' presented by others in interaction. According to Kimmel (1974), this aspect of the self, the I, is a

'fleeting, momentary, process self; it can never be observed or objectified because it exists only in moment-to-moment consciousness; it exists only in process. In some ways, it resembles the 'stream of consciousness' that James discussed – it is moment-by-moment awareness, everchanging and existing only in process'.

(Because it is process rather than content it is most easily identified by the 'ing' endings on words that describe its functioning: reacting, reflecting, experiencing, feeling, interpreting, responding, etc.).

Central to the notion of the 'I' is the fact that it responds to a situation in the immediate present experience and as such is always uncertain and unpredictable. It thus introduces the possibility of novelty and of change. 'The possibilities of the "I" belong to that which is actually going on, taking place, and it is in some sense the most fascinating part of our experience. It is there that novelty arises . . .' (Mead, 1934, p. 237).

The 'I' exists only in the present moment since it is ongoing; we are always feeling, responding, experiencing in this present moment. Sometimes we wish to examine our response to a particular situation and in so doing we are trying to grasp the 'I' of the past moment and make it a 'me' so that we may label, examine and talk about it as an object. Consider the following example: six-year-old Danny, a black child adopted by white parents, and attending an all-white school, had earlier told me that 'They call me Blacky Sambo at school, and I call them Pinky Face.' He clearly meant that the name they called him was a disparaging one. Then, a short time later we were watching television. A black runner was competing against several white runners and Danny pointed to the television and said, 'Look, there's me'. As the race drew to its climax and black and white runners contested the leadership, Danny shouted, 'Come on Blacky Sambo.' At that point he was developing an 'I' with regard to racial identity; his 'I' was overtly manifested at the brief moment in which he identified both with the black runner and the disparaging name which other children called him. Afterwards we asked Danny, 'Do you really think that you are a Blacky Sambo?' He pulled a face and said, 'I suppose so. That's what they call me.' Now, he had grasped the 'I' which had manifested itself during the excitement of the race; it had become part of his 'me', part of his objective self. It seems that Danny had internalised the racial attitudes of others, and now comes to see himself as they see him.

Our self is made up of these kinds of moment-by-moment interactions between the 'I' and the 'me' aspects of the self. Something is amiss when this kind of I–me interaction does not occur (as in some forms of schizophrenia). Most of us have a reasonable amount of interaction between what we experience and our perception of ourselves. As Mead (1934, p. 229) phrased it:

I talk to myself and I remember what I said and perhaps the emotional content that went with it. The 'I' of this moment is present in the 'me' of the next moment. There again I cannot turn around quick enough to catch myself. I become a 'me' in so far as I remember what I said . . . it is because of the 'I' that we say we are never fully aware of what we are, that we surprise ourselves by our own action.

This analysis of the self indicates that the individual's notion of himself is social in origin and as such is derived from his interaction with others who evaluate him in many differing ways. Sociologists such as Webster and Sobieszek have taken this a good deal further and suggest that the notion of the self is relational and specific. Self-evaluation, they say, is relative to the structure of the social situation. Both who the other is and what the situation is appear to be important. The self is an ongoing, changing, active processing characteristic of the individual.

Freud and his followers were among the first to develop psychological ideas about the self. Freud himself argued that there are three aspects of personal development, the Id (instinctual drives), the Ego (the adaptive part of the mind which brings it into conformity with external reality) and the Super-Ego (that which represents the demands of parents and society, guiding the Ego along a 'moral' path). Nash (1976) pointed out, however, that self did not form the central theme of Freud's work; it was his daughter, Anna Freud, who became one of the pioneers in emphasising the importance of self images in the individual.

'Identity' formed the core of Erikson's study which was published in 1968. He argued that the individual and the quality of his self-value was of greatest importance. The search for integrity involves the identification with figures in the culture (which could be presumed to include own racial figures); and this is supposed to be difficult in modern Western society where models for identification are weak and goals of the society are vague. The development of ego identity in Erikson's theory proceeds through eight stages. At each of the first seven stages, a particular problem must be solved before ego integrity is reached, in the eighth stage. Even in this eighth stage, however, ego identity is still threatened. The eight stages which unfold as the individual gets older, are: (1) trust versus basic mistrust; (2) autonomy versus shame and doubt; (3) initiative versus guilt; (4) industry versus inferiority; (5) identity versus role diffusion; (6) intimacy versus isolation; (7) generativity, 'doing things', versus stagnation; (8) ego integrity versus despair.

Another theorist, Abraham Maslow, has outlined a theory that for brevity is called the self-actualisation theory (Maslow, 1954). This is a multiple-factor theory which posits five levels of needs (whose development also coincides with certain age stages) arranged in a hierarchy. From lower to high levels they are: 'Physiological needs' such as hunger, thirst and warmth; 'Safety needs' such as security, stability and order; 'Belongingness and love needs' such as needs for affection, affiliation and identification (presumably this includes affection for, affiliation to and identification with one's own racial group); 'Esteem needs' such as needs for prestige, success and self-respect; 'Need for self-actualisation, or self-fulfilment'. The order in which these needs are listed is significant in two ways. This is the order in which they are said to appear in the normal development of the person. It is also the order in which they need to be satisfied. It might be expected then that people in affluent societies, such as Britain, will manage to satisfy the needs lower in the hierarchy and in many cases will be preoccupied with the need for self-actualisation. More and more studies point to strivings for the three last levels among many West Indian children and adolescents in Britain (see Weinreich, 1979; Bagley *et al.*, 1979b).

The relationship between self-esteem and personality is not made very clear by modern personality theorists. The works of psychologists such as Eysenck and Cattell do not appear to recognise 'self' as a basic concept. In their book on *The Structure of Human Personality* (1969), Eysenck and Eysenck make only a passing reference to self-actualisation, and no reference at all to self-esteem. Similarly, Cattell's idea of 'self-sentiment' formed only a small part of his work in *The Scientific Analysis of Personality* (1965). Gorsuch and Cattell (1977), however, offer a complex theoretical analysis of 'the self and the superego', emphasising cognitive and self-actualising aspects of self theory, ignoring 'the felt, experienced, introspected immediately acting self'.

Unlike the above personality theorists, others argue that the notion of the self is important and indeed central to personal functioning. Becker (1971), for example, argues that the dominant motive of man is the need for self-esteem. Hayakawa (1963) also suggests that the main purpose of all human activity is to enhance the self-esteem. It could be that personality theorists such as Eysenck and Cattell are measuring self-esteem indirectly, since for example, Eysenck's personality inventories ask questions about the self. Some of these questions are similar to those found in the inventory of Coopersmith, e.g. Eysenck asks 'Do you day-dream a lot?' (Eysenck Junior Personality Inventory), while Coopersmith invites a response to, 'I spend a lot of time day-dreaming' (Coopersmith Self-Esteem Inventory).

Scholars usually draw a distinction between self-concept and self-esteem. Self-concept involves an objective or cognitive appraisal of the self, while self-esteem involves an emotional appraisal of the self, reflecting self-confidence. We would argue, however, that since all descriptions of the self (except descriptions such as weight, height, sex) involve some emotional loading, that all self-conceptions are also expressions of self-esteem. Taking Eysenck's and Coopersmith's variable of 'day-dreaming' for example – to admit that one day-dreams is to admit to an undesirable behaviour. This statement is one of 'fact' but is inevitably involved with emotion in actually admitting it.

THE CONCEPT OF IDENTITY

According to Erikson (1959b), identity means a sense of continuity and social sameness which bridges what the individual 'was as a child and what he is about to become and also reconciles his conception of himself and his community's recognition of him'. He thus registers a certain impatience with what he calls the 'faddish equation of the term identity with the question "Who am I?"' (1965); nobody would ask himself this question except in a more or less transient morbid state, in a creative self-confrontation, or in an adolescent state sometimes combining both. The most pertinent question for most people is 'What do I want to make of myself – and – what do I have to work with?' This is indicative of a positive move and this awareness of inner motivation is quite important in not clouding or swamping the future with infantile wishes and adolescent defences. Thus identity contains a complementarity of the past and the future in both the individual and the society – a 'self-realization coupled with a mutual recognition' (1959).

Identity can be both personal (as in the case of James, 1920) or personal plus cultural (in the case of Freud) (1937). Many people never have a clear grasp of their identity (and can be said to have relatively little 'ego strength', 'self-esteem' or 'self-actualisation'). The average white Englishman has, perhaps, in the past had a relatively undeveloped sense of ethnic identity, simply because he had no need to reflect on his ethnic position except in terms of superiority. It seems to us that many English people are now, in collective or cultural terms, enduring an 'identity crisis' because the old ethnic and imperial superiority has been lost, and English people are forced to reappraise themselves as simply partners in a multicultural society. The reaction of many English people seems to be a racist one – an adaptation of 'premature identity foreclosure', in Erikson's term; this is a search for 'a purified identity', as Sennett (1970) puts it, in his adaptation of Erikson's identity theory to account for problems in the wider social structure.

Social change may force an identity crisis upon a particular group of people or cultural group, just as the onset of adolescence may impose an identity crisis on an individual. Oppressed minority groups may be thrown into an identity crisis if the onset of the oppression is sudden and unexpected. Kurt Lewin (1936) addressed himself to this problem, writing for the Jewish community at the time of growing Nazi oppression. His answer was to suggest that Jews accept their minority group position and that they make it a position of strength. He understood that the Jewish child's greatest need was solid social and psychic 'ground' on which to stand. Although the problems of the Jewish minority situation are in some ways different from those of other minority children, such as blacks, Lewin's guidelines for parents bear some generalisation. His proposals are that:

(1) The minority group child has to face the facts of his life.
(2) It is best for these facts to be faced squarely from the start, by involving the child in that knowledge.
(3) This applies under the best and the worst of minority group circumstances, since the conditions can and do change.
(4) The minority parent can thereby set up a situation in which the child has a definite sense of belongingness with other members of the minority situation. This minimises ambiguity, tension, and maladjustment.
(5) Minority parents should treat the minority problem not as an individual and private matter but as a social issue. This will prevent feelings of self-accusation and self-pity which can otherwise result from the contemplation of the minority experience.
(6) This sociological approach is especially important for the adolescent minority person. He needs to have a considerable reassurance concerning his belongingness. This is best provided through the interdependence of members of the minority group.
(7) Minority parents should not be afraid of overlapping loyalties. Belonging to more than one overlapping group is natural and necessary for everyone. The real danger lies in standing 'no-where' − in being a 'marginal man', and 'eternal adolescent'.

Black parents are more disadvantaged than Jewish parents in coping with problems of identity in their children. Unlike the Jewish community, they do not have a clearly defined religious basis for their culture, with an ancient tradition as well as literary and intellectual traditions. The base of the black parent is too often one of extreme economic oppression, and the cultural disorganisations imposed by slavery and its aftermath. Yet the tasks of the black parent in establishing an adequate sense of identity in their children are precisely the same as those set out by Lewin.

IDENTITY DEVELOPMENT

Erikson indicates that identity development has two complementing facts: (1) a developmental stage in the life of the individual, (2) a period in history (i.e. of the wider culture). There is thus a complementarity of what he calls 'history' and 'life-history'. The development of psycho-social identity is not feasible (according to Erikson) before the beginning of adolescence (just as it is not dispensable after adolescence). This is a time when, in the life of the individual, there is a sense of 'identity versus role diffusion', 'need for esteem' (Maslow's theory) and. a resistance to stereotyped views of the self in establishing one's own identity and feelings of self worth. Another feature of adolescence is as a time:

> when the body, now fully grown, grows together into an individual appearance; when sexuality, matured, seeks partners in sensual play and, sooner or later in parenthood; when the mind, fully developed, can begin to envisage a career for the individual within a historical perspective – all idiosyncratic developments which must fuse with each other in a new sense of sameness and continuity (Erikson, 1965).

How relevant are these studies of identity foreclosure in lower-class black adolescents in America for a consideration of the psychosocial development of black youth in Britain's deprived inner cities? There is some American evidence that with the rise of the 'black pride' movement in America, black adolescents no longer devalue themselves to the extent, and in the manner, which affected a previous generation (Coopersmith, 1975). But in some respects the situation in Britain with regard to black identity is similar to the American situation 15 or 20 years ago. Blacks in Britain do not have a united movement which emphasises black pride and black achievement, and there is no clearly successful black middle class. Blacks in Britain suffer· severe racial discrimination, especially in access to employment and housing (McIntosh and Smith, 1974), and the problem seems to be particularly severe among black school-leavers, amongst whom the unemployment rate is as much as four times that in white school-leavers. Whether recent movements of an aggressive and semi-political nature in which young blacks take a leading role (as in Bristol and Notting Hill) represent a reversal of this trend toward self-devaluation remains to be seen.

IDENTITY TYPES: POSITIVE AND NEGATIVE

In Erikson's theory, every person's psychosocial identity contains positive and negative elements (Erikson, 1965). The growing human being, throughout his childhood, is presented with negative prototypes (as by reward and punishment, parental example and by the community's typology).

It is clear, then, that many important components of one's identity tend to be resolved around this time. If one is not able, because of societal or personal reasons, to resolve these in a positive way, then 'identity confusion' may result. This is uncertainty about the role one is playing in the scheme of life. The resolution of this turning point or 'identity crisis' may be conscious and deliberate, perhaps partly reflecting the adolescent's newly acquired ability to think abstractly (the stage of 'formal operations' in Piaget's scheme of cognitive development). On the other hand, much of the resolution of this crisis involves emotional issues that may be relatively hidden beneath the surface of conscious awareness.

For some black adolescents this crisis is inevitable, since because of the structure of society and the pressures of the dominant culture, they are denied the necessities with which to build an adequate 'life-history' to combat their surrounding milieu. The notion of 'identity foreclosure' (which some black adolescents may experience) appears in Erikson's discussions of precursors of the adolescent crisis (Erikson, 1959b). In his writings of 1956 and 1963 Erikson referred to 'ego identity' and 'identity diffusion'. According to Marcia (1966), these refer to 'polar outcomes of the hypothesized psychosocial crisis occurring in late adolescence . . . "identity achievement" and "identity diffusion" are polar alternatives of status inherent in Erikson's theory'. Accordingly, an 'identity achievement' individual has experienced a crisis period and is now successfully committed to an occupation and ideology.

The 'identity diffusion' individual may or may not have experienced a crisis. He lacks commitment and unlike his 'achievement' counterpart, displayed the following attitudes in Marcia's study: he has neither decided upon an occupation nor is much concerned about it; seems to have little conception of his daily routine and gives the impression that his choice could be easily abandoned should opportunities arise elsewhere; is either uninterested in ideological matters or adopts the approach that any one outlook is as good as the other, and he does not mind sampling from them all.

Marcia also proposes two other states which fall roughly between 'identity achievement' and 'identity diffusion'. These are the 'moratorium' and 'foreclosure' statuses. Marcia describes the moratorium individual as one 'in the crisis period, with commitments rather vague'. He can be distinguished from the 'diffusion' individual by the appearance of an active struggle to make commitments. He seems preoccupied with issues which could be described as 'adolescent', and is constantly attempting a compromise between his parents' wishes, society's demands and his own capabilities. He gives the appearance of being bewildered and this possibly is the result of the many unresolvable issues which preoccupy him.

Erikson's analysis of 'identity foreclosure' suggests an arrest in ego development which assumes a 'progression through time of a differentiation of parts' (Erikson, 1959a). The pre-adolescent forms of ego identity are found in the latency period and it is during this time that the child is concerned about what Erikson calls 'competence' (1959a). For the development of competence, there should have been successful ego development in the periods preceding the latency stage, together with a facilitating environment within the latency period. Successful passage of these requirements leads to the emergence of 'a sense of industry' (Erikson, 1955). There is thus a sense of 'anticipation of achievement' in the next stage of ego development – adolescence.

If there is failure in this expectation of fulfilment the child may emerge with a sense of 'inadequacy and inferiority'. Associated with this failure, the child develops what is known as 'identity foreclosure', 'a premature interruption in the adolescent task of identity formation' (Hauser, 1971).

There appear to be two opposite forms in which this 'interruption' can be expressed – negatively, as the 'sense of inferiority, the feeling that one will never be any good'; or positively, when for example the child 'identifying too strenuously with a too virtuous teacher or becoming the teacher's pet . . . his sense of identity can become prematurely fixed on being nothing but a good little worker or a good little helper, which may not be all he could be'.

Hauser, in *Black and White Identity Formation* (1971), found that the type found most commonly among his black American subjects was the negative one. He found that themes of inferiority, mediocrity and degradation featured very much among them, both with regard to school and job opportunities, occasions 'where doors were slammed at you' in a social system of limited choice. Hauser's black subjects noticed this most directly in the area of work. There were few part-time and summer jobs available and availability appeared to be combined with distasteful kinds of work. Prospects of a better job after graduation seemed even more unlikely.

Hauser found that a second environmental constraint was in terms of 'heroes' i.e. positive figures whom the black subjects were interested in emulating. Not only did the subjects find the talents of men such as Joe Louis, Jackie Robinson, Sidney Poitier and James Baldwin, out of their reach, but it was noticeable that the numbers of observable heroes gradually diminished over time. Erikson argued that the individual belonging to an oppressed and exploited minority, and who is aware of the dominant cultural ideals but prevented from emulating them, is likely to fuse the negative images held up to him by the dominant majority with his own previously developed identity (Erikson, 1955, p. 155).

Hauser (1971) describes negative identity as

> the adolescent derivative of a failure to resolve the set of issues belonging to the developmental stage of conscience formation. It is the phase of ego development in which the conflicts between guilt and initiative become most prominent.

Hauser follows Erikson (1968) who argued that if guilt becomes predominant for the individual, the result is 'a self-restriction which keeps an individual from living up to his inner capacities or to the powers of his imagination and feeling'. This, of course, is the essence of identity foreclosure. Negative identity is, however, a specific type of identity foreclosure. It occurs where identity formation is prematurely arrested because of the individual's commitment to that which could be termed 'allied' to him. He thus makes a more or less total choice, a single set of identifications, with the values of the despised, and may consider himself as hateful, and totally undesirable. Erikson sometimes refers to this identity pattern as a 'total commitment to role fixation' (Erikson, 1968).

The alternative to an exclusive, unhistorical identity (Erikson, 1965) is the wholeness of a more inclusive identity. This has become a feature in many parts of the world, the struggle for more inclusive identities: 'What has been a driving force in revolutions and reformations, in the founding of churches and in the building of empires has become a contemporaneous world-wide competition' (Erikson, 1965). For blacks of the diaspora, this is the movement for an African identity, which incorporates the dignity of African cultures, the history of slavery, struggle, and the newly emerging black culture.

SELF-CONCEPT AND SELF-ESTEEM

Life in a multiracial society affects not only the attitudes and behaviour of minority group members toward the standard set by the dominant society, but also the responses to themselves and their groups. The way one looks upon himself is a product of his social experience with others. The nature of that experience profoundly influences the basic ego structure which is the central core of the self. This way of looking at one's self is defined by Coopersmith (1967) thus:

> Self concepts are symbols that blend together the enormous number of varied perceptions; memories and prior experiences that are salient in the personal life of the individual. This concept of one's self . . . is formed by the individual, and represents an organization of separate experiences into some pattern that provides meaning and order in his inner world.

He emphasises that although the terms self-concept and self-esteem are sometimes used interchangeably, they refer to markedly different phenomena: 'Self-concept is the symbol or image which the person has formed out of his personal experiences while self-esteem is the person's evaluation of that image'.

One's concept of the self is initially influenced by certain basic characteristics such as one's age, sex, colour, caste and in some cases, religion. These 'ascribed' characteristics impose upon the person's choice of others with whom he interacts and thus influence his answers to the questions: Who am I? What am I like as a person? Thus the answers to these questions come not in isolation from the society as a whole, but to a great extent in relation to the individual's position in the social structure. 'Position' and 'structure' as used here are important variables in that they are the phenomena to be examined when the 'self-concept' is being investigated. Social structure exists before the person is born and constitutes the milieu into which he or she is thrust. This social structure consists of individuals with certain beliefs, ideas and knowledge and thus each person has to see others as objects which must be taken into account in his or her conduct.

Before we can make an assessment of a child's self-concept and its relationship to identity we must know his world of 'objects' and the social arrangements of the family and community into which he is born. This includes beliefs and values found in the family, attitudes towards the child at school, among his peers etc., all of which are influenced by his position in the social structures, whether he is black or white, rich or poor, urban or rural, and in such areas where it may be salient, whether he is Catholic or Protestant.

In a complex society, 'objects' or significant others might be numerous and indeed present the child with conflicting values. This comes to the fore very much when the child starts school where the teacher's qualities conflict with those of the parents. This may prove problematic for the child not only by imposing limitations on the development of self-concept but on what Hewitt (1976) (reflecting Goffman) calls 'impression management' – how to live up to parental images and at the same time show qualities valued by outsiders whom the child may have to please if his goals are to be achieved. Indeed a 'bifurcation of the social worlds and of the self' might result.

The self-concepts which emerge within particular ethnic groups are not necessarily influenced just by beliefs and values within the group itself; they may emerge through the particular contrasts between one's own ethnic group and the 'others' (outsiders) that the members of the group choose to emphasise, (or which are forced on a group). To be black therefore is not simply to live up to a set of images of what blacks ought to be like, as defined by blacks, but also to avoid (or perhaps emulate in a subordinate fashion) certain qualities and beliefs which are presumed to be characteristic of white.

What avenues are open to individuals whose self-presentations make little or no difference to the way others view him? Firstly, the individual is free to regard the others as 'insignificant' and their evaluations as irrelevant. However, there are limits to how often and how many he can define as significant or otherwise, since there are some people whose opinions the individual cannot forever ignore, even if their evaluations are painful. These opinions continue to have an impact on the conception of the self as they continue to raise doubts where there were none before. For example, the child may regard his teacher as an 'insignificant other', but that teacher's appraisals have raised doubts about his competence and this doubt may affect his self-concept long after he has left school. On other occasions the individual with a positive self-concept may be in constant contact with others who do not share with him the image he has of himself. They are a constant reminder of the low esteem in which he is held not only by them, but others whom he might not yet have encountered.

Many of the child's earliest and most important feelings and attitudes about himself are developed within the family. Proshansky and Newton (1973) argued that for the black child in America the development of positive feelings toward the self could often be difficult because of the general feeling of resentment, anger and hopelessness that surrounds the child. The parents may in fact use the child for purposes of their own ego enhancement. However, the fate of the black child, whether in America or in England, is not entirely a lost one because of the development of group pride among blacks generally. Even during the time when Proshansky and Newton made their review of the literature, significant numbers of black parents were able to provide a strong supportive atmosphere for their children which helped to foster attitudes of self-worth. As the Ausubels (1958) rightly observe: ' . . . the consequences of membership in a stigmatised minority group can be cushioned in part by a foundation of intrinsic self-esteem established in the home'.

There are, too, social class differences in family life and attitudes towards the dominant society among blacks in America. This of course has differential consequences for the self-concept of the black child. For the ghetto child, studies by Rainwater (1966), Pettigrew (1964), and Drake (1965) depict a somewhat defeatist attitude towards the self. Rainwater suggests that for most children growing up involves developing feelings of mastery and competence over the environment, but for the slum child, this process is reversed. Such a child learns what he cannot do, about the difficulties of achieving his aims and about the futility of even trying.

MEASURING SELF-CONCEPT IN YOUNG CHILDREN

First of all it is important to point out the differing ways in which the 'feeling about one's self' is expressed. The terms range from self, self-image, self-identity, self-concept, through to self-regard; with each investigator claiming that each concept envelops a greater part of the personality, or the total being. A good deal of work has been undertaken on measurement of self-concept of the adolescent, but very little attention has been paid to measuring the developing self-concept of the young child aged between 4 and 7 or 8.

Many techniques for measuring self-concept have not been based on observational techniques of interaction, which though ideally necessary, are difficult to carry out (Rist, 1970, 1975). Researchers interested in black identity and self-concept have tended to investigate this in 'black – white' terms; but other researchers such as Samuels (1973) show that social class is a more important variable than race in determining black self-concept. Coopersmith (1975) points out that in addition to a global self-concept, developing individuals form specific self-concepts that are more limited and particularistic. Thus in investigating or describing black self-concept there needs to be a distinction between the global and the more localised self-image. It is worth noting that it has not yet been empirically shown whether certain basic attributes such as sex, race or size are so salient that they affect all aspects of the self-concept. Investigators such as Clark and Clark (1950), Kardiner and Ovesey (1951), Noble (1973), argued that feelings about racial identity are an inherent part of the experience of every black American. On the other hand, Rosenberg and Simmons (1973) suggest that the black person is generally more acutely aware of his blackness when he is among whites than when he is among blacks. They show that the self-image of black boys in a segregated setting is in fact more favourable than that found among their white counterparts. Bagley *et al.*, (1979b) review British evidence which points to the same conclusion.

RELATIONSHIPS BETWEEN IDENTITY, SELF-CONCEPT AND SELF-ESTEEM

The terms 'identity', 'self-concept', 'self-image', 'self-evaluation', and 'self-worth' are often used in the literature, sometimes interchangeably, but sometimes to imply different aspects of personality and personal functioning in social situations. Often self-concept is used to imply both cognition (knowledge of self characteristics) and emotional appraisal of those self characteristics.

Identity is clearly related to self-concept and self-esteem. As we argued earlier, Identity has both cognitive (knowledge) and affective (evaluation) aspects, and these two aspects are related to self-concept and self-esteem respectively. We prefer to use the concept *global identity* as the highest-order concept, involving both self-concept and self-esteem in an integrated whole. Within global identity are the parts of the self, related to one another in particular configurations representing varying degrees of ego integration. The degree and type of integration at any point in time depend on the degree to which the various develop-mental crises in Erikson's scheme have been solved, and the degree to which the parallel needs outlined by Maslow (e.g. for love and belongingness, and for self-esteem) have been met. The term global identity is equivalent to the notion of global self-concept outlined by Coopersmith (1975).

The hypothetical relationships of identity, self-esteem and self-concept are sketched in Figure 3.1. Cognitive identity is composed of both cultural identity (usually possessed by ethnic minorities and which was stressed by Freud) and personal identity (stressed by William James). Ethnic minorities, of course, have both personal and cultural identity. Indeed, the problem for ethnic group members is to have, within a global identity, an adequate balance of personal and cultural

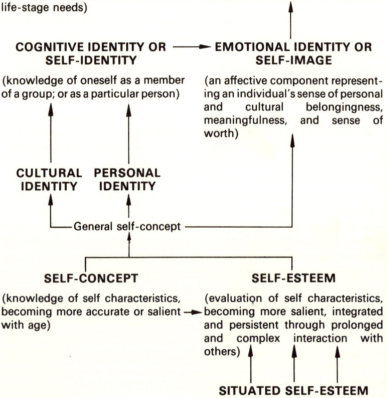

GLOBAL IDENTITY OR THE GLOBAL SELF-CONCEPT

(the parts of the self, related to one another in particular configurations representing varying degrees of ego integration, and differing degrees of success in the resolution of Erikson's life-crises, or fulfilment of Maslow's life-stage needs)

COGNITIVE IDENTITY OR ⟶ EMOTIONAL IDENTITY OR SELF-IDENTITY   SELF-IMAGE

(knowledge of oneself as a member of a group; or as a particular person)

(an affective component representing an individual's sense of personal and cultural belongingness, meaningfulness, and sense of worth)

CULTURAL   PERSONAL IDENTITY   IDENTITY

General self-concept

SELF-CONCEPT   SELF-ESTEEM

(knowledge of self characteristics, becoming more accurate or salient ⟶ with age)

(evaluation of self characteristics, becoming more salient, integrated and persistent through prolonged and complex interaction with others)

SITUATED SELF-ESTEEM

(evaluation of the self in various situations)

FIGURE 3.1   Relationships of identity and aspects of the self

identity, combined with positive evaluation of those aspects of identity, in combination again with a degree of mastery over environment, and self-actualisation.

We have used the term 'general self concept' as a lower-level concept which refers to knowledge of one's self characteristics as seen by others, and acceptance of the evaluations placed on those self characteristics by other people with whom one interacts. Hewitt (1976) distinguishes between situations (current interactions) and biographies (the sum total of internalised evaluations of the self) which make up the individual's current self-appraisal, self-worth, or self-esteem. Self-esteem is often dependent on the situation in which the individual finds himself, but there is also evidence to show that the older an individual gets, the more identity stages he has passed, the more complex his biography and the range of others he has interacted with, the more persistent a particular style of self-evaluation will be. It is important to stress that each individual has a unique identity, a unique configuration of knowledge about self, and evaluation of self characteristics based on interaction with others (a unique set of significant others some of whom he has chosen and some of whom he has had imposed upon him). He is unique, too, in the way in which he has solved his successive identity choices at various stages of development. This uniqueness of identity is close to the uniqueness of each human personality stressed by Allport (1968). According to Allport, personality is a consciously developing, goal-oriented insightful individuality that changes and develops at various stages of one's life. This concept is very similar to that of global identity or global self-concept. Allport (1968) illustrates this well in his discussion of the individual psychological development of William James. Allport argued that all psychology should ultimately come back to the study of the unique individuals in what he described as the morphogenic study of personality and persons. The richest and most important source of data about a person, Allport suggests, is that individual's own self-knowledge. He is here clearly referring to the global identity or personality of the individual, and he notes that in fact many studies of 'self-concept' are based on general and lower dimensions of personality (1968, p. 83).

There is an interesting analogy between the different types of 'intelligence', and various levels of identity and self-esteem. Intelligence A is supposed to refer to the 'true' but probably unmeasurable intelligence of a person; intelligence B is supposed to be the intelligence that various psychometric tests may measure; and intelligence C is the effective intelligence the individual uses in solving everyday problems

(Vernon, 1969). Global identity is analogous to 'intelligence A', an important higher-order concept which directly influences many other aspects of personal functioning, but is extremely difficult to measure in direct or global terms. Analogously to 'Intelligence B', general self-concept is the operational aspect of personal identity, and is measured in a variety of direct and indirect ways. Levels of self-esteem are also inferred in a variety of ways, and from a variety of types of interaction or of descriptions of self characteristics.

Perhaps a person's global identity can be measured by knowing how he construes himself and the world in various complex ways. Attempts have been made to measure these 'personal constructs' (Kelly, 1955; Bannister and Fransella, 1971) and it is noteworthy that Hauser (1971) and Weinreich (1979) have used adaptations of personal construct methodology to measure global identity. Weinreich has shown that level of self-esteem is part of a more complex identity structure, and in some black adolescents in Britain a high level of self-esteem is not matched by other aspects of identity integration.

It is important to stress that identity is a developmental concept. Identity and identity problems change as the individual gets older and experiences 'crises' associated with biological, social and role changes. For the young child of 3, the cognitive idea of himself as separate from others has emerged; he is learning, too, how he differs from others. The evidence indicates that knowledge of one's ethnic status is a salient trait which develops early. Such knowledge of ethnic or radical status is particularly marked in young children in minority groups, such as blacks in America. The child learns through a variety of interactions with others how to evaluate his self characteristics (which those same interactions have taught him are important or salient). For the young child, evaluations of self characteristics are relatively uncrystallised and are highly dependent on the situation in which he finds himself. Thus findings from doll studies, showing that young children negatively evaluate figures like themselves and effectively devalue their self characteristics, may be expressing attitudes which reflect a particular situation, rather than an embedded characteristic of the self. Negative feelings towards one's ethnic characteristics as a young child do not necessarily predict poor self-esteem in later years. They do, however, imply problems for the developing identity, for previous negative views of the self have to be resolved and incorporated with a new identity. It is the strength of that identity resolution, not the actual level of self-esteem, which is of overriding importance in the adolescent years and beyond.

Hewitt (1976), in trying to integrate the concepts of self and identity, develops a complex, 12-variable model (p. 81) in which he distinguishes between (1) 'situated self' (the self reacting in particular situations) and (2) 'biographical self' (the self as the sum total of previous interactions). The person is an object both to (3) himself, and to (4) others. Within each of four cells created by the interaction of the four aspects of the self there is a hierarchy of identity, self-image and self-esteem. This hierarchy is quite similar to the one we have developed in Figure 3.1, but certainly should not be regarded as definitive in any way. Indeed, a reading of Hewitt, who relies strongly on George Mead's theory of symbolic interaction, suggests that the matter is very complex. Hewitt poses the following set of questions:

> The person is thus a complex reality – an enduring object as well as one constituted from moment to moment, an object of his own acts and those of others, an object involved in social relationships, with attributed characteristics and with a sense of worth. To introduce order into this reality, we must pay attention particularly to the relationships between the situated and biographical aspects of the person. How are situated self-esteem, self-image, and identity related to situated social identity, situated images, and situated esteem? How does esteem influence situated self-esteem, and self-esteem? (Hewitt, 1976, p. 82).

The answers to these questions are not known; and indeed, they may not even be relevant questions. Hewitt's model may be unduly scholastic. What we can conclude with confidence is that self-esteem is crucially important in individual functioning, and that global identity is an overriding concept in which self-esteem is subsumed.

4 Ethnic Identification, Preference and Sociometric Choice[1]

A. G. DAVEY

INTRODUCTION

The work reported in this chapter forms part of a more comprehensive investigation[2] into the development of children's ethnic attitudes. The main study was designed to investigate the manifestations of racial awareness in young children at three levels: the perception of differences, the criteria employed to form person categories, and their attitudes towards members of other ethnic groups. In addition, a test of cognitive ability was included in the battery and a sociometric study was made of the children's friendship patterns. The parents of all the children were interviewed by own-race interviewers.

The present chapter is principally concerned with that part of the study which investigated the perception of differences. However, since some investigations have found that children exhibit more prejudice in projective tests than in reality-based situations (Radke *et al.*, 1950; Goodman, 1964) and that a lack of correspondence exists between doll choice and friendship patterns (Hraba and Grant, 1970) a comparison is included between the children's ethnic preferences and their sociometric choices.

METHODS

THE SAMPLE

Equal numbers of children at ages, 7, 8, 9 and 10+ were drawn from sixteen primary schools – eight in London and eight in industrial

Yorkshire. 256 children were white, 128 were of West Indian parentage and 128 were of Asian parentage.

A factorial design was adopted, as this has the advantage of sampling a wide range of possible relationships which can be used repeatedly in different combinations. In each region, north and south, two of the schools had 50 per cent, or more, Asian children; two had 50 per cent, or more, West Indian children; two had 20 per cent, or less, Asian children; and two had 20 per cent, or less West Indian children. In each school, a white child was paired by age and sex with an Asian or West Indian child so that each school unit was composed of: 2 races × 2 sexes × 4 ages × 2 children = 32. The total sample, therefore, consisted of:

2 regions × 2 densities × 4 schools × 32 children = 512.

MATERIALS AND PROCEDURE

For both the identification and preference tests professionally produced, full-length photographs of primary-school children, in approximately the middle of the age-range of the subjects, were used. The photographed children were identically dressed, the boys in jeans and sweaters, the girls in jumpers and skirts, in order to minimise the selection of irrelevant criterial cues. Black and white half-plate prints were chosen in preference to coloured photographs since skin shade could be a critical factor for West Indian children, and it was thought that good quality monochrome would allow them to freely project their preferred skin shade.

The children were seen individually in a quiet room in their school on two occasions, separated by some 4–6 weeks. An atmosphere of informality was aimed at and, in order to maintain interest, a procedure was devised, for the study as a whole, whereby the sessions were kept short (between 30 and 40 minutes) and the child was asked to participate in a number of different activities during each session.

The identification test was carried out during the first visit. The children were presented with three photographs of children of the same sex as themselves, one for each ethnic group, and asked: Which one looks most like you?

For the preference test, presented during a subsequent visit, the children were shown the same photographs, but this time the tester asked: If you could choose, which one would you most like to be?

In the sociometric test, the children were asked:

(1) Who are the two children you would most like to sit next to in this class?

(2) Who are the two children in the school you would most like to play with in the playground?
(3) Who are the two children in the school you would most like to invite home?

The sociometric item involved 3953 children, yielding some 23,718 individual pieces of data, since all the children in a sample child's class were asked the same three questions.

The full sociometric study will be reported elsewhere, but for the purposes of the comparison between ethnic preference and sociometric choice only the results from the schools in the high-density portion of the sample were used, where the ethnic ratio was approximately 50 : 50. This was done in order to give every ethnic group an equal opportunity of having exclusively own-race friends. In the Hraba and Grant study (1970), the proportion of black children in some of the schools was so low that it would not always have been possible for a child, who preferred black friends, to have behaved consistently with his choice on the projective test.

One southern, low-density Asian school did not complete the preference test, reducing the sample size for this test to 480. Otherwise, missing data due to absenteeism or removals is less than 3 per cent. Reduced *N*s, where employed, are clearly indicated.

RESULTS

IDENTIFICATION

A comparison of the proportion of children from each ethnic group who correctly identified with the appropriate photograph (Table 4.1), provides little support for the phenomenon of self-rejection amongst minority group children. If the West Indian and Asian results are pooled then, statistically, it can be said that it is no more probable that a black child will say that he looks like a white child than it is that a white child will say that he looks like a black child.

An interesting exception to the overall trend is provided by the white girls who are not only more likely than white boys to identify with an out-group photograph ($\chi^2 = 15.26$, 1 d.f., $p < 0.001$), but also more likely than West Indian girls to make an out-group response ($\chi^2 = 13.47$; 1 d.f.; $p < 0.001$). Their remarks during the test suggested that they ignored pigmentation and picked out similarities in small details of

TABLE 4.1 Percentage of children at each of four age levels making the correct response on the self-identification test

Race and sex of subjects
(correct response as percentage of group)

Age	White			West Indian			Asian			Total correct
	Boy	Girl	All	Boy	Girl	All	Boy	Girl	All	
7+	90.6	75	82.8	75	100	87.5	87.5	68.8	78.1	82.8
8+	93.8	62.5	78.1	93.8	100	96.9	93.8	75	84.4	84.4
9+	87.5	75	81.3	87.5	87.5	87.5	93.8	81.3	87.5	84.4
10+	93.8	78.1	85.9	100	93.8	96.9	93.8	81.3	87.5	89.1
TOTAL CORRECT	91.4	72.5	82	89.1	95.3	92.2	92.2	76.6	84.4	85.2
TOTAL INCORRECT	8.6	27.5	18	10.9	4.7	7.8	7.8	23.4	15.6	14.8
N =	128	128	256	64	64	128	64	64	128	512

hairstyle and dress – despite the fact that all the girls in the photographs wore identical clothing!

No consistent trend towards a stronger out-group orientation was found amongst either West Indian or Asian children in schools where they constituted only a small minority. The only reliable difference between the high- and low-density schools was provided by the Asian children. Significantly more Asian children in schools where the concentration of Asians was small, than in those where it was 50 per cent or more, chose their own-group photograph ($\chi^2 = 5.92$; 1 d.f.; $p < 0.025$).

Comparisons between schools in the north and the south also yielded significant differences for the Asian children but not for the other two groups. The Asians in the London schools made more own-group choices than those in Yorkshire ($\chi^2 = 11.6$; 1 d.f.; $p < 0.001$), but again, the girls were the principal contributors to the difference ($\chi^2 = 10.4$; 1 d.f.; $p < 0.005$), with the boys failing to approach the conventional significance level.

PREFERENCE

The results from the Self-preference test (Table 4.2) present a very different picture. The responses of both the West Indian and Asian children differ markedly from those of the white group. Whereas some 86 per cent of the white children preferred their own group, less than half the West Indian and Asian children made own-race choices ($p < 0.001$ for both differences).

Taken as a whole, the choices of the small proportion of white children, who preferred another group to their own, marginally favoured the Asians. This predilection was stronger for girls than boys, although none of the differences in the distribution of choices between West Indians and Asians was significant.

The pattern of the white children's preferences was remarkably consistent. The magnitude of their own-race preference was relatively unaffected either by the ethnicity of the group with which they were in contact or by the size of the group, relative to their own, in a particular school.

The out-group preferences of the two minority groups indicate that they have little desire to be like each other. Only 4 per cent of the Asian children preferred the West Indian photograph, and less than 5 per cent of the West Indians chose that of the Asian child. Overwhelmingly, their preference was for the picture of the white boy or girl.

Neither the size of the concentration of a particular group in a school,

TABLE 4.2 Percentage of children at each of four age levels making the own-race response on the self-preference test

Race and sex of subjects
(own-race responses as percentage of group)

Age	White			West Indian			Asian			Total
	Boy	Girl	All	Boy	Girl	All	Boy	Girl	All	
7+	93.3	76.7	85	37.5	37.5	37.5	42.9	35.7	39.3	61.7
8+	86.7	80	83.3	50	50	50	64.3	28.6	46.4	65.8
9+	83.3	90	86.6	37.5	50	43.8	71.4	21.4	46.4	65.8
10+	96.7	83.3	90	68.8	62.5	65.6	57.1	42.9	50	74.2
TOTAL	90	82.5	86.3	48.4	50	49.2	58.9	32.1	45.5	66.9
TOTAL OF OTHER RACE RESPONSES	8.3	15	11.6	46.9	50	48.5	37.5	62.5	50	30.4
MISSING DATA	1.7	2.5	2.1	4.7	0	2.3	3.6	5.4	4.5	2.7
N =	120	120	240	64	64	128	56	56	112	480

nor its location, north or south, appreciably affects the general pattern of ethnic preference. However, more West Indian girls in the high-density West Indian schools than in schools with a low concentration of West Indian children, would prefer to be white ($\chi^2 = 6.4$; 1 d.f.; $p < 0.02$), and more Asian children in the northern schools than the southern schools chose the white photograph ($\chi^2 = 5.33$; 1 d.f.; $p < 0.025$).

The results do, however, suggest that, for all groups, age brings a greater acceptance of one's own ethnicity, but only the difference between the 7- and 10-year-old West Indian boys is reliable ($\chi^2 = 8.16$; 1 d.f.; $p < 0.01$).

Girls, in general, tend to be more out-group-oriented than boys ($\chi^2 = 5.6$; 1 d.f.; $p < 0.02$), but within each ethnic group the difference between boys and girls only reaches significance for the Asians ($\chi^2 = 8.16$; 1 d.f.; $p < 0.005$).

An analysis was made of the West Indian children's preferences according to their skin shade. The light-skinned children, in contrast to the dark-skinned, made fewer own-race choices, but the difference just fails to reach the 5 per cent level of significance ($\chi^2 = 3.81$; 1 d.f.; $p < 0.10$).

WHY DO IDENTIFICATION RESULTS DIFFER FROM PREFERENCES?

As inter-group attitudes have become more intransigent there is increasing resistance in the minority communities to judging themselves by white values. Pressure from minority group leaders, churches, mosques and Saturday schools has encouraged children to develop a pride in their own culture which is reflected in identification results.

But self-pride and self-enhancement can only be achieved by comparison with the dominant group. This leads to a sharper perception of the dominant group's favourable status and the unequal competition in living standards, job opportunities, etc. This is reflected in the feelings which are expressed in the preference group scores. It is in this crevice between a heightened sense of personal worth and the sharpened perception of relative status that the seeds of inter-group hostility germinate.

PHOTO-PREFERENCE AND FRIENDSHIP

In order to explore the relationship between a preference test choice and a choice made from a known group, a comparison was made between the preference test results for those children who consistently chose own-race friends on the sociometric items, with the preference test choices of those children who had friends in ethnic groups other than their own, the hypothesis being that children who are ethnically exclusive in their friendship patterns are less likely to make other-group choices on the preference test.

It appears that in schools where the ethnic mix is such as to allow children a more or less equal opportunity of choosing own-race friends or other-race friends, only a minority wish to confine their friendships exclusively to members of their own group. Overall, 66.5 per cent ($N = 238$) prefer to have some other-group friends. This sentiment is most pronounced among the West Indian children (78.5 per cent, $N = 59$) and least often expressed by the Asians (55.4 per cent, $N = 58$) with the white children falling between the two (63.6 per cent, $N = 121$). Moreover, the fact that some 34 per cent of the children appeared to be exclusive in their friendship patterns does not necessarily mean that they had no other-race friends. It may merely mean that these friends were not ranked high enough to be named amongst the top two on any of the three criteria with which the children were presented.

However, those children who named no other-race friends were more likely to have chosen their own race on the preference test ($\chi^2 = 5.21$; 1 d.f.; $p < 0.025$). Considered independently, each of the ethnic groups exhibits the same trend, but the difference only reaches the 5 per cent level of significance with the white children.

Contrary to the findings of Hraba and Grant (1970), there is a positive relationship between the preferences expressed in the photo-choice situation and desired friendship. The relationship is a weak one. It would be disturbing if it were not so. It seems likely, as Teplin (1977) suggests, that when children choose between photographs of unknown individuals the choices will reflect their ethnic stereotypes, since only visual cues are available. In contrast, when a child chooses from a known group, as in the sociometric test, his choice is not necessarily restricted by ethnic considerations since additional sources of information, relevant to potential friendship, are open to him. A close relationship between imaginary photo-choice and choice in a real-life situation would imply that the children's stereotypes were already so inflexible that the children were no longer amenable to the discovery of characteristics which conflicted with their ethnic expectations.

DISCUSSION OF IMPLICATIONS FOR EDUCATION

Although our sociometric data, like that of Jelinek and Brittan (1975) shows that friendship is markedly ethnocentric, the fact that only a minority of children at this age confine their friendships exclusively to their own group suggests that this trend towards ethnocentricity is not irreversible.

The beliefs and practices of teachers are of crucial importance if this is to be achieved. It is not simply a matter of adjusting teaching techniques and curricula to meet the needs of children from different cultures, but of helping all children to understand those with whom they share their lives and enabling them to respond to the diversity of human groups without hostility or distrust.

The first step must be to help teachers, and teachers in training, to discover their own habitual ways of thinking about such social categories as race, sex, ethnicity and social class. This can be a delicate business.

A growing awareness that our concepts of other groups contain a large proportion of error can lead to the over-compensating assumption that all stereotypes of group differences are false, and by implication, that all groups are similar. We perceive the difference attributed to the out-group as the cause of the hostile attitudes and feel that if it were not for these imagined differences, the out-group would be loved.

But any form of programme designed to prepare children for a multiracial society which overtly or implicitly denies the existence of group differences could be as disastrous as it would be mistaken. Educationalists have always been too co-operative in processing children into categories which validate society's current notions of equivalence – academic children, technical children and the rest – but what should interest educators is not how much children are alike, but how much they differ.

To treat all children as if they were alike is perhaps the greatest of educational injustices. The task of the educator in a multiracial society should be conceived as one of bringing about an adjustment to diversity and social change rather than the elimination of difference.

If the educational system strove for the ideal of treating each person as an individual, the schools would not talk of a 'race problem'. There would, of course, be problems associated with poverty, overcrowding, defective language skills, retarded conceptual development and academic disenchantment, but these are problems in schools where no black or brown child has yet been seen. The truth of the matter is that the newcomers have thrown into sharp relief the fact that a sizeable proportion of the indigenous population has not been too well served by our educational system. Too many of them suffer from culturally induced backwardness, have their occupational aspirations tailored to fit the demands of the market, and live in decaying ghettos.

One of the long-term benefits of multi-racial schools could be to persuade us to re-examine the validity of our traditional courses, teaching methods and assessment procedures.

This means, I think, that we must scrutinise the way we group children together for different purposes, the manner in which we negotiate with them and the extent to which we are prepared to share authority with them. Purging the textbooks of black stereotypes, boosting the black child in our teaching materials and telling improving stories about children of other lands will not have the slightest effect on how children treat each other – if teachers make rules without explanation, if they command needlessly and assume their authority is established by convention. We learn to respect each other's individuality not by hearing about tolerance, or reading about tolerence, or even by discussing tolerence, but by being tolerated by others and being tolerant in return. In Trager and Yarrow's (1952) telling phrase – 'We learn that we live.'

Schools, of course, respond to society, and they cannot by themselves bring about a social reformation. Like Jencks and his colleagues at Harvard, I do not believe that schools can narrow the inequalities in society. To do that we must operate on society directly. I do believe, however, that if teachers recognised every child's need as equally legitimate, they would not only make schools more egalitarian, but make an immediate contribution to each child's well-being, and *that* is an end in itself.

NOTES

1. Paper presented at the Annual Conference of the British Psychological Society (Education Section) Conference, Oxford, September 1979.
2. The Project, financed by the SSRC (Social Science Research Council) was undertaken in collaboration with P. Mullin, V. Norburn, and I. Pushkin.

5 Ethnicity and Cultural Competence: Aspects of Interaction in Multiracial Classrooms[1]

GEOFFREY DRIVER

The comparison in methodology between those who develop and utilise test instruments to establish and to quantify certain theoretical constructs, and those who simply observe and describe behaviour by means of an internally consistent account, involves coming to grips with some rather basic philosophical and aesthetic differences. Such differences Kuhn (1962) associates with pre-paradigmatic and post-paradigmatic sciencing; in this chapter they relate to the ethnographer and the researcher who uses tests and questionnaires. Yet even if the gulf between the two sides is wide and common understandings and approaches few, there are still some areas where discussion useful to both can be developed. This seems to apply to notions of identity and self-esteem.

In this chapter the theoretical significance of these terms as part of a general theory of culture is discussed from the standpoint of anthropology. Self-esteem and identity, essentially psychological constructs, would appear to offer useful insights even when there are differences over method between researchers of the two disciplines, psychological testing and ethnography. It is argued here that self-esteem and identity, along with intelligence, are important aspects of a more general theory of culture and cognition relevant to our understanding of ethnic diversity. Secondly it is suggested that the range of attitudes and behaviours associated with self-esteem and identity are often projected quite differently in different social contexts, prompting the question as to whether it is not the generalised constructs but situational expressions of them (in the home, among peers, in the classroom, etc.) which can tell us the most about the meaning of subjects' behaviour. In order to develop these twin themes, it is necessary first to review the literature associated with identity and self-esteem, particularly as related to Black children in British and American schools.

SELF-ESTEEM AND IDENTITY

Various studies have indicated that self-concept is significantly related to academic achievement for 'disadvantaged' as well as other pupils (Coleman, 1966; Coard, 1971; Milner, 1975 and others). Most of these writers focus on self-concept, or self-esteem, as a sense of personal worth; they offer much less information on identity (i.e. an individual's feeling of being associated with other individuals or groups) though such writers as Milner (1975) and Weinreich (1979) speak of ethnic identity. They do so, however, without describing the social structures which would give cogence to such a term; so much so that one must question whether it would not be better for them to use the term 'ethnicity'.

Even if the term 'identity' is set on one side, readers will be aware that there have been a series of overlapping terms used to describe an individual's awareness, valuation and knowledge of his own competence and acceptability. As well as self-esteem, self-image, sense of personal worth and self-perception are among several other terms for which constructs have been developed to indicate the idea of self-concept. Many American studies cite theories of self and personality associated with the social philosophy of G. H. Mead; others link their theory with such writers as R. D. Laing.

By the early 1970s, self-concept was frequently put forward as a factor in school achievement. Particularly in the United States, it became an essential part of special programmes for the so-called 'disadvantaged' to include scope for the development of self-esteem. But research results in the area of self-concept need to be treated with caution for several reasons. Firstly a variety of instruments have been used and many of them lack evidence of reliability and validity. Secondly there is little evidence that they are measuring the same construct; as a result they cannot be viewed as equivalent measures. Instruments take a variety of forms: rating scales (e.g. McDaniel, 1967), semantic differentials (e.g. Caliguri, 1966), and doll and picture identification tests (e.g. Milner, 1975; Coard, 1971). In some cases self-assessment measures are used, while in others they are not. It seems therefore reasonable to suppose that self-esteem is not a unitary construct. No studies seem to have been done to establish construct validity (by using different instruments on the same population). It is my thesis that self-esteem should be conceived as a selection of perceived attitudes which an individual may display towards, for example, his (or her) physical appearance, friends, family, etc. This multidimensional position is borne out by the literature (see Andrews, 1970).

Related to this multidimensional view is the evidence that self-esteem is a context-dependent variable. Caplin (1968) found a significant difference between children in integrated and segregated settings with respect to their school-related self-concept, yet this difference did not carry over into their scores for perceived self-esteem in more generalised situations. Miller and Woock (1970) have remarked on this discontinuity in relation to school success and a generalised self-concept. They state:

> What seems to be involved . . . is a distinction between a *general* self-concept – in which disadvantaged youngsters may come off reasonably well – and a *self-concept of achievement* that is self-measured against the standards and achievements of the school as a middle class institution.

But even if it is accepted that the self-concept related to school achievement is to be distinguished from the more generalised self-concept (though it would appear that the latter is more difficult to determine in existential terms) there is still the problem of validity and reliability related to the different instruments used. This may help to account for the different results reported. Deutsch (1960) and Henton (1964) both reported that white American junior high-school students had a higher measure of self-esteem than their black counterparts. Subsequently Carpenter and Busse (1969), Gibby and Gabler (1967) and McDaniel (1967) reported no such difference. Later Zirkel and Moses (1971) indicated that the black American children in their study exhibited higher self-esteem than the white American children with whom they were compared.

Given the variation in the test instruments used it is perhaps also useful to inquire into the internal detail of one or other of these studies for more specific information related to specific sub-populations and the instruments themselves. Here it appears that, even though often there are no overall differences between the self-esteem of different ethnic categories, there are ethnic differences related to the sex, age and level of ability of subjects. For example Carpenter and Busse show that their black boys had a significantly higher self-esteem than their black girls. Gibby and Gabler, also studying Amercian white and black schoolchildren, indicated that on the one hand they found no significant differences in self-esteem between black and white boys and girls of high ability, sex and ethnicity did relate to self-esteem among their less able subjects.

A further reason for caution in the interpretation of self-esteem scores lies with the fact that subjects are relied upon to give honest answers about themselves. Long (1969) reported that some unexpectedly high self-esteem scores were registered by so-called 'disadvantaged' subjects allegedly because of the desirability of presenting a certain 'response set'. DeBlaissie and Healy (1970) found that their black American subjects were often defensive and tried to present favourable images of themselves. In contrast, Coopersmith (1967) maintained that the matter of response sets and defensive postures appears more critical in theory than in fact. With such a range of opinion, there is surely adequate scope for scepticism in interpreting the results obtained simply on the basis of what subjects choose to say about themselves.

While this chapter has concentrated on American research in coming to these conclusions, similar comments have recently been made by Bagley *et al.*, (1979c) with regard to the findings of various studies of self-concept carried out on English and West Indian children in Britain. Against this background of theoretical and methodological problems there seems adequate justification to assume that within any general population of boys and girls in school, whether in England or America, differences in self-esteem do not account directly for differences in school achievement (West and Fish, 1974). However as my own research in a West Midlands secondary school showed (Driver, 1977a), such differences do begin to appear significant when self-esteem scores for pupils of different ethnic affiliations take into account also their sex, academic stream and age; and even more so when self-esteem sub-scores linked with specific social arenas are used. Even when such relations are confirmed, the test instrument approach leaves researchers to speculate as to how the significant trends come about in fact. The answers given by a set of individuals to a series of externally devised questions continue to offer a range of possible and even contradictory explanations unless they are linked to a careful analysis of the structures and dynamics which individual subjects experience in different arenas of their social lives.

IDENTITY AND CULTURAL COMPETENCE

In ethnomethodological inquiry, much of the research interest centres on describing and analysing the worlds of meaning which appear to underlie observed behaviours and expressed attitudes. Human subjects are not only self-aware, but their social activity is likely to reveal a complex set of negotiated agreements in which meaning and identity are bound to be key elements. It is what an individual understands about himself and about his physical and social environment which can lead him to feel that he is able to act purposefully within it. As he feels more sure of his physical and social skills, as goals are established, as the individual feels he is developing a more shrewd knowledge of the way the world works, as relationships prove themselves, an individual may be more sure of his present status and more determined about his future plans. This will almost certainly involve new social alliances and conflicts for the individual concerned; and around him, every other individual is likely to be engaged, each on their own subjective terms, on a similar exercise, for the cultural process here described is a continuous one. Furthermore the process of reconnoitring, stratagem-development and negotiation is taken up anew as individuals move from one social situation to another in the course of everyday life. In modern urban society it may involve one individual during one short period in dealing with the family over breakfast, the neighbours on the street, the newsagent and his customers, the people in the bus queue, meeting the staff and other current clients of the local dental-school clinic, etc. Each social situation has its repertoire of socially relevant information, some of it highly specific and non-transferrable so that it cannot readily be understood by an 'outside' observer.

Obviously some situations, even entire rounds of life involving whole communities of people, require interpretation if they are to be seen as significant by non-participants. This has traditionally been the role of anthropologists: to interpret the exotic. However not all such exoticism is to be sought in remote, primitive tribes. The same anthropological methods, viewing all social relations as exotic, offers insight into the realm of negotiated meaning involved, the self-confidence which individuals demonstrate in dealing with others, and the shared identity which may be expressed in these relationships. Moreover where the learned repertoires of information and skills for dealing with others in one or more situations are not synonymous, as when people from different lands and ways of life relate with one another, the subtlety of understanding and the complexity of negotiation taking place in even the most routine activities of daily life are emphasised by the real difficulties which individuals demonstrate through their behaviours.

The capacity to weigh up one's choices and chances in any one of a series of 'social establishments' (Goffman, 1959), or for an individual to 'construe' (Kelly, 1963) subjective experience and then devise objectives and behaviour for the developing situation in which one or more others are similarly engaged, has been called 'cultural competence' (Driver, 1977a). It springs from the view of culture as negotiation about meanings taking place between individuals. Such a view has been articulated by several writers, anthropologists and psychologists, including Wallace (1961), Goodenough (1963, 1970), Spradley (1970) and Crissman (1975). These writers argue that a culturally competent individual is able to interpret and predict the responses which others will make to him to such an extent that he feels able to devise and develop his own interests through his dealings with them.

It is this competence, exercised in a series of social establishments, which seems to be connected in some definite way with the notion of self-esteem. However, since a positive sense of one's own ability to deal successfully with others is likely to arise out of specific situations, even specific incidents, then it is likely that individual feelings of self-esteem are related primarily to particular areas of an individual's experience (if not to even more limited sequences and events in which, on his own terms, he managed to carry himself off most successfully in negotiating with others).

The writer's own research, which was primarily an ethnographic study, led him to believe that West Indian boys and girls, adolescents attending a secondary school in a multiracial area in the Midlands, exibited different feelings of self-confidence about their dealings with others in different areas of their lives – with family, with friends and with teachers. In this, the two sexes seemed to differ from one another, and from non-West Indian boys and girls, in their general trends.

Later the intuition, first considered during fieldwork, was substantiated to some extent, given the limitations of the instrument, by the results of a self-esteem questionnaire administered to subjects. The data from the instrument, which was Coopersmith's Self-Esteem Inventory, when examined with respect to different categories of questions within the questionnaire as a whole, produced a number of significantly different statistics for questions dealing with parents, peers and teachers. Also the pattern of those differences varied for different sub-sets of the pupil studies – according to whether they were boys or girls, and whether they were English, West Indian, South Asian or of some other ethnic affiliation.

Table 5.1, dealing with the responses of 107 English and West Indian boys and girls aged 14+ and attending the multiracial school in the West Midlands, gives the means percentage of responses indicating positive self-esteem to all 58 items in a questionnaire, and to selected items dealing specifically with relations with teachers (6 questions) parents (8 questions) and peers (6 questions) within the questionnaire. The questionnaire used was a slightly modified version of Coopersmith's Self-Esteem Inventory, changes only being made to meet requirements of English language-usage in Britain as opposed to the US – for which it was originally devised. Since Coopersmith offered no pre-set interpret- ations of questions – responses from subjects, nor did he propose his own pre-set categories of questions within the instrument; such interpretations and categories were obtained by reference to the opinion of the School Counsellor at the school in question.

These results, while they show no significant differences between pupil categories in over-all terms, are however important when considered in terms of the sub-scores for each pupil category, and between pupil categories in the case of the 'school' sub-score. An analysis of variance showed that there was a difference significant at the 0.01 level of the sub- scores for each pupil category. In the other direction, the means of 'school' sub-scores between pupil categories were shown to be signifi- cantly different at the 0.05 level, though this was not so with the sub- scores for self-esteem with parents and peers.

In general, however, these patterns of responses for different social arenas of the lives of individual subjects give significant importance to variations due to the ethnicity and sex of subjects. They would, it seems, imply that for these subjects at this age and in given social contexts gender is far more influential than skin colour in establishing an individual's positive or negative self-esteem. These results, incidentally, are plainly at variance with Coopersmith's own findings. Coopersmith, dealing with a slightly younger age-group in North America, found no significant patterns in the sub-scores for different sets of questions within his Self-Esteem Inventory. Moreover, in accord with the work of Carpenter and Busse (1969) and of Gibby and Gabler (1967), the scores (and sub-scores) varied according to the level of ability and achievement in the school of the boys and girls in the fourth year of the writer's West Midlands school (Driver, 1977a, 1977b). Of course, the findings here also underline the different significance of gender for different ethnic communities for, despite the necessary scepticism about the self-esteem

TABLE 5.1 Means (and standard deviations) for positive responses to 58 self-esteem questions by 107 English and West Indian boys and girls aged 14+ at a West Midlands school

Category	Percentage over-all self-esteem (58 questions)	Percentage 'school' sub-score	Percentage 'parent' sub-score	Percentage 'peer' sub-score
All pupils (N = 107)	31.61 (±7.82)	49.45 (±23.76)	60.69 (±26.11)	70.17 (±20.63)
West Indian boys (N = 30)	32.67 (±6.58)	53.20 (±24.88)	57.47 (±26.01)	74.23 (±18.65)
English boys (N = 24)	34.79 (±5.38)	45.08 (±23.71)	63.96 (±23.86)	71.08 (±18.30)
West Indian girls (N = 31)	30.35 (±8.96)	54.26 (±24.98)	60.74 (±25.91)	72.61 (±21.47)
English girls (N = 22)	28.77 (±9.14)	34.68 (±17.57)	62.64 (±17.57)	70.55 (±26.94)

SOURCE: Driver, 1977a.

instrument, it confirms the striking difference in approach to school-work between English girls and West Indian girls which were noted ethnographically and subsequently portrayed in the 16 + results obtained by those pupils.

Clearly the questionnaire data served a useful function in helping to verify field observations. For its part, the ethnography was able to suggest appropriate ways in which questionnaire data could usefully be broken down, by referring to substantive characteristics of subjects in their observed social activities and relationships, and not simply to statistical formulae and precedent. The complementarity of the two approaches when data are considered in situation-specific terms, would tend to press home the point that self-esteem, self-concept and identity – maybe also intelligence – should not be taken so much as a generalised factor applicable to specific situations, but rather as a capacity (or capacities) generated in part at least by those specific situations, as well as by subjects who exercise some degree of self-awareness and autonomy in their behaviours.

CONCLUSION

There are one or two brief but important conclusions to be drawn from this point of view. First, it appears that there are good grounds to be wary of acknowledging the legitimacy of any generalised notion of self-esteem. As with intelligence testing the results are valid only for individuals doing a particular 'test' in particular circumstances. Hence there is a need to recognise the limitations in the data to be obtained solely by the use of particular self-esteem instruments on subjects of different ethnic affiliations. The evidence produced by descriptive accounts of social interaction would suggest that trends in self-esteem cannot disregard the specific social contexts and role-involvements to which they refer in the experience of different subjects – hence the cultural influence of socialisation as boys and girls grow up in different ethnic contexts and social environments. It would also suggest that each individual will self-consciously filter and focus the presentation he or she makes of self in everyday life, and that this also affects substantially what configurations of responses are made to self-esteem question-naires. These contextual elements must, I believe, be taken into account in interpreting self-esteem responses and would seem to make for great uncertainty and variability in making any generalised findings with regard to large populations of one age-group, sex or ethnic category (as the reported research results indicate).

Following from this, it is apparent that the use of such instruments to provide evidence of self-esteem in particular contexts which are already observed and documented by the researcher, offers a complementary methodological approach to field ethnography. For its part, the ethnography orients the investigator to the significance of the self-esteem data obtained from an instrument such as Coopersmith's. The mutual value of the two approaches in studying the social experiences of relatively small-scale populations is not, I believe, a restriction upon the self-esteem questionnaire approach, but the result of a more thorough and effective appraisal of its interpretive capability. Greater sensitivity to the significance of self-esteem as a factor of subjective attitudes in specific social situations can only help to understand better the people who are involved and how they seek to act competently and purposefully from their own points of view. In partnership with ethnography this can surely be achieved.

NOTE

1. Paper presented to the Annual Conference of the British Psychological Society, Oxford, September, 1979.

Part III
Studies of Disadvantage and Achievement

6 The Problems of Vocational Adaptation of 'Asian' Adolescents in Britain: Some Theoretical and Methodological Issues

GAJENDRA K. VERMA

INTRODUCTION

In recent years considerable attention has been focused on the problems of minority ethnic groups in Britain, especially on those who have settled in this country in the last 20 years. Interest in these problems is increasing because of the various educational and social issues which concern both the 'immigrant' communities and the 'native' population.

The debate concerning education of immigrants and children of immigrants has been centred around the problems of race relations, language, disadvantage and achievement. This debate concerning the process of schooling seems to me to be too restrictive. It assumes that equality of opportunity is an easily realised goal, and ignores the fact that the role of education is also a system of differentiation and classification of the working force in industrial society. The recent studies of Halsey and Goldthorpe (1980) have emphasised the relative rigidity of Britain's system of stratification.

Some observers point to the dubious relevance of the entire debate, given the context of hierarchical roles and extremely limited opportunity structure (Roberts, 1977). The focus on cognitive abilities as revealed through psychometric and educational measures of attainment also has weaknesses (Verma, 1977b, 1979); the affective aspects of human behaviour have often been ignored.[1] Some writers have, however, attempted to link important affective aspects of behaviour and personality such as self-esteem, prejudice and performance to certain aspects of social structure (Bagley *et al.*, 1979c; Bagley and Verma, 1979; Verma and Bagley, 1979b). The importance of this interdisciplinary approach is often underestimated, but it seems to us to be the most genuine approach to the problem of situating individual consciousness within complex sets of social forces.

Rutter and his associates (1979) have demonstrated a high degree of correlation between certain organisational and procedural indices on the part of the school, with behavioural and attainment indices on the part of groups of pupils attending 12 London secondary schools. The results of this study also showed that differences between the schools studied were not just a reflection of the quality of intake but many of the effects of secondary schools were associated with their characteristics as social organisations. Driver (1977a) found that the 'cultural incompetence' of many teachers in British schools, their failure to achieve a communicative mode of instinction with black teenagers, also led to underachievement.

The study of the present writer[2] was designed to explore the nature and determinants of the vocational aspirations, choices and achievements of adolescents from a South Asian background in two major industrial cities in the North of England. It was hoped that, by studying the experience of one particular minority group, the findings would not only throw light on the problems of our 'target group' (i.e. young South Asians), but also on disturbing aspects of the British educational system. In orthodox terms, these problems might be referred to as 'over-aspiration' and 'underachievement' of Asian adolescents. Both phenomena have been ascribed to 'cultural' factors in the literature (Gupta, 1977; Beetham, 1967; Baker, 1978).

The purpose of this chapter is to outline the programme of research relating to its context, and to describe the main issues of theory and method which arose out of this work. A small segment of our total experience gained from this research is also included in the chapter.

CONTEXT OF THE STUDY

The different ethnic groups in Britain fall into four broad categories:

Blacks: West Indian, African;

Asians: Pakistanis, Indians, Bangladeshis, Sikhs, Malaysians;
Chinese;
Italians, Cypriots and Greeks, Poles, Hungarians.

Each 'immigrant' group is distinctive in its background, its cultural characteristics and the historical context in which it settled in Britain. Thus, each of the immigrant groups relates in different ways to educational, social, occupational and cultural life in British society. For instance, there are at least five distinct cluster of Asian communities (as mentioned above) in Britain who do not form a single cultural and social group. They differ in terms of language, values, customs, and social class. There are over 18 major languages with totally separate scripts, about 10 main religions, several castes and hundreds of sub-castes. Thus, among sub-populations of Asian communities there are certain dimensions of difference that are to be found between immigrant groups in general. However, given the time and resources it was not feasible to study more than one major immigrant group at the level required to meet the objectives of this research. Therefore, the particular case of south Asians in the Bradford and Leeds area has been examined. It was hoped that a study of this group from the Asian population would throw light on the problems of vocational adaptation of immigrant groups in general.

Although the precise number of South Asians currently resident in Britain is difficult to estimate, they (Indians, Pakistanis and Bangladeshis) form the largest single immigrant group. An article by Derek Humphrey in *The Sunday Times*, London (January 1977) gives the following figures: Asians 618,000; West Indians 236,000; Chinese 81,000; Africans 30,000. It is estimated that 1.9 million people from the New Commonwealth Countries of Asia and Africa now live in Britain (The Franks Report). The bulk of the migration from Asia started in the early 1950s, but over half the immigrant South Asians arrived in the United Kingdom between 1960 and 1965; the vast majority of these first immigrants were young people, many single men, who left their families and dependents behind. During the same period there was a marked increase in the number of children arriving. To these have been added, particularly since 1967, sizeable groups of Asians who were forced to leave East Africa as a result of Africanisation. They are composed of Gujaratis, Sikhs and Goans. In general, these East African Asians tended to settle in areas where friends and relatives had settled previously. A small number of Asians came from the West Indies whose experiences in their country of origin were similar to the East African

Asians. They have been urbanised, better educated and have had a better standard of living than, say, the average Pakistani or Bangladeshi immigrant. A large majority of Asian communities have settled in Leicester, Luton, Bradford, Leeds, Walsall (the Midlands) and Southall in London.

To many Asians, Britain was a foreign land whose language, customs, religion and way of life were totally alien. The social structure of the Indian sub-continent is characterised by village, kin and caste. Being predominantly agricultural, the village community with its cohesiveness and control is the mainstay of society. Coming to Britain, for Asian immigrants, thus involved very substantial changes in environment: changes in the cultural climate and occupational context of their lives. Such a massive discontinuity in the way of life of the 'immigrant' poses major problems of adaptation. Of the range of such problems mentioned by South Asians, one of the principal sources of difficulty in our experience is that of *vocational adjustment*.

While the problem seems plain enough, it has remained stubbornly intransigent. The process of adaptation to British life for the immigrant is poorly understood because of the complexity of the process, its manifestation in so many aspects of life, and because very little research has been carried out in this field of human adaptation. Furthermore, the individuals concerned are, in many respects, disadvantaged (Smith, 1976); until recently their problems have been opaque to the British community; but with the 'Immigration Acts' since 1964, the problems of ethnic minority groups have received some attention.

VOCATIONAL ADAPTATION AND ETHNIC MINORITIES

According to Brody (1969), 'adaptation in the psychological sense refers to the process of establishing and maintaining a relatively stable reciprocal relationship with the environment'. In examining the vocational adaptation of the youngsters of South Asian migrants such a perspective was preferable to the more usual concept of 'assimilation' which implies a one-way process. It is too seldom recognised that the presence of migrant workers in Britain is a product of the adaptation of the British society and economy to its changing employment structure. As Allen and her colleagues (1977) point out, in this analysis not enough attention is paid to the 'demand' side of the migration equation. In the 1950s Britain was desperately short of both unskilled and skilled labour for its economic revival.

There is a small, though growing, body of literature concerned with the formation of vocational orientations among 'Asian' and 'West Indian' adolescents. Most of the research and reports about immigrants has been concerned with the first generation of immigrants (Rex and Moore, 1967; Burney, 1967; Patterson, 1968; Rose *et al.*, 1969). Research findings indicated that black workers entering the metropolitan 'mother' country were discriminated against at a variety of levels and were incorporated into underprivileged roles within British society. However, the attitudes and responses of the second-generation ethnic minorities towards British society do appear to be different from that of their parents. Young West Indians and Asians interpret their future situation in Britain less optimistically than their parents (John, 1972).

There is also a belief that the children of immigrants (second generation) face similar adjustments to those of their parents, but they are less resistant to assimilative pressures than first generations. An explanation of this similarity and difference might be that the adaptation processes of 'first-generation immigrants' mediated through a diffuse net-work of interpersonal and institutional mechanisms (e.g. networks of friends and family, community-based self-help systems and perhaps less significantly government agencies), whilst 'second-generation' individuals are exposed to the institutionalised and culturally complex socialisation system of schools and career preparation.

For the native British child the values of home and school are likely to be congruent with those in the society at large. But for the new generation of Black and Asian British this congruence cannot be assumed, and is likely to vary in ways which are significant for the process of vocational adjustment. It cannot also be assumed that congruence is achieved solely by adjustments on the part of ethnic minority populations.

Cause-and-effect relations in the area of value orientation are notoriously difficult to establish. Many of the immigrants to this country have been compelled to negotiate the problems of vocational adaptation at a personal level. Since the cultures of Britain and the Indian sub-continent are different in many respects, the juxtaposition of similar and contrasting elements makes possible the exploration of the relationships between cultural values, educational institutions and vocational choice.

The adaptation of the native British youth's employment aspirations to British market conditions is relatively well understood, and has recently become an object of increased interest (Willis, 1977). The present study was initiated in the light of those studies, in order to throw new light on the general problem of the vocational aspirations, choices and achievements of adolescents from a South Asian ethnic background.

THE CONCEPT OF DIFFERENTIAL ASPIRATION

The concept of differential aspiration was first introduced in the work of Beetham (1967). He offered a detailed analysis for the phenomenon of aspiration on the part of 'immigrants', particularly 'Asians'. According to his explanations 'Asians' use a limited set of occupations, entry to which required qualifications 'beyond their reach'. His interpretations included:

(a) a lack of acquaintance with the full range of occupations available in British society;
(b) a fascination with mechanical jobs natural for those who came from the country where mechanisation was not highly advanced;
(c) a reluctance to enter the lower occupations endured by an earlier generation;
(d) the considerable influence exerted by parents whose conceptions were based on the occupational structure of the country of origin:
(e) the tendency to aim for jobs which would provide money or status in the event of the family returning home.

Beetham also pointed to the 'surprising diffidence' of 'English' children who saw substantial obstacles in the way even of their modest ambitions and aspirations. Following Veness (1962) he points to the particular nature of the socialisation fostered by the 11 + examinations, streaming, and in particular, the secondary-modern school. Hence his model has achieved a degree of sophistication in its balance between 'cultural factors' derived from interaction with the British educational system.

However, there seems to be a somewhat ethnocentric aspect in the explanations of Beetham. He views 'depressed aspiration' in white working-class children as the rational norm, and considers the ambition on the part of the South Asians as 'unrealistic', a phenomenon to be modified by the appropriate agents of social policy. This aspect of his work was most severely criticised (e.g. Hiro, 1968), but which paradoxically was also enthusiastically followed up by teachers and other researchers.

An evaluation of Beetham's study shows a number of flaws. Firstly, whilst attributing much of the characteristic of 'over-ambition' to the conditions or attitudes in the country of origin, he failed to subdivide his sample according to the area of origin. Secondly, he did not give detailed descriptions of the sorts of social factors giving rise to these attitudes. Thirdly, little mention was made of the phenomenon of discrimination in British society, and its impact on the aspirations of Asians Hiro (1968), criticising Beetham's work, perhaps rightly suggests that so-called unrealistic aspirations might be a recognition on the part of a discriminated minority that they must have a higher aim than the majority population in order to have a chance of achieving at the same level.

A glance through the literature clearly suggests that 'culturally determined' over-aspiration has become a prevailing conceptual framework amongst teachers and careers officers. Often a simple reference to the 'culture of immigrants' is used as an explanation for a whole complex area of occupational entry. It featured in evidence to the Select Committee on Race Relations and Immigration (DES, 1973, vol. 2, *Evidence of Wolverhampton Principal Careers Officer*) and filtered through to a wide 'grass-roots' acceptance. 'We all have a laugh about the Paki who want to be a brain surgeon', commented one teacher from one of our Project schools in a staff-room conversation. The following extract from a teacher in another Project school emphasises the point more articulately:

I spend a good deal of my time writing references for certain Asian youngsters that are in actual fact a waste of time, and I know it before I send the reference off to college, and the youngster in a sense, I think, knows it, but won't accept it. There is a certain tendency amongst some of them to believe that knowledge and ability can be boxed and taken down from a shelf, and the ingredients of that box can be put in front of them and all they do is soak it up, recharge themselves like a battery with academic standing, that's very sad because there's a great tendency to believe among the Asian community to think sheer diligence is sufficient and it is not.

Whilst certain sections of the Youth Service and the Youth Employment Service are willing to accept the existence of discrimination (e.g. Committee of the Youth Service Development Council), others have refused to admit or deliberately ignored its existence and suggest crude versions of Beetham's findings as answer to any problems encountered in vocational work with South Asian adolescents (D.E.S.: Select Committee on Race Relations and Immigration, 1973).

An example of this superficial approach is the surprise expressed by a careers officer (interviewed in our Project) that many 'Asian' teenagers did not wish to take up agriculture as a career, although 'many of them came from a rural background'. This careers officer had specialised in 'immigrant problems' for three years, but he disregarded the fact that parents of these children had migrated from a particular sort of village life; and indeed farming in Punjab and Kashmir is not the same as in West Yorkshire. At first one may feel surprised at such stereotyping in a profession which relies so heavily on sensitive dealings with people. Yet, this may be due to the pressures which careers officers have to face in confirming the validity of individual choice in an employment opportunity structure which provides ever-decreasing scope for it. As Allen and Smith (1975) found in their Yorkshire studies:

> Difficulties in placing black school-leavers tended always to be attributed to the failures of black individuals themselves. The situation is aggravated if the teacher makes 'patient' and 'persistent' efforts and still does not meet with 'success'. Stereotypes are thus confirmed.

Thus, intensified careers advice, starting at an earlier stage in the curriculum, as recommended in the Select Committee's Report on Education, may prove to be of little assistance if it is based on the premise that the required objective is 'cultural adaptation', and assumes that racial discrimination in employment is largely absent. It has already been established that discrimination in employment is fairly widespread, and is based not on cultural origin or foreignness, but on skin colour (McIntosh and Smith, 1974; Ballard and Holden, 1975).

One aspect of our research programme has been to test the empirical validity of *ad hoc* opinions that South Asian children tend to (a) over-aspire, and (b) aspire to a restricted category of jobs (careers officers and teachers responsible for careers education we interviewed seemed to be absolutely certain that they did).[3] The results of our study indicate that some South Asian youngsters did admit to having had fantasy aspirations, but it also appears that these were similar to the fantasies admitted to by indigenous adolescents.

Much of the debate on the issue of occupational aspiration has centred on the way in which South Asians deviated from the obscure model of aspiration favoured by the British system of education. Some researchers (e.g. Gupta, 1977) found that 'Asians', both male and female, expressed significantly higher educational and vocational aspirations as compared with the 'English' sample. Those researchers attributed this differential aspiration to parental attitudes and 'ethnic coloured minority status'. Other studies have also discussed the relevance of 'cultural' influences to occupational entry (CRE, 1978b; Baker, 1978). Fowler and her colleagues (1977) reported a stereotyped viewpoint on the part of a youth employment officer in Glasgow, where so-called over-aspiration was seen as a barrier to appropriate job-choice for South Asian youths. The researchers found that this was an inadequate theoretical framework for explanation of disappointment and failure in the world of work. They drew attention to the *nature* of the job market itself and proposed the existence of a dual labour market, within the secondary sector of which the Asian population was confined. An interesting aspect of their study was their examination of young Asians working within an 'Asian economy' even when they had explicitly rejected this option before leaving school.

Thus, the theme of 'over-aspiration' on the part of South Asian youngsters has been backed up by opinions expressed both at the grass-roots level and at the academic level. What has been lacking from most analyses and explanations is an adequate treatment of the way in which these aspirations are socially and psychologically constructed, or similarly the precise social and psychological consequences of failure to meet them. The problem facing immigrant parents and their children, the schools and the community at large have ramifications on many different planes: economic, psychological, social, educational, cultural, religious and governmental. A research design which artificially re-stricted the problems to only one or two of these planes must leave the major issues untouched in many of their essential features. The ways in which aspirations of South Asians are differentiated from those of indigenous adolescents are multidimensional, and reflect the complexity of the social situation which migrants from the Third World have to negotiate in metropolitan society.

The vocational adaptation project has been concerned specifically with the following aspects of these concepts:

(1) Whether adolescents of South Asian origin under-achieve, relative to their white indigenous counterparts.
(2) How far aspirations are in keeping with performance as compared with their indigenous peers.
(3) The factors influencing their aspirations.

The 'selective migration' hypothesis (Eisenstadt, 1954; Kemper, 1977; Berger and Mohr, 1975) has been examined in our study with the use of 'need for achievement'. Other explanatory models particularly relevant to the South Asian group are based on the prevalence of a religious culture, placing high emphasis on prestige (Alavi, 1972; Anwar, 1977; Aurora, 1967; Verma *et al.*, 1980), the lack of acquaintance of a rural population with the occupational structure in Britain, and the internalisation of the overt meritocratic values in the British educational system by adolescents and their families. In the interpretation of results data collected in a 2-year Indian-based empirical research (Verma *et al.*, 1980) have been utilised. The findings of research in India showed that the teenagers in urban schools are on the whole highly motivated to do well in academic work with some degree of anxiety at the possibility of lack of success in the occupational sphere.

(4) The degree to which employers in West Yorkshire view Asian and black adolescents in negative or positive terms, and the degree to which some employers practise racial discrimination.
(5) The impact which interaction involving discrimination has on individuals' and groups' perception of the host community as a whole, and the world of work in particular.

The negative responses engendered by this factor amongst young blacks and Asians have been well documented, and cited as a cause for concern to us on numerous occasions by teachers, educators and policy-makers. These youngsters may also increasingly come into conflict with an education system which does not provide them with qualifications to compete with their white peers (Bagley, 1973a, 1976; Brittan, 1976).

(6) The values inherent in the normative conception of a 'correct level of aspiration'; the extent to which education 'downgrades' the expectations of working-class 'British' adolescents and acts as a filtering process by which the system of stratification is reproduced (Bowles and Gintis, 1976; Willis, 1977; Jenkins and Shipman, 1976). In evaluating this aspect data gathered from a sample of 'white' adolescents has been employed.

METHODS AND TECHNIQUES

Methods employed have been both quantitative – the gathering of statistical data on employment, vocational aspiration, size and geographical location of the immigrant settlement – and qualitative – individual in-depth interviews with selected adolescents (both South Asian and indigenous), parents, employers, teachers, members of the community, careers officers and policy-makers, and observation of educational process.

In order to answer the above six questions the study was conducted at two levels. The first was concerned with large-scale data-collection. In order to examine the relevant aspects of the vocational aspirations and expectations of South Asian youth, a questionnaire was designed, and administered to over 1000 teenagers (20 per cent were of South Asian origin) from the 1978 fifth forms of the seven schools in Bradford and Leeds cooperating in the project. The objective was to obtain a sample across ethnic and ability ranges. Data concerning cultural and socio-economic variables with a theoretical bearing on their occupational aspiration were collected. At the second level of research we had used a smaller cohort of 150 youngsters from the 1979 fifth forms, and the work undertaken with them has been far more extensive, covering a wide range of techniques, from intensive interviews to the administration of standardised measures of academic motivation, self-esteem and achievement motivation. This second stage of the sample included both males and females (over 80 adolescents were of a South Asian origin).

Due to the complex nature of the data it is not possible to offer the results in this chapter. Moreover, the main purpose of this chapter has been to communicate to the reader some theoretical and methodological issues of our study. The complete findings of our 2-year research will be reported in book form containing a full range of phenomena, perspective and judgements. However, the following section presents a small segment of our experience gained in the project.

DISADVANTAGED POSITION AND DIFFERENTIAL ASPIRATION OF SOUTH ASIAN TEENAGERS

The continued underprivileged position of ethnic minority groups in British schools has created considerable feelings of alienation and resentment. Common problems in black teenagers include those of differential identity, alienation and self-esteem bases (Bagley, 1976; Bagley *et al.*, 1979b; Verma and Bagley, 1979b) and a progressive decline in achievement in some black pupils as they advance, in an atmosphere of increasing alienation, through the British school system (Bagley *et al.*, 1979a).

In dealing with the subject of 'disadvantage, opportunity and differential aspiration' in our study we were faced with two distinct types of information – one dealing with the global picture about the educational and social disadvantages of the 'target group' (i.e. South Asian youths) which pointed to the extent to which their pre-educational and educational experience predisposes them to occupy an unenviable position in the world of work; the other type of information dealing with the question of how their experience is translated in individual and group terms into a perception of the world.

A number of studies have shown that whilst the transition from school to work (or further and higher education) may be the fulcrum for the distribution of 'life chances' between individuals and social groups, the various kinds of disadvantages experienced by some people in the early years of their lives can predetermine their success at this level (Wedge and Prosser, 1973; Rutter *et al.*, 1976).

It is not intended in this chapter to discuss the social background of South Asians living in Bradford and Leeds. However, according to the classic criteria of housing, income levels and family size, the 'Asian' population of Bradford and Leeds seems to experience considerable deprivation, which one would expect to have an adverse effect on their self-esteem, educational performance and motivation. However, the fact that there is some differentiation in 'cultural' norms between the South Asian population and their equivalents in the 'indigenous' population balances the problem; the mutual support networks in the South Asian communities were also noted in our research which is in line with other investigations in this area (Anwar, 1977; Saifullah Khan, 1975). It is also interesting to note that our South Asian sample from the Leeds and Bradford area seemed to have levels of self-esteem no different from those of indigenous adolescents.

However, the differentiation in cultural norms between South Asians and the white population can also create its own problems. For example, there may be problems in reconciling the experience and interpretation which a migrant worker develops concerning his host society when his children arrive after socialisation in the education system; alternatively the socialisation at home may clash with the socialisation demanded at school. In either of these two cases, it is the children who are most likely to experience difficulties. The most serious of these difficulties arises from language deficiency which not only provides educational disadvantages but which can, as a result of the organisation of the educational experience, cause additional problems of identity.

A survey in November 1977, concerning language problems of ethnic minority pupils in Bradford schools, revealed the extent of the language problem faced by South Asian teenagers, particularly in their early school years (see Table 6.1). The problem may be enhanced by the practice of streaming in upper schools. As can be seen from the table, at the age of transfer, 20 per cent of the 'Pakistani' group still suffer from a severe language problem. This may mean that they are not able to use their talent in scientific subjects if the streaming system utilises ability in English as a basic criterion for *all* subjects.

Thus, many circumstances serve to differentiate young South Asians as a social group. Where there is a reinforced consciousness of this fact, the cause of separateness may be increased, with a consequent effect on identity (see Weinreich, 1979). The 'over-aspiration' of South Asian youngsters has often been described in the literature as culturally determined, but it may simply be a reaction to the group experience of South Asians in work situations which has been predominantly unpleasant. This point has been emphasised by several respondents from the second stage of our sample. As mentioned earlier, about 250 youngsters were interviewed using a semi-structured interview schedule (20 per cent of this sample were of a South Asian origin):

He doesn't [father] want me to go into textiles because he says he doesn't think much about it, and I don't want to go to work in a mill either. He says it's not good there – you have to work all night and you don't get any sleep and you come home and you have to sleep at daytime and there are kids making a noise and they don't let you sleep (Pakistani boy).

They never thought I would work in a factory, they have always had high hopes for me and my brother. They thought he was going to study on, but he didn't, and they were let down by him – that's why they don't expect too much of me. He regrets not staying on now – he thinks there is nothing in just getting a job anywhere (Pakistani girl).

They [parents] wouldn't like me to have a dirty job because my father was a mechanic first and if you come from Pakistan – the main reason my parents have really come here was to get a job and to get the children a good education, so if they returned they would have something to show for it; a high job (Pakistani boy, Barkerend Road).

It should be emphasised that the explicit rejection of the type of factory work their parents did was highly marked amongst South Asian youngsters, particularly Pakistani teenagers. This does not essentially

TABLE 6.1 Language problems of 'ethnic minority' children on roll in Bradford schools, November 1977

Origin of child and/or parent	5 and Under		5–9		9–13		13–16		16+		Total		
	ES	NES	ES	NES	ES	NES	ES	NES	ES	NES	ES	NES	All
Pakistan	153	378	1870	910	1285	360	532	111	115	17	3955	1776	5731
Bangladesh	–	13	30	33	139	22	15	17	–	–	184	85	269
India	163	105	1008	156	951	41	533	21	92	1	2747	324	3071
West Indies	45	–	320	3	491	8	372	9	17	1	1245	21	1266
Asians from Africa	12	9	70	16	68	8	84	10	17	2	251	45	296
Other Commonwealth	6	4	59	6	25	3	24	–	4	–	118	13	131
SUB-TOTAL 'ASIAN'	379	509	3357	1124	2959	442	1560	168	245	21	8500	2264	10764
	328	492	2948	1082	2394	431	1164	159	224	20	7137	2230	9367

ES = English-speaking.
NES = Non-English-speaking. In the teacher's opinion – to the extent that he/she cannot follow the teaching appropriate to his/her age group.

mean that they were unrealistic about their future career – 90 per cent of our second-stage sample foresaw great difficulties in the way of attainment of their goals. But they were highly motivated, and seemed anxious to succeed in their academic work.

The interaction of this high motivation with the socialisation system can be viewed as highly problematic, which partly accounts for the derivation of the term 'over-aspiration'. The most obvious explanation is the existence of discrimination and prejudice which interprets the ambition on the part of Asian and black people as 'unrealistic'. It was evident from interviews with many teachers and careers officers (as quoted earlier) that racism was of primary importance.

In view of the over-all resistance to the idea of entering the textile industry we noted in our South Asian sample (particularly Pakistani in Bradford) that a disproportionate number do, in fact, find themselves obliged to obtain work in textiles – 45 per cent in textile and distribution as compared to 29 per cent of all male school-leavers (Bradford Metropolitan Council, 1979). The alternative to employment in textiles appears bleak, particularly in the present economic climate.

It is evident from the foregoing discussion that the vocational adaptation of South Asian youngsters studied is an issue closely bound up with larger social issues, and therefore cannot be considered in isolation. The hard core of racism affecting Asian minorities survives, as can be seen in many aspects of life (Bagley and Verma, 1979; Bagley *et al.*, 1979c). Thus, youngsters have to face the added problems of discrimination and multiple deprivations as members of the minority community.

NOTES

1. For a further discussion of some of the issues see Chapter 11 in this volume, by Verma and Mallick, on tests and testing in a multiethnic society.
2. The study was conducted over a period of two years (1977–79), and was funded by the Leverhulme Trust Fund, London. The Project was based in the Postgraduate School of Studies in Research in Education, University of Bradford, and was directed by the present author.
3. We interviewed 12 teachers and four Careers Officers.

7 A Case of Non-Achievement: West Indians and ESN–M Schooling[1]

SALLY TOMLINSON

The discovery and classification, during the twentieth century, of more and more children considered to be 'defective', 'handicapped', have 'special needs' or 'learning difficulties', has generally been regarded as enlightened advancement and an obligation placed upon civilised society to care for its weaker members. In contrast to this view, it can be held that the social categorisation of weaker social groups always serves the specific interests of the dominant definers and categorisers. To be categorised out of the normal education system, and offered instead a special education (ESN–M), represents the ultimate in non-achievement in present-day industrial society. It means being at a total disadvantage in a society in which the education system offers a seemingly democratic currency of credentials and qualifications. Furthermore, when educational advancement or exclusion is controlled by ostensibly 'fair' meritocratic testing, resulting social hierarchies appear to be legitimately based on intrinsic gifts and skills (Bourdieu and Passeron, 1973).

This chapter questions the way in which one social group – children of West Indian origin – come to be 'over-referred' for ESN–M schooling and offered what is in effect a 'non-education' – reviews some current explanations for the process, and offers a further small piece of evidence to explain over-referral and placement. It also suggests that the general poor level of achievement of West Indian children in normal schools and their non-achievement through special schooling is not necessarily due to factors intrinsic to the children or their families, but is partly the result of the way the educational administration and practitioners are currently dealing with black children. Liberal pedagogic ideologies are at present being stretched to their utmost in assuming that West Indian chidren are 'equal' to white children in most of the educative processes, and over the 'ESN issue' the administration has to date largely been able to ignore what is perceived by the West Indian community and others to be a substantial social problem (observations on the Report by the Select Committee on Race Relations and Immigration; DES, 1978).

As a preliminary, the view of special schooling taken here is that its major function since the 1890s has been to allow for the removal from normal schools of children who were troublesome – in the sense of exhibiting learning difficulties teachers could not cope with, or behaviour they could not control.

Special education has functioned as the 'safety-valve' of the normal education system, removing certain kinds of undesirable children (Tomlinson, 1981). The process is dynamic; normal schools are now seeking more ingenious ways of ridding themselves of non-conformist and undesirable children. Historically, children who received a special education have been excluded from most occupations (Collman, 1956), and from chances of social mobility, and their placement in the lowest social class has been ensured. It is not surprising that these children have always been predominantly working-class children – higher social classes have usually been able to provide for and incorporate their 'dull' children (this was pointed out in 1908 by the Royal Commission on the Care and Control of the Feeble-Minded), who do not need to be controlled or legitimated as of low status. This view turns back to front the literature on ESN–M children which attempts to trace causal explanations for educational subnormality in low socio-economic status or cultural disadvantage. Total exclusion from the education system is a powerful form of social control not acceptable to, or needed by, higher social classes. It is by viewing special education as a product of dominant vested interests, rather than as catering for the 'needs' of certain children, that it becomes possible to question the grounds for categorising 'too many' West Indian children as ESN–M.

Since the settlement of black immigrants and their children in Britain, a 'racial' dimension has been added to the class and control dimensions of the ESN–M category. The over-referral and placement of children of West Indian origin in ESN–M schools, in proportion to their numbers in the total school population, has been a matter of concern to the West Indian community for a number of years. It symbolises the general under-achievement of West Indian children in schools, and contributes to anxieties amongst first-generation immigrants that their children may be destined, through educational failure, to inferior employment and status – as a witness to the Select Committee on Race Relations and Immigration remarked in 1976, 'This is one of the very bitter areas for West Indians.'

The anxiety concerning over-referral was expressed as early as 1965 by the North London West Indian Association, who lodged a complaint of discrimination with the Race Relations Board in 1970. An ILEA (Inner London Education Authority) survey of ESN schools in 1967 had noted that the schools felt a 'misplacement' was four times more likely in the case of 'immigrant' children. Bernard Coard's polemical paper *How the West Indian Child is made Educationally Sub-normal in the British School System*, published in 1971, publicised the issue and the black media have continued to express concern throughout the 1970s. A DES letter to Chief Education Officers in 1973 indicated that children of West Indian origin were indeed over-represented in ESN–M schools while Asian children were 'under-represented' (see Appendix 1 to this chapter). The Select Committee on Race Relations and Immigration (DES, 1973) collected evidence from 16 official bodies over the 'ESN issue' for their report on *Education* in 1972–73, and in 1976 nine official bodies gave evidence on the issue when the Committee reported on *The West Indian Community*.

From a long-term point of view the West Indian community can be regarded as the first pressure group to sustain a protest and demand more clarity over the criteria used to decide ESN–M placement. It is at this point, however, that any protest comes up against the ambiguous nature of the criteria used to ascertain children as ESN–M. The referral and assessment criteria are discretionary and often unformulated, and are based on professional judgements which are themselves influenced by social and political processes. It is difficult to 'prove' or refute any explanation for the over-referral of a particular group of children, or indeed to demonstrate clearly that any child is misplaced in ESN–M schooling (Tomlinson, 1981).

The West Indian concern has largely been based on the supposition that ESN–M schools are only for children of low 'innate' intelligence and that testing procedures are unsuitable for black children. The educational administration can validly reply that the referral criteria have always been concerned with 'other factors' and that no cause need be established before children are given a special education (Ministry of Education, 1946).

The kinds of explanation offered about the over-referral of West

Indian children for special schooling have tended to merge with explanations for their general underachievement in school. Overt references to innate 'inferiority' are not currently popular, although they do receive some academic and political support[2] and there are also some subtle indications that practitioners do tend to regard the problems of West Indian children as 'natural' and therefore innate (Brittan, 1976). Migration stress, family difference and disorganisation, child-minding and cultural differences have all been offered as explanations (Kitzinger, 1972; Nicol, 1971). More recently explanations have been sought in schools and teachers, particularly teacher expectations and stereotyping of West Indian children (Giles, 1977; Bagley *et al.*, 1979a) and there is a growing literature on identity and self-esteem (Verma and Bagley, 1979b). Behaviour considered unsuitable for normal schools has long been a referral criterion for special schooling, and the 1973 DES letter to Chief Education Officers suggested that teacher inability to discipline West Indian children was possibly leading to referral. Some research has linked learning difficulty with poor behaviour (Yule *et al.*, 1975) while other explanations have focused on overt racial hostility in schools. Verma and Bagley (1979b) recently suggested that what they called 'response to alienation' on the part of West Indian children might lead to referral for ESN–M schooling. Unsuitable assessment procedures have sporadically been offered as an explanation for the over-placement of West Indian children in ESN–M schools and 'culture-fair assessment' has been erratically pursued (Hegarty and Lucas, 1979). However, this explanation has always been logically dubious in view of the 'under-representation' of Asian children in ESN–M schools.

As part of a study concerned to question the epistemological status of the concept of mild educational subnormality (Tomlinson, 1981) an attempt was made to substantiate the notion that beliefs about West Indian children were closely linked to the referral criteria for ESN–M schooling. The study followed 40 children – 18 of immigrant parentage – through their referral assessment (and placement in 28 cases). All the professional people who had made a decision on the children were interviewed.[3] Initially, a series of 'accounts' purporting to describe and explain ESN–M children were abstracted from the literature on educational subnormality (see Appendix 2 of this chapter). The professionals were asked about the criteria they use to refer, recognise or assess ESN–M children. In the conclusions to the study the different accounts offered by the professionals were calculated as a percentage of their total replies and shown in histogram form. Appendix 3 shows that referring Heads overwhelmingly use functional and behavioural criteria in accounting for potential ESN–M children. (Educational Psychologists disagree with Heads over the behavioural criteria – they tend to use functional accounts 'explained' by statistical, social and school accounts.)

The professionals were also asked what they considered the school-related problems of West Indian children to be. Appendix 4 demonstrates that referring Heads' perceptions of the problems of West Indian children correspond very closely to their referral criteria for ESN–M schooling. Further, the Heads in this study considered that West Indian children possessed 'natural' functional and behavioural handicaps. They were 'bound to be slower – it's their personalities'; 'a representative bunch, slow and low-functioning'; 'the usual problems – hyper-active and anti-authority'. They felt that the learning process was slower for West Indian children; they lacked ability to concentrate, were 'less keen' on education, impeded by Creole dialect, were likely to be boisterous and disruptive. The close correspondence between the Heads' referral criteria for ESN–M schools and their beliefs about the 'natural' problems West Indian children, made it highly probable that as a group the children would be likely candidates for ESN–M referral. If learning and behaviour problems are also regarded as 'natural' and therefore as intransigent, it is less likely that Heads would attempt to find solutions within the school and more likely that they would press to have the children removed from their schools, although Heads who felt their schools had 'low standards' were less likely to refer. In contrast, Appendix 5 shows that the Heads' perceptions of the problems of Asian children are totally different from those of West Indian children. Asian children do not meet the referral criteria for ESN–M schooling and their functional problems, particularly language, are not thought to be natural or intransigent.

An interesting point in this study was that, once in the ascertainment process, 'immigrant' children were more speedily placed in ESN–M school than indigenous children. The indigenous children waited a mean of 2 years between referral and placement in special school; immigrant children waited only 11.4 months. Decisions appeared to be made more speedily concerning immigrant children than concerning indigenous children.[4]

As a further general conclusion in the study, Educational Psychologists and Medical Officers, although more cautious than Heads in attributing characteristics to West Indian children, did seem more likely to proceed with assessment on the basis of their beliefs. Although testing was noted as a problem, only one psychologist had refused to test a West

Indian child, and, despite their considerable power in the assessment process, psychologists could still be influenced by schools to 'get rid' of troublesome children. Psychologists who relied more on IQ test results, and believed that West Indian children had family problems and different developmental norms, might be more likely to recommend ESN–M schooling. Those who did not rely over-much on test results, and were dubious about the value of ESN–M schooling, might be less likely to recommend placement. The doctors felt freer than other professionals to mention racial hostility but in some cases they appeared to have taken over the school definition of West Indian children as behaviour problems; 'They have ebullient natures'; 'they can go berserk at school'. One doctor rejected the claim that West Indian children were over-represented in ESN–M schooling, and generally the professionals were not well informed about the issue.

Paradoxically, the failure to examine the whole referral and assessment process as it affects black children in a white society may have led to the continual issue of West Indian children in ESN–M schools. Normal schools may, as Bernard Coard asserted, 'make' West Indian children ESN, but the way the beliefs of Heads about West Indian children accord so neatly with their referral criteria, and the way the other professionals act in the assessment process, would certainly seem to work towards an over-referral and placement of this group of children. The suggestion made in the Warnock Report (1978) that former remedial and disruptive children become, together with the ESN–M category, 'Children with Learning Difficulties', has serious implications for the schooling of West Indian children in Britain. Given the number of remedial (and disruptive) West Indian children in normal schools, special education might cease to be of symbolic significance only. 'Special Educational provision' could become a major form of educational provision for children of West Indian origin.

NOTES

1. Paper presented at the British Psychological Society Annual Conference, Oxford, September 1979.
2. Since the publication of *Race, Intelligence and Education* in 1971, Eysenck has been held to support genetic explanations of racial difference in intelligence. The National Front overtly uses the view in its literature.
3. Interviews were carried out with referring Heads, educational psychologists, Senior Clinical Medical Officers, Special School Heads, parents and 'others' in 1976.
4. The study was in no way statistically 'valid' – the point is raised for discussion only.

APPENDIX 1

Children attending ESN−M schools as a percentage of their numbers in the total maintained school population, 1972

	(i) total school population	(ii) No. in ESN school	(ii) as a percentage of (i)
All children	846,629	60,045	.7
West Indian children	101,898	2,972	2.9
Asian children	86,813	453	.5

SOURCE: adapted from appendix to DES letter to Chief Education Officers, November 1973.

NOTE: Collection of statistics by ethnic origin was discontinued after 1972. More recent information must consist of speculation based on unofficial estimates. This paper estimates that, despite a reported decrease in over-all referral and placement, 2 per cent of children of West Indian origin, as against 0.5 per cent of children in the total school population, are in ESN−M schools.

APPENDIX 2

Accounts of Educational Subnormality (M)

1. *Functional*	1. Child cannot do X (X may be social, educational, technological, but is usually connected to 'learning' or intellectual functioning).
	2. Child cannot communicate adequately.
2. *Statistical*	1. Child has a 'low' IQ as measured on standardised tests.
	2. Child falls into lowest 1 per cent (or 20 per cent) of school population in school achievement.
3. *Behavioural*	1. Child is disruptive, troublesome, uncontrolled.
	2. Child exhibits bizarre, odd, non-conformist behaviour.
	3. Child unable to behave 'appropriately'.
4. *Organic*	Child has:
	1. Genetic disorder or 'innate capacity'.
	2. Pre-natal or birth 'damage'.
	3. Organic or metabolic disorder.
	4. Medically demonstrable 'illness' or 'condition'

5. *Psychological*	Child is 'emotionally disturbed'.

6. *Social*　　Child has:
1. Family with low socio-economic status; father semi- or unskilled.
2. Family 'disorganised' – poor maternal care; single parent; working mother, etc.
3. Poor or different socialisation techniques.
4. Adverse material factors – poor housing, bad physical environment.
5. Cultural deficiency – poor cultural milieux; poor preparation for school.

7. *School*
1. Unsatisfactory school conditions.
2. Normal school rejects child.
3. Child rejects school, i.e. truants.

8. *Statutory*　　Child may be 'certified' as in need of special education.

9. *Intuitive*　　Child has 'something wrong with him'.

10. *Tautological*　　Child is in need of special educational treatment.

APPENDIX 3
Referring Heads' accounts of ESN–M children

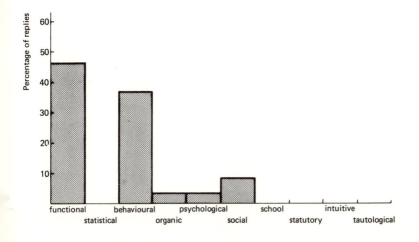

APPENDIX 4
Referring Heads' perceptions of the problems of West Indian children

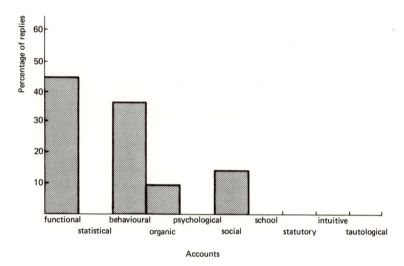

APPENDIX 5
Heads' perceptions of the problems of Asian children

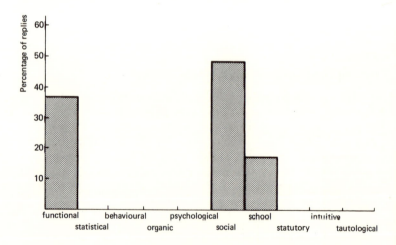

8 Achievement, Behaviour Disorder and Social Circumstances in West Indian Children and Other Ethnic Groups

CHRISTOPHER BAGLEY

Although there is evidence that some children of West Indian parents are underachieving, and are also seen by their teachers as manifesting problems of behaviour in the classroom (Little, 1975; Varlaam, 1974; Bagley, 1975b) it is by no means clear what social factors if any underlie this apparently deviant performance. Nor is it clear the extent to which social and behavioural factors connected with the educational performance of young West Indian children have an enduring effect into adolescence and young adulthood. As Phillips (1979) in reviewing these problems has observed, all evidence, even that from surveys carried out in the 1960s, is valuable because it may help to establish the extent and direction of change over time, which is an issue of central importance.

The data on which the present study is based were collected as part of the National Child Development Study of the National Children's Bureau in London, and were obtained from the SSRC (Social Science Research Council) Data Archive. The study which produced these data produced longitudinal measures of a cohort of all children born in one week in March 1958 (Davie *et al.*, 1972). Investigations were carried out at birth, and when the children were aged 7, 11 and 16. Data from the 16-year-old 'sweep' had not been made available in the SSRC Data Archive for secondary analysis in 1979 when the present work was undertaken, and we have therefore analysed selected variables (some 450 in all) relating to medical and social characteristics at birth, and educational, social behavioural and health data when the children were aged 7 and 11. By the time they were aged 7, more or less complete data existed on some 14,000 children (Davie, 1968), 91.3 per cent of the subjects participating in the inquiry at this stage, and 90.9 per cent of those contacted in the 11-year-old sweep (Griffiths, 1977). At each sweep systematic attempts were made through the educational system to trace children who were born in the relevant week, but who were not included in the earlier sweeps of the survey for some reason. One major reason was that the child was born overseas, and had migrated to Britain since 1958. The largest proportional increment for any group was in those described as 'coloured' and with parents born in India and Pakistan – only 25 such children were included in the sweep at 7 years, compared with 72 at 11 years. The numbers of black children in the survey whose parents were born in the West Indies increased from 77 to 121 between 1965 and 1969, while the number of white children with parents born in England, Scotland and Wales (the areas covered by the survey) increased from 10,480 in 1965 to 10,779 in 1969.[1]

TYPES OF DATA AVAILABLE FOR ANALYSIS

Various kinds of information, including educational test data and tests of achievement administered in the classroom, are available in the survey. The main source of data in the birth sweep is a district midwife, and includes much medical data concerning the period of pregnancy and birth. Later data collected when the children were 7 and 11 concerns home conditions, educational achievement, and various health and behavioural indicators. The informants were parents, teachers, health visitors, doctors and the children themselves.

The information on child behaviour at ages 7 and 11 is derived from teachers and parents. Teachers completed the Stott Social Adjustment Guides (Stott, 1966) which gives scores on a number of 'syndromes' relating the behavioural schemata of Professor Dennis Stott (Stott *et al.*, 1975). The Stott questionnaires are not often used in British schools at the present time, having been largely replaced by the Rutter scales for completion by teachers (Rutter *et al.*, 1969). There is a general assumption that the Rutter scales are equally valid, and rather easier for teachers to complete. Stott developed his scales in Britain, but in the late 1960s went to Canada to establish the Centre for Learning Disabilities at the University of Guelph. His continued research, indicating the reliability and validity of the behavioural scales, is largely Canadian-based (Stott, 1966, 1978; Hale, 1978), although a number of British studies have indicated the usefulness and validity of the Stott measures, or ones related to them (Chazan, 1968; Wight and Norris, 1970; J. Wilson, 1973; Toms, 1979; Thomson, 1978).[2]

Analysis of the Stott data in the NCDS has been reported by Davie (1968) who found significantly more behavioural difficulties in boys, and in children in lower SES groups. Ghodsian (1977) found that the 12 subscales in the Stott guide when factored broke down into two main components, labelled 'restless, outgoing and anxious' and 'withdrawn, anxious and inhibited'. This factor structure was invariant across sex and social class groups. These two major syndromes are similar to those which have emerged in many factor analytical studies of child behaviour, including the Rutter scales, and it is likely that the Rutter and the Stott scales are measuring the same underlying dimensions of behaviour (Wilson, 1973; Stott *et al.*, 1975; Hale, 1978). While the Rutter scales were developed from a clinical base, the context of the development of the Stott scales was to aid children with learning disability, the assumption being that much learning disability is associated with behavioural difficulty of various kinds (Chazan, 1968; Stott, 1978).

THE DATA ON ETHNIC MINORITY GROUPS

Ethnic minorities in the NCDS survey are defined in two ways: by physical features (European or Caucasian; African or Negroid; Indian or Pakistani; and other) described by the medical authorities examining the child; and by birthplace of parents, according to the parents themselves. Defining ethnic groups rigorously, by the birthplace of both parents *and* by the physical appearance of the child, yields five groups with sufficient numbers for a meaningful statistical analysis. The first group consists of children of European appearance both of whose parents were born in England, Wales or Scotland. The second is of children of European appearance whose parents were born in 'Ireland' (both Eire and Ulster). The third group is of children of European appearance, with both parents born in the continent of Europe – no other information is available on this heterogeneous group, but it is clear that the majority of parents are relatively recent immigrants to Britain, and frequently speak a language other than English at home. Presumably these parents come from both northern and southern Europe. The fourth group is of children described as of 'Indian or Pakistani appearance' whose parents were born in India or Pakistan. There are too few individuals so defined for analysis in the 7-year-old sweep, but because of substantial immigration from India and Pakistan between 1965 and 1969 reasonable numbers for analysis were obtained for the 11-year-old sweep. The fifth group contains children of African or Negro appearance, both of whose parents were born in the West Indies.

Classification on this basis excludes children one of whose parents was born in Britain and one overseas, and children for whom data on parental birthplace are missing. A less rigorous classification of ethnicity by ethnic appearance only yields some 200 children in the 'African or Negro' category, and this group contains, besides those with parents born in the West Indies, those with parents born in Africa, some children of 'mixed' marriages, and children for whom data on birthplace of one or both parents were missing. The main data analysis has examined ethnic groups defined both by child's appearance and birthplace of parents, but occasionally when larger numbers are required for analysis we have analysed data on groups defined by ethnic appearance alone. In fact, the patterns of disadvantage which emerge in the examination of data on the West Indian group also emerge in the analysis of data for the larger 'black' group.

There is in some sense an imbalance in numbers in the different ethnic groups – over 10,000 in the indigenous group, and less than 100 in some other ethnic groups. We have tried to balance this by firstly accepting a very high level of significance in the chi-squared analyses in Tables 8.1 – 8.6 for non-random distribution across groups: only differences occurring by chance one time in a thousand were considered. Secondly, in some analyses we have taken a random sample of the indigenous group to produce a group of size rather similar to that in some of the children of immigrant parents.

The most recent data we possess on this sample (the 11-year-old sweep) were collected in 1969.[3] The question arises: to what extent can the data be used to generalise to the situation of ethnic minority children in 1980? This is a difficult question to answer, since now many ethnic minority children aged 11 are, because of the restrictive curbs on immigration from 1966 onwards, second-generation, indigenous children. It may be that the social situation of minority groups has improved in the past decade (though Smith's survey in 1976 of 'the facts of racial disadvantage' do not give much ground for optimism in this respect in comparison with Davison's 1966 survey). What we would suggest is that if we can show that social disadvantage is related to educational underachievement and behavioural deviance in minority

TABLE 8.1   Variables in the National Child Development Survey for which there is a differential incidence across ethnic groups significant at the 0.1 per cent level of significance, in the survey when the children were 7 years old

School and educational variables, age 7	Proportions in children of:			
	Native white parents (N = 10,480)	Irish-born white parents (N = 182)	European-born white parents (N = 87)	West Indian parents (N = 77)
Variable 35 Child receives help in school because of educational or mental backwardness; or child in special school already	11.9	20.8	18.8	37.5
Variable 37 Teacher thinks child would benefit now from attendance at special school	3.2	3.5	7.0	11.8
Variable 38 Teacher thinks child would benefit from special schooling in next 5 years	4.6	5.8	4.8	19.4
Variable 43 School reports that mother shows little or no interest in child's education	42.6	56.5	37.0	48.4
Variable 44 School reports that father shows little or no interest in child's education	35.1	36.0	30.5	41.5
Variable 46 Proportion of group in a school class with more than 36 pupils	51.3	77.1	61.3	69.4
Variable 65 Teacher estimates that child's oral ability is excellent, or above average	26.7	22.5	18.4	11.0

TABLE 8.1   *(Contd.)*

	Proportions in children of:			
School and educational variables, age 7	*Native white parents (N = 10,480)*	*Irish-born white parents (N = 182)*	*European-born white parents (N = 87)*	*West Indian parents (N = 77)*
Variable 67 Teacher estimates that child's 'world-awareness' is exceptional, or above average	23.8	13.7	18.8	5.9
Variable 68 Teacher describes child as a wide and fluent reader, or above-average reader	32.1	24.2	24.1	15.0
Variable 70 Teacher describes child's number work as extremely good, or above average	21.7	19.2	18.4	8.2
Variable 81 Teacher's estimate of reading standard by book number – beyond basic reading scheme, or on last book	58.2	48.3	46.5	32.4
Variable 88 Teacher considers child is difficult to understand because of poor speech	10.0	9.9	14.9	32.9
Variable 89 Teacher considers that child has poor or imperfect grasp of English	1.1	1.1	38.8	26.0
Variable 90 Proportion of children in group with problem arithmetic scores in lowest quartile for whole group	26.9	30.7	32.6	61.0
Proportion of children in group with problem arithmetic scores in highest quartile for whole group	15.6	13.9	17.5	2.8

TABLE 8.1   *(Contd.)*

School and educational variables, age 7	Proportions in children of:			
	Native white parents (N = 10,480)	Irish-born white parents (N = 182)	European-born white parents (N = 87)	West Indian parents (N = 77)
Variable 92 Proportion of children in group with Southgate reading test scores in lowest quartile for whole group	25.8	31.9	43.3	50.1
Proportion of children in group with Southgate reading test scores in highest quartile for whole group	19.7	14.8	18.6	8.6
Variable 105 Proportion of children who attended a local authority day nursery before age 5, for at least a month	9.2	7.3	19.5	20.3
Variable 111 Proportion of children who started infant schooling full-time before their fifth birthday	54.9	35.7	45.7	45.5
Variable 179 Mother reads to child at least once a week	50.0	42.0	34.5	56.5
Variable 180 Father reads to child at least once a week	37.1	34.7	25.3	26.9
Variable 186 Mother reads book or technical journal most weeks	35.3	17.1	23.2	31.9
Variable 194 Mother stayed at school beyond statutory leaving age	22.8	22.7	40.3	28.3

TABLE 8.1   (*Contd.*)

School and educational variables, age 7	Proportions in children of:			
	Native white parents (N = 10,480)	*Irish-born white parents (N = 182)*	*European-born white parents (N = 87)*	*West Indian parents (N = 77)*
Variable 227 English is mother's usual language in the home	90.3	90.6	28.6	95.7
Variable 382 Child has normal vision for school tasks	86.7	72.7	79.3	79.0
Variable 389 Child has hearing impairment	4.9	2.9	6.1	9.1
Variable 403 Child has mild mental retardation (doctor's judgement) not needing special treatment	0.5	0.6	0.0	3.1
Child has mental retardation of type requiring ESN schooling (doctor's judgement)	1.2	0.0	0.0	6.0
Variable 1840 Score on Draw a Man test in lowest quartile for whole group	27.7	27.6	34.7	41.7
Score on Draw a Man test in highest quartile for whole group	26.0	33.0	44.4	27.1
Variable 1813 Identification of gifted children using Draw a Man test (score 37+)	1.1	0.6	1.2	4.3

Educational variables which have no significant variation in the 7-year-old sweep across ethnic groups:

Variable 20   Type of school attended.
Variable 39   School refers to specialist agency because of difficulties in school.
Variable 116   Parents want further education for child.
Variable 618   Child's laterality for eyes, hands and feet.

group children, similar relationships may pertain in the present generation if social disadvantage itself remains persistent.

What is most important is that the population of West Indian children born in March 1958 and described in the NCDS survey are very likely, given the nature of the sample, to be born in similar social circumstances to West Indian children born in Britain in 1957, 1958 and 1959. We may be able to generalise with some accuracy also to the circumstances of children born in the West Indies who came to Britain between 1958 and 1965. It is most likely that we have an accurate profile of the childhood circumstances of West Indians in Britain now in their early twenties, and it is for this population that generalisations are most appropriate. The actual long-term significance of childhood circumstances and performance and behaviour for this group of young adults is a matter for further inquiry, but it is worth noting that a brief report of the data on minorities in the 16-year-old sweep reported by the NCDS (Essen and Ghodsian, 1980) does point to the persistent underachievement of West Indian children in the sample.

The data describing the characteristics of the different ethnic groups (Tables 8.1–8.6) have been classified according to age of child (7 or 11) at the time of the sweep or inquiry; and by type of data – 'school and educational', 'health and behavioural' and 'social and demographic'. The original NCDS code numbers have been retained, and it will be seen that some of the variables contained in the 7-year-old sweep data file were in fact collected at the time of birth.

The educational data at age 7 show underachievement by all of the children of immigrant parents; but the West Indian children in particular seem to show massive underachievement. Much of this information is gathered, however, from teachers' reports, and may therefore reflect negative labelling. It is certainly extraordinary that teachers should consider that 19 per cent of West Indian children aged 7 would benefit from special schooling in the next 5 years (variable 38), and that so many were referred for ESN schooling (variables 35 and 37). Teachers have a very negative perception of black children and their parents (variables 43 to 89), and this is reflected in the scores of these children on group tests of achievement. Over half of black children have reading scores in the lowest quartile for the whole group; similarly in the highest 'quartile'.[4] The achievement of the black children was less than 50 per cent of that of the indigenous group. Scores of the black children on the test of arithmetic were even more depressed. Three times as many black children were described as having poor speech, in comparison with which indigenous children, and over a quarter of black children, were described as having an imperfect grasp of English, compared with only 1 per cent of indigenous children (variables 88 and 89). Clearly teachers have great difficulty coping with the Creole dialect of many West Indian children. It is likely, as Townsend (1971) has demonstrated in his surveys, that much of the supposed failure and the false referral to ESN schooling which West Indian children suffer is based on this failure of English teachers to cope with Creole and its British forms.

Such difficulties are not encountered by teachers in dealing with the children of European parents, for although nearly 40 per cent of such children 'have a poor grasp of English' this is not reflected in their test scores, and in a number of important respects such as number work these children are achieving at a level which is equal to, or greater than, that of their indigenous counterparts. We must hypothesise, therefore, a specific failure on the part of teachers in coping with the cultural background and educational needs of West Indian children.

Black children are more likely than others to have attended a day nursery (reflecting the fact that their mothers frequently worked), but they were less likely than others to have attended infant school before they were 5. Once in school, black children were placed in larger classes than were white children (variable 46), 69 per cent of black pupils being in classes with 36 or more pupils.

Table 8.2 shows the degree to which teachers have labelled their 7-year-old black pupils as behaviour-disordered, using Stott's Bristol Social Adjustment Guide. Black children were twice as likely to be seen as behaviour-disordered as white children. The picture of black children as withdrawn, hostile, depressed and fidgety in the classroom was *not* matched by parental reports of disturbed behaviour. Black parents described their children as rather solitary, but not as aggressive or hostile.

The disadvantages suffered by West Indian children began before birth. Their mothers attended antenatal clinics later; their present pregnancy often came less than 2 years after a previous pregnancy; mother frequently worked late into pregnancy; conditions at delivery were less advantageous; and the West Indian children were more likely to be of low birthweight. Only in respect of mother smoking during pregnancy were West Indian children advantaged.

It is technically possible that the higher levels of mental retardation reported on the doctor's examination in West Indian children (variable 403) might be to some extent sequels of earlier impairments of the central nervous system which occurred before, during and shortly after birth; it could be too that various kinds of disturbed behaviour are a

TABLE 8.2 Health and behavioural variables in the National Child Development Survey for which there is a differential incidence across ethnic groups significant at the 0.1 per cent level of significance, in the survey when the children were 7 years old.

Health and behavioural variables, age 7	Proportions in children of:			
	Native white parents (N = 10,480)	Irish-born white parents (N = 182)	European-born white parents (N = 87)	West Indian parents (N = 77)
Variable 83 Teacher describes child as 'squirmy or fidgety'	24.5	26.6	18.6	37.5
Variable 86 Teacher describes child as, 'Often running or jumping about, hardly ever still'	26.8	28.6	26.7	43.9
Variable 130 Mother reports that child has poor appetite	15.9	17.9	23.8	30.4
Variable 122 Child rarely meets other children outside his household – mother's report	7.2	12.2	20.3	26.0
Variable 134 Child prefers to do things on his or her own – mother's report	21.7	27.5	18.1	32.4
Variable 404 Doctor reports moderate or severe emotional maladjustment in child	1.1	1.8	1.2	6.0
Variable 434 Child withdrawn – teacher's report using Bristol Social Adjustment Guide	18.8	21.9	18.1	37.0
Variable 436 Child depressed – teacher's report using Bristol Social Adjustment Guide	24.0	24.1	26.5	47.9

TABLE 8.2   *(Contd.)*

	Proportions in children of:			
Health and behavioural variables, age 7	Native white parents (N = 10,480)	Irish-born white parents (N = 182)	European-born white parents (N = 87)	West Indian parents (N = 77)
Variable 440 Child hostile to adults – teacher's report using Bristol Social Adjustment Guide	15.7	16.3	14.4	35.6
Variable 444 Child anxious to be accepted by other children – teacher's report using Bristol Social Adjustment Guide	18.8	18.0	19.3	38.4
Variable 446 Child is hostile to other children – teacher's report using Bristol Social Adjustment Guide	15.2	11.2	15.7	27.4
Variable 455 Bristol Social Adjustment Guide (teacher's report) total score: First quartile, score 0 or 1	21.4	14.6	19.2	10.9
Fourth quartile, score 13+	25.9	25.2	27.6	48.0
Variable 500 First antenatal visit before 15th week of mother's pregnancy	52.8	37.1	39.9	27.1
First antenatal visit after 28th week of mother's pregnancy	6.8	8.5	14.7	10.9
Variable 504 No previous pregnancies before this one	37.1	28.7	39.8	19.5
Five or more previous pregnancies	4.3	8.4	1.2	11.7

TABLE 8.2   (*Contd.*)

Health and behavioural variables, age 7	Proportions in children of:			
	Native white parents (N = 10,480)	Irish-born white parents (N = 182)	European-born white parents (N = 87)	West Indian parents (N = 77)
Variable 509 Problems of toxaemia in pregnancy, interpartum haemorrhage, or Caesarean section in previous pregnancy	9.0	13.0	4.8	12.0
Variable 532 This pregnancy occurred less than 2 years after previous pregnancy	33.9	58.3	31.4	42.4
Variable 533 Delivery problems in present pregnancy (forceps needed on face and brow in vertex presentation; Caesarean section; breech birth; other abnormality)	13.6	16.5	14.5	18.2
Variable 543 Mother worked 40 hours or more a week, giving up work in 25th–32nd week of pregnancy	25.9	27.9	43.6	44.4
Mother worked 40 hours or more a week, giving up after 33rd week of pregnancy	5.7	18.0	15.4	15.9
Variable 557 No trained person present at birth; or trainee only without full medical supervision	2.0	2.2	1.2	5.2
Variable 646 Child's birthweight below the median for the whole group	50.8	57.8	49.2	65.0

TABLE 8.2   *(Contd.)*

Health and behavioural variables, age 7	Native white parents (N = 10,480)	Irish-born white parents (N = 182)	European-born white parents (N = 87)	West Indian parents (N = 77)
			Proportions in children of:	
Variable 639 Mother a medium smoker or heavy smoker after 4th month of pregnancy	17.2	22.6	6.3	1.3

Health and behavioural variables which have no significant variation in the 7-year-old sweep across ethnic groups:

Variable 82   Poor hand control
Variable 84   Poor co-ordination
Variable 85   Clumsy child
Variable 87   Child over-dependent on mother (teacher's estimate)
Variable 238   Child referred to specialist service because of eye problems
Variable 239   Child has condition requiring physiotherapy or remedial exercise
Variable 240   Child has been referred to a child guidance clinic
Variable 241   Child has been referred for speech therapy
Variable 242   Child has been referred to specialist service because of hearing problem
Variable 274   Child suffered febrile convulsion(s)
Variable 275   Child has had a fit after first year of life
Variable 276   Child has petit mal epilepsy
Variable 279   Child manifests tics or habit spasms
Variable 280   Child has suffered concussion or head injury
Variable 283   Sibling or parent has congenital abnormality
Variable 292   Child has a squint
Variable 293   Child has other eye problem
Variable 294   Child has had glasses prescribed
Variable 299   Child's single or multiple birth
Variable 300   Child has been referred to a children's department
Variable 301   Child has been referred to a voluntary children's society
Variable 345   Child has mouth or palate abnormality
Variable 352   Child has ear deformity

TABLE 8.2   *(Contd.)*

Variable 362	Child has suffered hernia
Variable 367	Child has suffered cerebral palsy
Variable 372	Child has lower limb malfunction
Variable 376	Quality of right eye vision (doctor's report)
Variable 377	Quality of left eye vision (doctor's report)
Variable 401	Child has general motor handicap
Variable 402	Child has disfiguring condition
Variable 415	Child has epilepsy
Variable 416	Child has other central nervous system disorder
Variable 438	Child is anxious (teacher's report) according to Bristol Social Adjustment Guide (BSAG)
Variable 450	Inconsequential behaviour (teacher's report according to BSAG)
Variables 481 to 487	Health problems – physical disorder (BSAG)
Variable 505	Previous aborted or ectopic pregnancy
Variable 519	Mother's haemoglobin level during pregnancy of study child
Variable 520	Foetal distress or cord prolapse during delivery of study child
Variable 625	Bleeding reported during pregnancy of study child
Variable 627	Toxaemia reported during pregnancy of study child
Variable 629	Mother's age when child was born

concomitant sequel, as Stott (1978) has found in work in Scotland and Canada. Various causal possibilities are briefly considered later in this chapter.

Table 8.3 shows the significant differences across the ethnic groups of various social and demographic factors. West Indian children come from larger families; fathers are predominantly working class; and the mothers in West Indian families were seven times as likely as white mothers to have worked when the child was aged less than 5. Even though black families are more likely than others to be buying a house or flat, parts are frequently sublet and sharing of facilities is common. The homes of black families are crowded, and fathers are non-resident in over a quarter of cases. The black families live predominantly in the West Midlands or in the London region. Irish families in this sample share some of the disadvantages associated with large families and manual working-class parents, but it is clear too that the situation of the large majority of the West Indian families in this sample is extremely disadvantaged, and their situation seems rather similar to the conditions

TABLE 8.3   Social and demographic variables in the National Child Development Survey for which there is a differential incidence across ethnic groups significant at the 0.1 per cent level of significance, in the survey when the children were 7 years old

Social and demographic variables, age 7	Native white parents (N = 10,480)	Irish-born white parents (N = 182)	European-born white parents (N = 87)	West Indian parents (N = 77)
Variable 101 Child has three or more siblings	12.4	21.7	12.0	24.5
Variable 183 Father plays small or no part in managing child	9.9	13.1	15.7	23.2
Variable 190 Father in Social Class I or II	18.3	1.3	11.1	1.4
Father in Social Class IV or V	20.6	37.8	36.3	40.6
Variable 197 Mother worked full time when child aged less than 5	7.6	10.4	30.9	54.4
Variable 199 Family in a whole house	89.6	67.2	90.2	56.5
Family live in rented rooms within a house	1.3	12.2	3.7	29.0
Variable 200 Family own or are buying house or flat	42.7	28.9	71.1	65.2
Family rent council house or flat	40.8	43.3	15.7	5.8
Family live in privately rented accommodation	11.3	23.3	7.2	27.5
Variable 201 Accommodation has two rooms or less	2.3	9.0	3.6	13.0
Accommodation has three rooms or less	13.3	21.8	9.7	26.0

TABLE 8.3   (*Contd.*)

Social and demographic variables, age 7	Proportions in children of:			
	Native white parents (N = 10,480)	Irish-born white parents (N = 182)	European-born white parents (N = 87)	West Indian parents (N = 77)
Variable 419 Household contains more than nine persons	3.5	11.8	4.8	18.2
Variable 492 One parent family, or no husband resident	1.8	2.9	3.9	27.9
Variable 524 Mother's father belonged to Class I or II	9.7	3.8	17.6	3.0
Variable 539 If mother worked when starting this baby, proportion in Class IV or V	30.7	56.0	57.9	71.7
If mother worked when starting this baby, proportion in Class I or II	11.3	3.4	7.9	0.0
Variable 549 Mother has seven or more siblings	13.4	45.5	14.7	31.8
Variable 607 Percentage of families living at a density of more than 1.5 per room, when child born	13.4	30.5	8.6	34.8
Percentage of families living at a density of more than 2.0 per room, when child born	2.8	12.4	4.9	16.6
Variable 609 Father in non-manual occupation when child born	32.9	10.2	22.9	6.0

T ABLE 8.3   *(Contd.)*

Social and demographic variables, age 7	Proportions in children of:			
	Native white parents (N = 10,480)	*Irish-born white parents (N = 182)*	*European-born white parents (N = 87)*	*West Indian parents (N = 77)*
Variable 621 Family had sole use of bathroom, indoor lavatory, and hot water supply when child born	83.1	66.5	72.6	48.5
Family shared bathroom, lavatory and hot water; or had no use of up to two facilities when child born	5.4	15.1	8.3	39.4
Variable 623 Family live in London or South-East	15.9	36.6	22.0	53.2
Family live in Midlands	8.9	17.8	12.1	23.4

Variables which have no significant variation across ethnic groups:

Variable 103   Child cared for by mother substitute
Variable 104   Child cared for by father substitute
Variable 175   Number of periods of separation from mother before child aged 5
Variable 177   Number of periods of maternal separation since age 5
Variable 228   Sex of child

of disadvantage described by Wedge and Prosser (1973) in the analysis of data for the 11-year-old sweep in the NCDS.

Tables 8.4–8.6 present data from the 11-year-old sweep; by this time a further 54 West Indian children had been added to the sample, the large majority of these having been born in the West Indies. Children from the West Indies added to the sample at this stage had significantly poorer achievement and significantly more teacher-described behaviour disorder than children who were born in Britain and who thus were included in the birth sample, to which Tables 8.1–8.3 refer. Because of this the overall position of the West Indian sample appears to be

TABLE 8.4 Educational variables in the National Child Development Survey for which there is a differential incidence across ethnic groups significant at the 0.1 per cent level of significance, in the survey when the children were 11 years old

School and educational variables, age 11	Proportions in children of:				
	Native white parents (N = 10,779)	Irish-born white parents (N = 225)	European-born white parents (N = 99)	Indian and Pakistani parents (N = 72)	West Indian parents (N = 121)
Variable 824 Child in special school, day or residential	1.1	0.0	0.0	0.0	6.3
Variable 848 Child in a class in which teacher considers less than 10 per cent of children are fit for academic education	10.4	10.0	11.0	35.9	27.1
Variable 849 Parents have not approached school on any matter in school year	40.5	40.8	47.3	71.9	57.5
Variable 850 School has initiated discussion with parent in school year	42.8	50.0	37.8	19.7	47.7
Variable 851 School sees father as having little interest in child's education	16.2	19.8	13.5	27.0	28.8
Variable 852 School sees mother as having little interest in child's education	12.4	15.0	11.1	26.7	25.0
Variable 853 Child receives special help in school because of educational backwardness	8.7	13.9	15.9	32.3	18.3
Variable 857 Would benefit now from special education, or in ESN school already	3.3	2.4	1.1	4.7	10.8

TABLE 8.4   (*Contd.*)

School and educational variables, age 11	Proportions in children of:				
	Native white parents (N = 10,779)	Irish-born white parents (N = 225)	European-born white parents (N = 99)	Indian and Pakistani parents (N = 72)	West Indian parents (N = 121)
Variable 858 Child is at present receiving free school meals	9.0	16.0	5.4	3.1	14.9
Variable 876 Teacher rates child's general knowledge as very limited, or below average	27.5	34.3	37.3	67.7	61.7
Variable 877 Teacher rates child's number work as very limited, or below average	35.3	39.7	44.6	51.6	64.2
Variable 878 Teacher rates child's use of books as very limited, or below average	21.2	23.7	22.3	57.0	43.5
Variable 879 Teacher rates child's oral ability as very limited, or below average	20.3	22.2	26.6	68.8	46.1
Variable 881 Teacher describes child as squirmy or fidgety	20.8	24.0	22.6	21.3	42.8
Variable 883 Teacher describes child as often running or jumping about, hardly ever still	25.3	26.5	18.4	25.4	41.6
Variable 884 Teacher describes child as difficult to understand because of poor speech	9.2	12.1	14.0	38.1	31.3

TABLE 8.4 (*Contd.*)

School and educational variables, age 11	Proportions in children of:				
	Native white parents (N = 10,779)	Irish-born white parents (N = 225)	European-born white parents (N = 99)	Indian and Pakistani parents (N = 72)	West Indian parents (N = 121)
Variable 885 Teacher describes child as having imperfect grasp of English	3.1	1.5	27.7	61.5	23.7
Variable 886 Teacher describes child as having some outstanding ability in field of creative writing, drawing, chess, modelling, music, science, sport, etc.	21.9	20.4	26.1	9.2	28.7
Variable 887 Teacher considers that child has serious weakness of personality or character (delinquent, rebellious, aggressive, or easily led)	6.2	7.3	7.6	10.8	20.9
Variable 887 Teacher describes child as rebellious	1.5	1.0	1.1	1.5	10.4
Variable 917 Score on non-verbal test of general ability in lowest quartile for whole group	26.8	34.2	27.8	57.9	67.0
Score on non-verbal test of general ability, in highest quartile for whole group	26.4	23.4	27.8	12.8	3.5
Variable 920 Score on general ability test, (verbal and non-verbal parts) in lowest quartile for whole group	25.3	32.0	34.2	61.0	67.0

TABLE 8.4   (*Contd.*)

School and educational variables, age 11	Proportions in children of:				
	Native white parents (N = 10,779)	*Irish-born white parents* (N = 225)	*European-born white parents* (N = 99)	*Indian and Pakistani parents* (N = 72)	*West Indian parents* (N = 121)
Score on general ability test, (verbal and non-verbal parts) in highest quartile for whole group	26.8	22.8	20.3	6.4	4.3
Variable 923 Score on reading comprehension test in lowest quartile for whole group	23.0	23.8	39.5	66.1	56.4
Score on reading comprehension test in highest quartile for whole group	24.9	21.4	16.1	9.6	5.3
Variable 926 Score on mathematics test in lowest quartile for whole group	25.0	31.5	37.2	62.9	65.3
Score on mathematics test in highest quartile for whole group	25.3	15.1	24.7	8.0	3.6
Variable 929 Score on copying designs test in lowest quartile for whole group	18.6	27.2	13.9	43.5	39.9
Score on copying designs test in highest quartile for whole group	19.3	17.2	25.5	14.5	14.8
Variable 932 Pupil anticipates doing full-time study on leaving school	29.4	21.6	40.7	48.3	38.0
Variable 958 Child anticipates doing a professional or semi-professional or managerial job at age 25	21.2	20.6	32.3	27.5	21.1

TABLE 8.4 (*Contd.*)

School and educational variables, age 11	Native white parents (N = 10,779)	Irish-born white parents (N = 225)	European-born white parents (N = 99)	Indian and Pakistani parents (N = 72)	West Indian parents (N = 121)
	Proportions in children of:				
Child anticipates doing a skilled or semi-skilled manual job at 25	16.2	15.7	12.9	15.5	21.1
Variable 1135 Child has changed school twice or more since age 5	15.2	18.2	14.4	15.5	29.6
Variable 1439 English is mother's usual language when speaking to child	97.4	97.7	24.2	19.7	95.0
Variable 1476 Local authority has decided child needs special educational treatment, or exclusion from school	2.7	2.3	2.1	0.0	9.5
Variable 1477 Child considered ESN and in special school, or recommended for one	1.6	1.3	1.0	0.0	7.7

Educational variables which have no significant variation in the 11-year-old sweep across ethnic groups:

Variable 813 Sex of child's class teacher
Variable 832 Numbers of teachers at child's school
Variable 845 Age of school buildings
Variable 855 Child receives special help because of behaviour difficulties in school
Variable 856 Child receives special help because of physical or sensory disability
Variable 880 Poor control of hands in writing, drawing, etc.
Variable 882 Poor physical coordination in running, jumping, etc.
Variable 1061 Problems in school attendance
Variable 1136 Parents would like child to stay on at school after minimum leaving age
Variable 1137 Parents would like child to undertake further training or education
Variable 1137 Child referred to education authority for special help with psychological or welfare problem (doctor's report)
Variable 1263 Child has always had good hearing in both ears (doctor's report)
Variable 1268 Child has speech difficulty (doctor's report)
Variable 1481 Child wears glasses (doctor's report)
Variable 1482 Child has impaired hearing (doctor's report)

TABLE 8.5   Health and behavioural variables in the National Child Development Survey for which there is a differential incidence across ethnic groups significant at the 0.1 per cent level of significance, in the survey when the children were 11 years old

	Proportions in children of:				
Health and behavioural variables, age 11	Native white parents (N = 10,779)	Irish-born white parents (N = 225)	European-born white parents (N = 99)	Indian and Pakistani parents (N = 72)	West Indian parents (N = 121)
Variable 930 Child is often or sometimes bored in spare time (pupil's report)	69.5	64.2	67.0	47.5	56.9
Variable 974 Bristol Social Adjustment Guide, Unforthcomingness syndrome:					
No sign	45.3	47.6	36.2	28.8	31.6
Marked sign (score 5 +) teacher's report)	10.2	12.8	21.4	30.2	17.6
Variable 977 Bristol Social Adjustment Guide, Withdrawal syndrome:					
No sign	79.6	76.7	75.5	71.2	71.1
Marked sign (score 3 +) (teacher's report)	2.7	3.0	5.4	1.5	6.1
Variable 980 Bristol Social Adjustment Guide, Depression syndrome:					
No sign	55.1	56.3	51.1	51.5	33.3
Marked sign (score 5 +) (teacher's report)	3.8	3.0	2.2	4.5	8.0
Variable 986 Bristol Social Adjustment Guide, Hostility to Adults:					
No sign	79.6	70.4	69.1	75.8	36.0
Marked sign (score 5 +) (teacher's report)	5.3	5.4	6.4	0.0	21.1

TABLE 8.5   (*Contd.*)

Health and behavioural variables, age 11	Proportions in children of:				
	Native white parents (N = 10,779)	*Irish-born white parents (N = 225)*	*European-born white parents (N = 99)*	*Indian and Pakistani parents (N = 72)*	*West Indian parents (N = 121)*
Variable 989 Bristol Social Adjustment Guide, 'Writing off' Adults and Adult Standards:					
No sign	58.6	56.3	59.6	51.5	35.1
Marked sign (score 5 +) (teacher's report)	4.6	4.9	5.3	1.5	12.3
Variable 995 Bristol Social Adjustment Guide, Hostility to other children:					
No sign	84.1	80.6	90.4	84.8	62.3
Marked sign (score 3 +) (teacher's report)	3.7	2.5	2.1	0.0	6.1
Variable 998 Bristol Social Adjustment Guide, Restlessness:					
No sign	83.7	80.6	83.0	86.4	62.3
Marked sign (score 2 +) (teacher's report)	4.3	5.4	4.3	4.5	13.1
Variable 1001 Bristol Social Adjustment Guide, 'Inconsequential behaviour':					
No sign	47.0	43.7	48.9	47.0	24.6
Marked sign (score 6 +) (teacher's report)	5.7	9.7	3.5	6.0	9.6
Variable 1004 Bristol Social Adjustment Guide, Miscellaneous symptoms (childish, bullied, truanting, destructive etc.):					

TABLE 8.5 (*Contd.*)

	Proportions in children of:				
Health and behavioural variables, age 11	*Native white parents (N = 10,779)*	*Irish-born white parents (N = 225)*	*European-born white parents (N = 99)*	*Indian and Pakistani parents (N = 72)*	*West Indian parents (N = 121)*
No sign	65.0	63.1	64.9	40.9	50.9
Marked sign (score 3 +)(teacher's report)	5.6	6.3	6.4	10.6	7.1
Variable 1008 Bristol Social Adjustment Guide, grand total for all syndromes:					
Score in first quartile for whole group (score 0 or 1)	25.0	22.9	18.0	17.3	14.0
Score in highest quartile for whole group (score 13 +)	23.9	23.6	25.5	25.6	41.4
Extremely disturbed (score 26 +) (Teacher's report)	5.2	6.0	5.6	1.5	18.7
Variable 1095 Bristol Social Adjustment Guide, 'Size' estimation;					
Tall for age	17.7	14.1	23.9	9.5	28.7
Small for age	15.6	17.1	18.1	22.2	13.0
Variable 1268 Child has speech difficulty at present (parental report)	4.0	3.1	1.0	5.6	10.8
Variable 1301 Child has missed less than a week in total from school because of physical illnesses (parental report)	62.0	64.0	58.6	81.9	75.2
Variable 1353 Child has had tonsils removed	20.4	17.4	27.6	7.0	10.8
Variable 1398 Child has never stayed in hospital overnight	54.5	49.8	55.6	81.7	62.5

TABLE 8.5 (*Contd.*)

Health and behavioural variables, age 11	Proportions in children of:				
	Native white parents (N = 10,779)	Irish-born white parents (N = 225)	European-born white parents (N = 99)	Indian and Pakistani parents (N = 72)	West Indian parents (N = 121)
Variable 1448 Child frequently prefers to do things on his/her own (parental report)	29.2	40.4	32.7	33.8	45.2
Variable 1450 Child sometimes destroys own or other's belongings at home (parental report)	6.8	7.1	10.2	14.9	21.0
Variable 1453 Child frequently worries about many things (parental report)	14.2	15.6	9.2	3.0	4.4
Variable 1454 Child is never irritable or aggressive (parental report)	46.3	49.5	36.5	56.7	59.3
Variable 1460 Child is almost always obedient at home (parental report)	48.6	55.8	53.6	69.6	63.0
Variable 1482 Child has never had impaired hearing (doctor's report)	88.9	93.3	95.9	88.4	93.3
Variable 1507 Child has congenital or acquired condition or handicap, including conditions impairing normal functioning (doctor's report)	8.7	4.9	6.2	14.1	14.7
Variable 1510 Height in inches: in first quartile for whole group	23.3	27.8	21.5	33.4	14.1

TABLE 8.5   *(Contd.)*

	Proportions in children of:				
Health and behavioural variables, age 11	*Native white parents (N = 10,779)*	*Irish-born white parents (N = 225)*	*European-born white parents (N = 99)*	*Indian and Pakistani parents (N = 72)*	*West Indian parents (N = 121)*
Height in highest quartile for whole group (doctor's report)	23.7	16.9	32.0	5.6	36.6
Variable 1515 Weight in pounds: in first quartile for whole group	24.4	29.2	16.4	28.0	19.3
Weight in highest quartile for whole group (doctor's report)	24.1	19.1	37.9	6.6	37.5
Variable 1568 Child has abnormality or clumsiness of balance, gait, or in performing finger— nose or finger-tapping test (doctor's report)	12.1	6.6	20.7	17.8	26.9

Health and behavioural variables which have no significant variation in the 11-year-old sweep across ethnic groups:

Variable 983	Bristol Social Adjustment Guide (teacher report): Anxiety for Acceptance by Adults
Variable 992	Bristol Social Adjustment Guide (teacher report): Anxiety for Acceptance by Children
Variable 1005	Bristol Social Adjustment Guide (teacher report): Miscellaneous 'Nervous' Symptoms
Variable 1088	Bristol Social Adjustment Guide (teacher report): Poor Physical Health
Variable 1263	Child has good hearing in both ears (parental report)
Variable 1271	Child is completely dry at night (parental report)
Variable 1278	Child has suffered fracture of bone or skull (parental report)
Variable 1293	Child has had serious illness (parental report)
Variable 1306	Child has asthma (parental report)
Variable 1307	Child has had convulsions of various types (parental report)

TABLE 8.5 *(Contd.)*

Variable 1341	Child has recurrent headaches or migraine (parental report)
Variable 1342	Child has had hay fever (parental report)
Variable 1343	Child has had recurrent vomiting or biliousness (parental report)
Variable 1369	Child has had appendix removed (parental report)
Variable 1391	Child has seen specialist for hearing problem (parental report)
Variable 1396	Child has seen specialist for disturbed behaviour or emotional problem (parental report)
Variable 1444	Child has been reluctant to go to school in past 3 months (parental report)
Variable 1445	Child has bad dreams or night terrors (parental report)
Variable 1447	Child has difficulty in settling to anything for more than a few moments (parental report)
Variable 1449	Child is bullied by other children (parental report)
Variable 1451	Child is miserable or tearful (parental report)
Variable 1452	Child is squirmy or fidgety (parental report)
Variable 1453	Child worries about many things (parental report)
Variable 1455	Child sucks thumb or finger during day (parental report)
Variable 1456	Child is upset by new situations (parental report)
Variable 1457	Child has twitches or mannerisms (parental report)
Variable 1458	Child fights with other children (parental report)
Variable 1481	Child usually wears glasses (doctor's report)
Variable 1482	Child has suffered impaired hearing (doctor's report)
Variable 1501	Child has been referred for psychiatric or psychological opinion or treatment (doctor's report)
Variable 1533	Child has abnormalities of skin, hair or nails (doctor's report)
Variable 1536	Child has neurological, muscular or orthopaedic abnormality (doctor's report)
Variable 1552	Child wears hearing aid (doctor's report)

somewhat worse in several areas in the 11-year-old sweep. While at age 7 the achievement of black children was approximately half of the standard achieved by white children with parents born in Britain, with rates of school-based behaviour approximately double those of the white children, at the age of 11 achievement of black children was overall only about a quarter of the level of that of white children.[5] Teacher-described behaviour disorder was still markedly higher in black children at the age of 11. Eleven per cent of black children were recommended for transfer to schools for the educationally subnormal, or were in such schools already, compared with 3 per cent of white children. Although Indian and Pakistani children were particularly likely to receive special help in the school (presumably because of language difficulties), they were not particularly likely to be referred for ESN schooling (variables

TABLE 8.6 Social and demographic variables in the National Child Development Survey for which there is a differential incidence across ethnic groups significant at the 0.1 per cent level of significance, in the survey when the children were 11 years old

Social and demographic variables, age 11	Native white parents (N = 10,779)	Irish-born white parents (N = 225)	European-born white parents (N = 99)	Indian and Pakistani parents (N = 72)	West Indian parents (N = 121)
Proportions in children of:					
Variable 858 Child is receiving free school meals	9.0	16.0	5.4	3.1	14.9
Variable 962 Family live in London or South-East	15.4	37.4	26.6	30.3	52.6
Family live in Midlands region	8.7	17.0	11.7	28.8	21.1
Variable 1112 Relationship of family informant to child: mother	96.1	96.0	88.9	63.9	92.5
Variable 1116 Household contains six or more people	31.7	60.4	25.5	70.9	62.0
Variable 1117 Household contains five or more children	13.2	19.1	8.1	40.5	34.5
Variable 1118 Child has three or more older siblings	8.1	17.7	6.2	25.0	17.5
Variable 1132 Child looked after for more than 3 months by someone other than mother (excluding hospitalisation) since age 7	6.4	11.6	10.2	8.6	42.5
Variable 1133 In local authority care now or in the past	2.2	4.1	2.0	1.4	6.7
Variable 1145 Mother takes child on walk, outing, visit, etc. most weekends	55.4	50.9	36.1	28.6	29.4

TABLE 8.6   *(Contd.)*

Social and demographic variables, age 11	Proportions in children of:				
	Native white parents (N = 10,779)	*Irish-born white parents (N = 225)*	*European-born white parents (N = 99)*	*Indian and Pakistani parents (N = 72)*	*West Indian parents (N = 121)*
Variable 1146 Father takes child on walk, outing, visit, etc. most weekends	53.0	44.1	34.7	29.0	25.5
Variable 1147 Father takes a big part, or equal part with mother, in child care	66.8	57.8	63.4	68.8	62.3
Variable 1150 Family has moved house three or more times since child was born	20.4	30.2	26.2	33.8	48.1
Variable 1151 Family live in a whole house	91.2	75.1	91.9	84.7	70.0
Family live in self-contained flat	7.7	21.8	4.0	4.2	16.7
Family live in rented rooms	0.6	2.7	3.0	8.3	13.3
Variable 1152 Family own, or are buying on mortgage, their dwelling	46.2	29.3	73.5	85.9	65.0
Family rent from council	42.0	55.1	12.2	1.4	15.0
Family rent accommodation privately	6.8	3.1	8.2	11.3	18.4
Variable 1153 Front door is either below street level, or on first floor or above	7.9	18.2	3.0	11.1	11.7
Variable 1156 Accommodation has three rooms or less (excluding bathroom and kitchen)	8.3	10.7	7.1	14.1	20.9

TABLE 8.6   *(Contd.)*

	Proportions in children of:				
Social and demographic variables, age 11	*Native white parents (N = 10,779)*	*Irish-born white parents (N = 225)*	*European-born white parents (N = 99)*	*Indian and Pakistani parents (N = 72)*	*West Indian parents (N = 121)*
Variable 1157 Child shares bedroom with two or more people	15.8	29.0	13.3	39.4	41.7
Variable 1158 Child shares bed with one or more people	16.3	26.3	27.3	38.0	43.3
Variable 1159 Bathroom is shared with other families	0.9	1.8	4.0	9.7	16.7
Accommodation has no bathroom	4.8	8.0	4.0	15.3	9.2
Variable 1160 Outdoor lavatory, sole use	29.3	32.9	42.4	59.7	47.3
Outdoor lavatory, shared with other families	1.1	1.4	0.0	7.5	5.5
Variable 1161 Indoor lavatory shared with other families	1.0	3.6	3.0	4.3	14.2
Variable 1162 Cooking facilities shared with other families	0.4	0.4	2.0	4.2	7.5
Variable 1163 Shared hot water supply, or no hot water	3.4	7.6	6.1	13.9	20.8
Variable 1164 Family is 'rather dissatisfied' or 'very dissatisfied' with housing	11.1	22.9	10.2	6.7	22.1
Variable 1171 Father in Registrar General Class I or II	23.8	6.2	14.1	12.5	4.9
Father in Registrar General Class III (skilled manual)	41.7	49.3	39.4	27.8	47.1

TABLE 8.6 (*Contd.*)

	Proportions in children of:				
Social and demographic variables, age 11	Native white parents (N = 10,779)	Irish-born white parents (N = 225)	European-born white parents (N = 99)	Indian and Pakistani parents (N = 72)	West Indian parents (N = 121)
Father in Registrar General Class IV or V	21.8	37.8	40.3	48.6	36.3
Variable 1215 Mother has undertaken some paid work outside home since child aged 7	61.4	61.4	64.3	27.5	76.5
Variable 1215 Mother worked full-time in past 12 months, for 50 + weeks	13.8	12.7	26.8	21.5	35.9
Variable 1215 Mother worked in previous 12 months:					
Intermediate non-manual grade	9.5	9.0	3.2	5.3	16.5
Manual grade	32.6	44.8	66.1	68.4	65.9
Variable 1437 Mother arrived in Britain, before 1960	N.A.	59.2	48.0	24.3	72.9
Mother arrived in Britain after 1965	N.A.	2.8	1.0	38.5	1.7
Variable 1438 Father arrived in Britain before 1960	N.A.	93.8	87.9	36.6	78.4
Father arrived in Britain after 1965	N.A.	1.7	0.0	5.6	0.0
Variable 1681 Family have sole use of bathroom, WC and hot water supply	88.8	80.4	86.9	56.5	63.3
Family share all three, or has no access to one or more facility	2.5	3.6	4.0	8.7	17.5
Variable 1683 Crowding: density less than 1 per room	62.1	32.0	72.4	26.8	29.2

TABLE 8.6   *(Contd.)*

Social and demographic variables, age 11	Proportions in children of:				
	Native white parents (N = 10,779)	Irish-born white parents (N = 225)	European-born white parents (N = 99)	Indian and Pakistani parents (N=72)	West Indian parents (N=121)
Crowding: density more than 1 per room	10.9	24.4	4.0	43.7	30.8
Variable 1685 Father in manual occupation	63.4	87.0	78.9	76.9	91.4
Variable 1691 Child resides with both own parents, when aged 7 and 11	94.4	94.9	94.0	81.5	85.9
Variable 1692 Mother not married to child's father when child aged 7 or 11	0.5	0.1	0.0	0.0	12.7

853 and 857). Nevertheless, teachers judged that nearly a third of black children at age 11 had 'poor speech' (variable 884) – presumably a negative comment on West Indian dialect. The many negative comments which teachers make about black children again lead us to infer that negative labelling reflecting teacher bias or inadequacy may be taking place, and that black children are being labelled in the terms described by Rosenthal (1973).

Some evidence that the true ability of black children is not being represented adequately by conventional tests and teacher descriptions comes from the results of the Draw-a-Man test administered when the children were 7 (variables 1840 and 1813). This test, which involves no verbal skills at all, was used by Hitchfield (1973) for the identification of gifted children, and it will be seen that although the West Indian group has more low scorers on this test it also has more high scores (as do the Irish and European groups) than the group of white British children (i.e. in this case standard deviations did differ significantly across ethnic groups). What is most interesting is that 4 per cent of the West Indian children fell into the highly gifted group, a higher proportion than in any of the other four ethnic groups. Teachers' estimates of ability in West

Indian children failed to account for the potential of these 'gifted' children. It will be noted that teachers do identify a higher proportion of black children as having high potential (variable 886); but this 'high potential' is not reflected in black children's scholastic achievement, and almost certainly refers to the identification of sporting abilities. Black pupils themselves at age 11 are more likely than whites to want to do further study, and to have occupational aspirations similar to whites (variables 932 and 958). But the schools which many of them attend are often disadvantaged (variable 848), and West Indian children are also more likely to have changed school than other groups (variable 1135).

With regard to behaviour, teachers see black children as seven times more likely to be rebellious than white children (variable 887). Similarly, on the Bristol Social Adjustment Guide teachers see black children as four times as likely as whites to show marked hostility to adults (variable 986). We would surmise that by the age of 11 many black children are becoming alienated from school, as teacher failure contributes to further negative labelling, and in turn to a confirmation of these negative expectations. While parallel evidence would support this view (Bagley, 1979b) we must stress that no data from the NCDS survey can bear directly on this hypothesis.

On the grand total for all syndromes in the Bristol Social Adjustment Guide, black children have scores nearly twice those of white children, and some 19 per cent of black children have been categorised as having scores of clinical dimensions (variable 1008). However, when we turn to parental reports of behaviour, we find that on many dimensions West Indian children are significantly *less* likely than whites to show disturbance – they are less aggressive, more obedient and less worrisome at home, although more solitary and sometimes more destructive; but on many behaviours about which parents were questioned, black children had similar profiles to white children (variables 1444 to 1460). Nor are black children any more likely than white children to have been referred to a specialist because of emotional or behaviour disorder (variable 1396).

We are forced to conclude from various pieces of evidence that the high scores which black children have on the Bristol Social Adjustment Guide, an instrument completed by teachers and referring to behaviour in school, do not generalise to other situations, suggesting that if the scores are accurate (teachers could of course simply be biased in their perceptions of normal behaviour of black children, which is interpreted in stereotyped terms), they reflect a reaction to a specific social situation in the classroom. It is probable that, as Varlaam (1974) has suggested, many children are reacting adversely to their underachievement. Such underachievement must, in our opinion, be attributed to the failure of teachers to teach properly, and not to the failure of black children to learn properly.

Table 8.6 shows the massive degrees of social disadvantage suffered by 11-year-old black West Indian children and their parents, in terms of poor, overcrowded housing, coupled with large families. Some disruption of normal family life has been experienced by the black children, including care by someone other than the child's mother (variable 1132), often associated with the prior migration of the child's mother. West Indian children are more likely, too, to be in one-parent families (variable 1692).

ACCOUNTING FOR THE DIFFERENCES IN ACHIEVEMENT AND BEHAVIOUR BETWEEN WEST INDIAN AND BRITISH WHITE CHILDREN AT AGE 11

We have tried to account for the differences on achievement and behavioural variables observed between West Indian and British white children in the following way. A random sample of the 10,779 British white children was drawn, being 2.5 per cent of the main group. Added to this number were those children added to the group between the ages of 7 and 11, giving in total 370 white, British children. This number was added to the 121 black British children (with West Indian born parents) giving 491 11-year-olds for analysis. Variables selected for analysis (a) explained a significant amount of the variance (based on a correlation of more than 0.15) in the dependent variable within each of the two groups (white British and black British) considered separately; and (b) showed a differential incidence to the disadvantage of the black British group. Some of the variables were re-ordered either as binary variables or as ranked variables, to give reasonable approximations to linear distributions. This was done to enable correlation coefficients, on which the multiple regression technique is based, to be calculated. The stepwise multiple regression technique employed calculates, in a series of steps, the correlation of each predictor variable with the dependent variable, controlling for correlation with each of the remaining variables. The analysis is terminated when no further significant variables can be added to the regression set, which forms the basis of the multiple correlation with the dependent variable (Hope, 1968). Since the order in which the variables enter the regression analysis determines the significance of subsequent variables, we decided to enter achievement and behaviour in the two analyses respectively after all other variables had been entered. It is noteworthy that achievement and behaviour retain significant links, so the mutual variance of behaviour and underachievement is not fully explained by socio-economic factors underlying both variables.

In Table 8.7 it can be seen that being West Indian rather than white is a significant predictor of teacher-designated behaviour disorder both before and after controlling for the influence of various socio-economic factors. Crowded home conditions, mother's SES, frequency of domestic moves, an atypical domestic situation, and being added to the sample

TABLE 8.7   Multiple regression with total score on the Bristol Social Adjustment Guide at age 11 as dependent variable, in 491 black West Indian and native-born white children in the National Child Development Survey

Variable number	Variable name	Correlation with social adjustment	
		Before multiple regression	*After multiple regression*
–	Ethnicity: West Indian	0.32	0.17
1122	Parental situation (both own parents at 7 and 11/other)	0.30	0.18
–	Child added to sample between ages 7 and 11	0.26	0.20
1683	Number of people per room in child's house	0.20	0.16
1212 and 1225	Mother's work situation (I, II, III/IV, V, other/not working)	0.21	0.16
1150	Number of times family has moved house since child was born	0.17	0.10
1157	Number of people child shares bedroom with	0.17	0.04
1152	Tenure (own house/council/other)	0.16	0.06
932	Reading comprehension test score	−0.35	−0.21
–	Multiple correlation	–	0.65
–	Proportion of variance explained in BSAG total score		42.25 %

NOTE: Correlations of 0.16 and above are significant at the 5 per cent level or beyond.

after age 7 (reflecting birthplace overseas) retain a significant correlation with behaviour disorder. Poor reading also remains a significant predictor of behaviour disorder after controlling, and the combination of factors account for 34.8 per cent of the total variance in the dependent variable. Thus over half of the variance in behaviour disorder scores in this combined sample of white British and West Indian children remains unexplained.

Table 8.8 shows the results of a similar regression analysis with scores on the reading comprehension test at age 7 as the dependent variable. Again, West Indian children have significantly poorer scores on this test

TABLE 8.8   Multiple regression with reading comprehension test score at age 11 as dependent variable, in 491 black West Indian and native-born white children in the National Child Development Survey

Variable Number	Variable name	Correlation with Before multiple regression	Reading Score After multiple regression
–	Ethnicity: West Indian	−0.34	−0.21
–	Child added to sample between ages 7 and 11	−0.25	−0.18
1122	Parental situation (both own parents at age 7 and 11/other)	−0.24	−0.19
1135	Number of schools attended since age 5	−0.23	−0.14
1683	Number of people per room in child's house	−0.21	−0.18
1681	Full use of bathroom, indoor toilet, hot water supply/other	−0.17	−0.14
1212 and 1225	Mother's work situation: (I, II, III/IV, V, other/not working)	−0.16	−0.15
1008	Bristol Social Adjustment Guide, total score	−0.35	−0.23
–	Multiple correlation		0.59
–	Proportion of variance explained in reading comprehension test score		34.8%

NOTE: Correlations of 0.16 and above are significant at the 5 per cent level or beyond.

even when a range of social factors has been controlled. Many of these socio-economic factors retain a significant correlation with poorer reading after they have been controlled on one another, and the correlation of behaviour disorder with poor reading remains significant even when the effects of ethnicity and social factors have been taken into account. What this implies, and what is in fact the case (as further cross-tabulations indicate) is that even West Indian children born in Britain, and in relatively advantaged social situations, have somewhat poorer reading, and higher scores on the measure of teacher-described behaviour disorder, than their white counterparts. Neither poor achievement nor teacher-attributed behaviour disorder can be fully explained by survey variables, and other factors such as the negative experience of multiracial schooling (Bagley and Coard, 1975), hostility of white children (Bagley and Verma, 1975) and teacher inadequacy and even prejudice (Brittan, 1976; Tomlinson, 1979) have to be considered.

DISADVANTAGE, BEHAVIOUR AND UNDERACHIEVEMENT IN WEST INDIAN CHILDREN: ENDURING EFFECTS FROM BIRTH TO 11?

Work on social disadvantage seems to show the relatively enduring effects on social handicap on later adjustment and behaviour (Robins, 1978). Indeed, a report of social disadvantage in all children in the NCDS at age 11 by Wedge and Prosser (1973) was titled, *Born to Fail?*, implying perhaps that circumstances early in life are powerful determinants of attainment and behaviour at age 7, and perhaps later in life. Later analysis of scholastic attainment by the National Children's Bureau shows that attainment at age 7 is a good predictor of attainment at age 16 (Hutchison, *et al.*, 1979).

Analysis of the data on the West Indian children shows many significant links in data gathered at birth, and when the child was 7 and 11. These links are numerous and complex in sociological implication, and imply that different patterns of relationship exist in different subgroups within the West Indian sample. It should be pointed out that this over-time analysis has been carried out only for those who were present at the three study periods, and not for the immigrant children in the West Indian group.

A non-parametric correlation matrix was created for all variables in the analysis which could be meaningfully ranked, and linkage and cluster analyses (cf Wilson, 1973) were carried out (tables not shown). A major basis of classification, predicting different linkages across time, was mother's social class position. If her husband was in Social Class V (the lowest class) or was not present at the time of her baby's birth, adverse perinatal and social factors seemed to be particularly significant for later development of the child. Just over 40 per cent of West Indian mothers in the birth sample fell into this lowest social class group. In this class group, being in a special school (usually an ESN school) at 11 had a significant correlation of 0.32 with foetal distress during the child's birth. The method of delivery in this group (unusual methods such as forceps ranked highest) correlated 0.27 with some measures of intellectual achievement at age 7.

Mother being in a low social class, having to work in a low status occupation until late in pregnancy, coming late to antenatal clinics, experience of a difficult birth, and lower birthweight were all intercorrelated to a significant degree. These perinatal variables, singly or in combination, significantly predicted some social disadvantage at age 7, which in turn explained some (but by no means all) of the variance in measures of achievement and behaviour at 7. Social disadvantage at 7, and poor scholastic achievement, were significant predictors of underachievement and social disadvantage at 11. Over-all, significant correlations ranged up to 0.35, so it is clear that disadvantage at birth, although significant, was by no means the only predictor of underachievement and related behaviour disorders at age 11. Other educational and social factors, many of them not measured in this survey, have to be invoked to provide the fullest explanatory picture.

In order to illustrate the complexity of relationships, we would cite as an example hearing problems detected in the medical examination at age 7. Such problems in West Indian children were significantly linked to difficulties and problems in pregnancy and birth and to educational underachievement at 7 and 11. They correlated, too, 0.48 with mother's marital status at birth, and negatively with the child's height and weight at age 11, but positively with indices of social disadvantage at 11, such as overcrowding.

We would tentatively conclude from this analysis (which will be pursued more fully in a later paper) that a small but significant part of the variance in educational underachievement at 7 and 11, including being sent to ESN schools, on the part of West Indian children can be attributed to extreme social disadvantage suffered by mothers when they were pregnant, and when their children were born. Such early disadvantages will be compounded by the forces of institutional racism in

British society, and by the negative perceptions which many teachers may have of black children.

DISCUSSION

The picture that has emerged of West Indian parents and their children in the NCDS survey is rather similar to that which emerged in a south London study, based on screening a large sample of 10-year-olds using the Rutter questionnaire, and interviewing the parents of a sub-sample of high and low scores (Bagley, 1975b). It was found that although West Indian children had very high rates of school-based behaviour disorders, they had low rates according to parental description. This is precisely the finding which has emerged in the NCDS data, and implies not only that the school is the main arena of the alienation and hostility of black children, but perhaps the main source also. We have pointed to the alienation of the aspirations of young West Indians in school and elsewhere (Bagley, 1976, 1979b), and it seems to us that, as Varlaam (1974) suggests, educational failure on the part of black children may lead to resentment and hostility to the school, to teachers, and to other pupils concomitantly with underachievement. Black children who are in a minority in a school or in a school classroom are particularly likely, too, to suffer aggression from other pupils, and diminishment of self-image (Bagley *et al.*, 1979b) which may have important consequences for learning.

Whether educational failure precedes or follows classroom-based behavioural disorders is a 'hen or the egg' question (McMichael, 1979), and various studies have reached different conclusions (Leach and Raybould, 1977). The evidence from the present study seems to suggest that teacher-described behaviour disorders and underachievement emerge more or less simultaneously, although this must remain a speculation, since data for the crucial period 5 to 7 years is lacking. Although certain socio-economic factors can explain in some part the emergence of behaviour disorder and underachievement, by no means all of the variance can be explained by these social factors using the technique of multiple regression.[6]

At the present time, the most likely explanation seems to us to be that the negative views which some teachers had of these black children in the 1960s led quickly (by the age of 7) and in a mutually reinforcing cycle, to the emergence of behaviour disorder and underachievement in many children. This led in a significant minority of cases to placement in ESN schools, since the data show that such designation was likely to be based on both behavioural and scholastic grounds.

A number of the West Indian children in the present study, now young adults, will have children of their own who will begin school soon. Will many of them experience the same fate as their parents?

NOTES

1. These figures refer to those children for whom information on birthplace of both parents is available.
2. One Rutter item, 'squirmy, fidgety child' was included in the NCDS 11-year-old sweep. This single item from the Rutter scale correlates 0.58 with the BSAG 'Inconsequential Behaviour' syndrome, and 0.50 with the BSAG 'Syndrome Total' score. Yule (1968) found a correlation of 0.93 between the Rutter and Stott scales.
3. Data from the 16-year-old sweep will be available from the SSRC Data Archive some time in 1980, according to information given by the National Children's Bureau.
4. These quartile groups were based on the nearest division which test scores would allow.
5. These comparisons assume that the standard deviation around the mean for each parameter does not significantly differ between groups, an assumption borne out by various within-group analyses (tables not shown).
6. We are exploring log-linear models to see if clearer causal explanations can be elicited.

9 Teaching in the Multiethnic, Multicultural School

KANKA MALLICK and GAJENDRA K. VERMA

Post-war migration from the New Commonwealth countries in the Caribbean, Africa, India, Pakistan, Bangladesh and South-East Asia has created a new dimension in the historic continuation of different ethnic groups in British society. The majority of these immigrants have settled in the major conurbations in London, the Midlands and West Yorkshire where they found availability of both work and housing.

The New Commonwealth immigrant groups on average are young and their fertility is somewhat higher. Thus, there has been a rapid increase in the number of black and Asian children in British schools. Given the age structure and social–cultural patterns of these immigrant groups, the numbers of ethnic minority pupils in British schools are likely to rise. Although pupils with 'New Commonwealth' origins still constitute a small proportion of the total British school population, their concentration in certain urban areas means that there are large proportions of ethnic minority pupils in many inner-city schools. It should be noted that a large majority of ethnic minority pupils are British-born and have never seen their parents' country of origin.

These changes in the urban school population have posed challenges for educational planners, administrators and teachers. The nature of these challenges varies from one area to another. Teachers can no longer ignore the fact, whether or not they happen to teach in areas with large numbers of ethnic minorities, that there are certain issues which are of great importance in education and therefore the concern of *all* schools. Regrettably not many of the schools are willing or ready to accept that there have been significant social changes over the last two decades. The

149

Bullock Report in 1975 rightly stated that 'many schools in multicultural areas turn a blind eye to the fact that the community they serve has radically altered over the last ten years and is now one in which new cultures are represented'.

In this paper we will examine the extent to which teacher-training institutions in Britain have been aware of the challenges that the education of ethnic minority pupils can pose and how they can contribute to the evolution of a multiracial, multicultural society. We will also consider some of the crucial issues which may underlie these challenges.

TEACHER EDUCATION: SOME ISSUES IN THE EDUCATION OF ETHNIC MINORITY PUPILS

The Department of Education and Science (DES) published two surveys (1971; 1972a) concerning the education of 'immigrant' pupils. The 1971 survey stated that:

> the work of colleges in preparing students to teach immigrant children contains two main elements, one concerned chiefly with attitudes, the other with knowledge and skills. A student should honestly examine the premise that a multi-cultural society in twentieth century Britain is both right and natural. If his attitude to a racially mixed class is wrong, no amount of knowledge, no mastery of techniques will make him effective as a teacher of immigrant children. Conversely, right attitudes alone are not enough when a teacher faces a group of non-English speaking children.

The DES report clearly suggests that the consideration of teacher-training should include both the questions of teacher attitudes and those of professional techniques.

Some of the issues which at present concern teachers in multiracial schools are language, minority cultures, curriculum content, teacher attitudes and expectations, teaching of race relations. These are closely bound up with the concept of multicultural education.

No-one would deny that the acquisition of English language and literacy is crucial for the children of immigrants if they are to enjoy equal chances of success both at school and in the world of work in British society. In so far as questions of language ability have entered into educational thinking, attention has been directed towards the different problems that the two main immigrant groups[1] (i.e. children of West Indian origin and children of Asian origin especially from the Indian sub-continent) pose as learners of standard English.

In 1966 the Schools Council sponsored a project on 'Teaching English to Immigrant Children' at the University of Leeds. This was a 3-year English language teaching curriculum development programme to meet the needs of pupils of Asian, African and southern European origin, initially for those aged 7–13, and subsequently for older children and infants. The project produced the material *Scope*, [2] for teaching English to non-English-speaking children. Another Schools Council project, based at Birmingham University, was concerned with 'English for West Indian Children'. The objective of this project was the provision of materials to help West Indian pupils write standard English, with particular emphasis on the areas where their dialect created special difficulties in learning standard English. It soon emerged, however, that linguistically disadvantaged indigenous children had many problems in common with West Indians. Materials developed by both projects are in use in many schools and form the basis of some in-service and initial teacher-training courses.

In 1971 a survey of Head Teachers found that some 43,000 officially designated 'immigrant' pupils were unable to follow a normal school curriculum because of language difficulties (Townsend, 1971). The provision of language teaching at the time of this survey varied greatly between local education authorities which served the ethnic minorities. The survey showed that some authorities with substantial ethnic minority pupils provided no special language teaching at all. The argument was that non-English-speaking pupils would soon acquire a knowledge of English through interaction with indigenous pupils.

Although there is some emphasis in teacher training on the study of language, particularly language acquisition and the role of language in learning, a large majority of students leaving teacher-training institutions seem to have little skills in language development work with *all* children. Many new teachers are likely to be in classrooms containing not only Asian (non-English speakers) and West Indian (Caribbean dialect speakers) pupils but also those indigenous pupils who have linguistic handicaps because of social deprivations or for other reasons. In writing about the Schools Council 'Language Teaching Project' Candlin and Derrick (1972) pointed out that:

Something much deeper than the principles or methods of teaching English as a second language has been called for. These principles and methods only make sense to a teacher who has an understanding of what language is . . . It is seen as providing them with new insights into language that relate to their professional life as a whole. But why, they often asked, have these insights been slipped into their training, as it were, under cover of something else? They should be available *to all teachers in training* whether they are involved with immigrant children or not.

The value of language development work cannot be overestimated, and it should be regarded as a practical necessity for all teachers to have studied the role of language in education, but so far there is little evidence that this has been considered as an essential part of teacher-training courses.

The Council of the EEC (European Economic Community), on 25 July 1977, adopted the directive that ethnic minorities have a right to the maintenance of their home language and culture through the school system of a member-state. The aim of this philosophy is for each cultural group in a multicultural situation to feel proud of their language and culture while learning to respect the culture of other groups with whom they interact. It has not been the practice in the existing school curriculum in Britain to recognise that the majority of the ethnic minority pupils are in practice bilingual. It is interesting to note that precisely the same point was made in the Bullock Report (1975):

> when bilingualism in Britain is discussed it is seldom if ever with reference to the inner city immigrant population, yet over half the immigrant pupils in our schools have a mother tongue which is not English, and in some schools this means that over 75 per cent of the total number on roll. The language of the home and a great deal of central experience in their life is one of Indian languages. . . . These children are genuine bilinguals, but this fact is often ignored or unrecognized by the schools.

The argument for and against mother-tongue teaching seems to be clouded by discussion over whether ethnic minority groups in Britain are 'migrants' or 'immigrants'.

Evidence from Canada and the United States suggests that the learning of a second language is improved when the pupil has a good knowledge of, and ability to use, his mother-tongue (MacNamara, 1979). In Britain it is now officially recognised that children in Wales whose mother-tongue is not English but Celtic, the language of Britain's ancient culture, should be fostered rather than suppressed. Recent research evidence (Price, 1978) shows that bilingualism in no way educationally handicaps Welsh children who come to school at the age of 5 speaking Welsh, and learn English as a second language. Experiments, financed jointly by the EEC and the DES, have now been undertaken with Asian children in British schools in this direction; there is, however, still much resistance to the widespread acceptance of this policy from British teachers.[3]

Another fundamental issue in teacher-training institutions is the need to give student teachers some insight into the cultures of minority groups now living in Britain. After 20 years or so of having ethnic minority pupils in British schools, after several reports and research findings about racial discrimination and disadvantage, the educational system has not come to terms with the fact that Britain is a plural society. Britain has a multiracial population, and minorities within that population experience particular problems of discrimination, because of their skin colour and distinctive cultural and linguistic characteristics. This fact seems to have very little impact on Government policy in the field of education. A very small number of local education authorities have made special provision for ethnic minority pupils drawing up government money as authorised in section 11 of the 1966 Local Government Act. As one might expect, the DES has been responding in a *laissez-faire* way. However, this policy or non-policy of the DES and the continued underprivileged position of ethnic minority pupils in British schools has no doubt created considerable feelings of alienation and resentment on the part of young West Indians and Asians in British society. Common problems in black teenagers include that of differential identity bases (Bagley *et al.*, 1979b; Verma and Bagley, 1979b), and a progressive decline in educational achievement in black pupils as they advance, in an atmosphere of increasing alienation, through the British educational system. A Community Relations Commission (CRC) report revealed that 'Over two out of three young Asians believe that young people in the Asian community have difficulties not shared by their white contemporaries' (CRC, 1976).

The Race Relations Act of 1976 requires local education authorities to take positive action to eliminate discrimination and promote equal opportunities, understanding and good relations between different racial/cultural groups in the community. It is hard to assess how far attempts have been made by local education authorities to implement this directive through the educational channel.

In this very complex situation, most teachers might claim to support the Jenkins[4] concept of 'integration' but in practice they seem to be working towards 'assimilation'. Large doses of lip-service have been paid to the idea that children from ethnic minority groups should be allowed to retain their parents' culture and maintain their cultural heritage and ethnic identity. However, the ability to tolerate this diversity necessitates that student teachers should develop an awareness of some form of cultural pluralism as the goal of education.

Countries such as the Netherlands have long practised a positive policy of pluralism, giving particular attention to the cultural autonomy and personal identity of ethnic minority groups (Bagley, 1973c). This direction has been based on the assumption that this is necessary as a policy of basic tolerance, and it also ensures that the minority groups are socially, politically and economically on equal footing with the indigenous population. On the other hand, identity and cultural conflicts can diminish the capacity of any group for successful economic and social adaptation (Bagley, 1973c).

Returning to the British situation, there seems to be no traditional policy of supporting cultural pluralism as there is in the Netherlands. Yet, in order to attain social justice the policies of cultural pluralism and multicultural education need to be accepted by both the immigrant and host communities, particularly by educational planners, administrators and teachers. Unfortunately there has been very little curriculum change to make this possible. A survey by Her Majesty's Inspectors (HMIs) (DES, 1972a) of 54 secondary schools in 16 boroughs, all with a high proportion of immigrant pupils, showed that there was little evidence of curriculum modification to take account of minority pupils. In its broadest interpretation multicultural, multiracial education implies a reorganisation of the curricula of all the schools to recognise the fact that we live in a multiracial Britain, whether we are brought up in Bradford or Bournemouth. Jeffcoate (1979) comments that:

If children are to be adequately educated for adulthood in a multi-racial society, a constant and pervasive intervention across the gamut of everyday learning experiences will be needed which can be sustained from the beginning to the end of statutory schooling. We formulated this conclusion as a curriculum principle asserting that the regular curriculum should be 'permeated' with a multi-racial 'constant'.

There is much in the cultures of minority groups now living in Britain that can be utilised in a positive and creative way to broaden and enrich the curriculum of both teacher-training institutions and schools. Student teachers should be given the opportunity to understand the social and cultural diversity of ethnic minority groups. The Bullock Report (1975) suggested that 'this should receive attention in both initial and in-service teacher training'. Teacher-training institutions should design the curriculum in a way which would give student teachers an opportunity to study the history, literature, religion, customs and traditions of minority groups. Millins (1973) has rightly interpreted the implication of the James Report that an understanding of the multicultural nature of society is:

> not merely a series of lectures or seminars, but rather the organization of experiences which would allow students to meet individuals and community groups whose conventions and values might contrast sharply with their own . . . [which] should enable them to start to adjust to a wide range of diversity in human beings.

While discussing problems of research in *Teaching about Race Relations* Stenhouse (1975) wrote continuing this theme:

> the teacher should be an example of a person critical of prejudiced attitudes and opinions held by himself and by society at large and trying to achieve some degree of mutual understanding and respect between identifiably different human groups.

It would be unrealistic to think that, in Britain, which is basically a white racist society (Bagley and Verma, 1979), many student teachers would not have unbiased attitudes towards ethnic minority groups of New Commonwealth origin. Thus, the results of a survey undertaken by the National Foundation for Educational Research (NFER) showed that a significant proportion of the overwhelmingly white native teaching force perceive minority ethnic groups in Britain in hostile and stereotyped terms (Brittan, 1976). In fact, at least half the population in Britain express prejudiced attitudes to a serious degree (Bagley *et al.*, 1979c; Bagley and Verma, 1979).

Evidence shows that there are very large numbers of West Indian children in schools for the educationally subnormal (ESN) (Coard, 1971). In 1967 a survey[5] by the Inner London Education Authority (ILEA) revealed that five of their secondary ESN schools had more than 30 per cent 'immigrant' pupils. The 1970 statistics were even more alarming, for even though 'immigrant' pupils comprised only 17 per cent of the normal school population, approximately 34 per cent of the ESN school population was 'immigrant'. And *four* out of every *five* 'immigrant' children in these ESN schools were West Indians. There are many reasons for this state of affairs. One of the significant factors, we suggest, is the attitude of the many teachers towards the black child. Most teachers have absorbed the cultural symbols that many individuals in British society accept without question – that black people are inherently less intelligent than white people. Therefore, the black child is expected to do less well in school. The scientific racist Professor Arthur Jensen, the Enoch Powell of the academic world, has added credence to the popular myth of black racial inferiority by openly asserting that black people are inherently less intelligent than whites (Jensen, 1980).

A teacher can seriously affect the performance and achievement of a black pupil in two main ways: by being openly prejudiced in his or her interaction with the black child; and by having low expectations of the child's abilities and achievement. Both these attitudes can be found among white teachers in British schools (Giles, 1977). There are in our experience many teachers who are condescending towards ethnic minority pupils. Adults may fail to realise that children are very perceptive, and understand the true meaning of these attitudes and feel highly aggrieved; many black children build up deep resentment and develop behavioural problems and severe emotional blocks to learning (Goldman and Taylor, 1966; Giles, 1977). When this happens, the 'self-fulfilling prophecy' has been fulfilled.[6]

It is well known that the West Indian children have higher than average scores on behaviour rating scales (Widlake and Bell, 1973), and that a very high proportion of West Indian children are underachievers (Coard, 1974; Giles, 1977). It has been shown that disadvantages are greater for the male than the female children of West Indian immigrants. Driver (1977a), for example, found that the West Indian boys do indeed have more trouble than the girls with English teachers; that a higher proportion of girls obtain school qualifications and persist longer with their studies, and that more boys are assigned to the schools for the educationally subnormal. His results further showed that the 'cultural incompetence' of many British teachers, their failure to achieve a communicative mode of instinction with black teenagers, also led to underachievement. Our study of pupils in 39 English schools found that the level of self-esteem among male West Indians was lower than that of both female West Indians and of male whites (Bagley *et al.* 1979b).

It is now well established that teachers' attitudes and expectation-significantly influence the ability and achievement of pupils ((1) Rosenthal and Jacobson, 1968; (2) Pidgeon, 1970; (3) Nash, 1973). This is perhaps even more so in the case of pupils from ethnic minority groups who are often stereotyped as being different and to some extent inferior, which in turn influences teachers' attitudes and behaviour towards them. On the other hand culture and ethnicity are often deliberately ignored by some teachers who insist on imposing values of the dominant culture on all children.

Accumulated research in the United States has substantiated that teachers' expectations of student achievement sometimes function as self-fulfilling prophecies (Rosenthal and Jacobson, 1968; Brophy and Good, 1972; Rosenthal, 1973). It has often been found that some teachers have rather definite expectations about the ability and achievement of different children, based on little or no evidence, or on evidence which the teacher incorrectly thinks to be valid for predicting individual achievement.

In Jonathan Kozol's remarkable study (1967) *Death at an Early Age*, for example, there are many incidents that demonstrate that white teachers at the Boston school he describes had negative expectations of black children which they communicated in their behaviour. A number of researchers have obtained similar findings. Rubovits and Maehr (1973), for example, observed that white teacher-trainees provided different patterns of attention and praise to two groups of children in grades six and seven arbitrarily designated as 'gifted' (containing white pupils only) and 'non-gifted' (black pupils).

In Britain J. K. Richards, reporting on the efforts of a Coventry school to provide genuinely multicultural education, concludes that 'schools profess their aim to be equality of opportunity for all and yet guide these non-white pupils into factory and office, where they are not really wanted'.[7] It is important for teachers to gain an understanding and knowledge of the child's background, which might help them to avoid making assumptions about the ability of ethnic minority pupils on the basis of their racial or cultural characteristics.

It is widely accepted that elimination of prejudice is an extremely difficult task. However, a proper approach to curriculum innovation should prove useful, as shown by a number of studies (Stenhouse, 1975; Verma, 1977a; Verma and Bagley, 1978, 1979a) aimed at reducing prejudice amongst students. It seems important for teacher-training institutions to redesign their courses in such a way as to promote in all their students an awareness that they live and will teach in a multiracial society. They should also be provided with the opportunity to explore the cultural, social and religious backgrounds of ethnic minority groups in relevant academic and professional options in greater depth.

INITIAL TEACHER TRAINING

It is extremely difficult to assess the contribution of the teacher-training institutions in preparing students to teach in a multiracial society. However, there seems to be some evidence that with a few exceptions these institutions have paid only cursory attention to studies concerned with multicultural education. Their inability or reluctance to prepare students to teach in a multiracial society should be evaluated in the context of some of the current historical pressures within teacher education.

Following the McNair Report (McNair, 1944) most colleges of education have been associated with universities through university institutes of education or departments of education, and in some cases are members of university schools of education. The extension of the initial training course from 2 years to 3 in the early 1960s, and the marked growth for the B.Ed. degree (Bachelor of Education) from the late 1960s has led to an improvement in academic standards.

Although the pattern of curriculum varies from institution to institution, in general a student offers a 'main subject' and a 'traditional' school subject, together with education and professional or curriculum studies. The work of the education department within colleges has been concerned with the organisation of academic subjects, e.g. philosophy, psychology and sociology. These courses have tended to enjoy high status whereas some important practical classroom problems have received very little attention. In June 1966, 88 colleges replied to a short questionnaire of the National Committee for Commonwealth Immigrants, in which they were asked to indicate whether they were trying to promote among student teachers an understanding of the problems experienced by 'immigrants' in Britain. Fifteen per cent replied that they had established, or were intending to establish, courses for the 1966–67 session (NCCI, 1966). The 1971 NFER survey, however (Townsend and Brittan, 1972), found that only 11 per cent of probationer teachers had received specific training in this area.

In the second half of the 1960s some colleges of education began to pay a little attention to the needs of the multiracial schools. However, the Report of the Robbins Committee, published in 1963, declared that one of the aims of higher education was 'the transmission of a common culture and common standards of citizenships'. It was clear that the Robbins Committee had only the indigenous community and its standards in mind, and saw no need to relate the aims of education to a multicultural society.

The Report of the James Committee of Inquiry (DES, 1972b) into the education and training of teachers indicated specifically the necessity of preparing all pupils for a multicultural society and recommended that 'an understanding of the multicultural nature of society should feature in any general education'; but it included no guidance, in any form, of how this should be achieved. However, a wider interpretation of the James Report implies that many of the disciplines in the college curriculum should be re-examined in order to meet the challenge of the Committee that

> the teaching of almost any subject, to intending teachers and other students alike, should be illuminated by some awareness of its relationship to other areas of knowledge, and its reference to the social, political, economic, cultural and technological conditions of contemporary society (DES, 1972b).

Attempts to train teachers through short courses have not proved very successful. The NFER survey by Townsend and Brittan (1972) showed that from January 1968 to December 1970 only 15 per cent of the primary teachers and 3 per cent of the secondary had attended studies related to immigrant children. This constituted 7 per cent of the total teaching force. The researchers commented that: 'Comparatively few teachers attend substantial periods of in-service training on the subject of immigrant pupils, and in secondary schools very few teachers attend even the shortest courses on this important topic.' Although the James Report recommended that in-service courses for teachers in multiracial schools should be conducted in suitably placed institutions (DES, 1972b), no reference was made in the Report about the need for in-service education for a multicultural society. The advance summary of the Labour Party's policy document on education also contained no apparent awareness of this crucial issue.[8]

It is most surprising that some 10 years after the Robbins Report, the Parliamentary Select Committee on Race Relations and Immigration (DES, 1973), still advocated the view that 'all students on initial and postgraduate courses can and should be made aware that, wherever they teach, they will be doing so in a multi-cultural society'. It is obvious that nothing had been done until 1973 in spite of various recommendations and reports. The majority of organisations which gave evidence to the Select Committee were of the opinion that all future teachers should be given specific preparation for working in a multicultural society. It should, however, be remembered that such training takes place then within what the James Report describes as 'hubbub of competing priorities'. The Select Committee on Race Relations and Immigration Report on Education (DES, 1973, Vol. 1) in its chapter on teacher training pointed out that:

(1) in-service was inadequate and L.E.As should, with the co-operation of educational institutions, expand in-service courses for teachers in multi-cultural schools and arrange for specialist training of teachers in those schools;
(2) further training was needed for teachers and lecturers to be able to provide realistic effective courses for multi-cultural education;
(3) there was a serious shortage [based on their enquiry] of teachers who were able to teach English as a second language and teachers to train them, and actions must be taken to meet this need;
(4) there should be more 'immigrant' teachers, since their numbers were not proportionate to the 'immigrant' population, and that their own experiences and insights would make them valuable as teachers in multi-cultural schools;
(5) all students on initial or post-graduate courses could and should be aware that wherever they would teach, they will be doing so in a multi-cultural society.

As far as the initial teacher training is concerned, it seems obvious that a large proportion of student teachers do not wish to take up their first posts in multiracial schools. On the other hand those few who do take up posts in multiracial schools are often still not well equipped to meet the challenge of multiracial classrooms.

In 1970 the Community Relations Commission (CRC) (now called the Commission for Racial Equality) published an analysis of the impact of the multiracial character of many of the British schools on the syllabuses of colleges of education. Their findings showed that by 1968, 'a significant number of colleges were paying systematic attention in their courses to the problems of immigrants'. This report seems to have presented a more optimistic picture than subsequent published and unpublished reports seem to suggest. For example, the experience of the joint effort by the CRC and the ATCDE (Association of Teachers in Colleges and Departments of Education) in arranging conferences for lecturers in colleges and departments of education shows that those lecturers with an active interest in multiracial education were still a very small fraction of the profession, and that a very small number of students emerging from training colleges have had any training in understanding the problems they would encounter in multiracial urban schools. Perhaps even more disappointing is the fact that far too few of the postgraduates from university departments of education who have entered the schools in recent years have been aware of the severe challenge that the education of ethnic minority children can pose for teachers of even long and successful experience (McNeal and Rogers, 1971).

In 1974 a Joint Working Party of CRC and ATCDE produced a report entitled 'Teacher Education for a Multi-cultural Society'. The report recommended that all students in colleges of education should be given an awareness of the educational implications of a multicultural society, and that this awareness should also be incorporated in courses for other categories of students studying in reorganised institutions of higher education. It also recommended that specialist options should be provided in initial training for those students who plan to teach in multiracial areas. The report further suggested that colleges of education should use their expertise and resources to provide varied in-service courses in cooperation with local education authorities.

The CRC and ATCDE Report seems valuable in the sense that at least it provides categories for the discussion of aims and objectives, and describes some courses currently in operation in colleges of education. Further, it gives a number of suggestions as to how these institutions might improve their training of student teachers who would be able to teach in a multicultural society. In spite of various reports and recommendations there is little evidence that these institutions are approaching the training of teachers for a multicultural society in any systematic way. The need is not so much for additional courses in the teaching of ethnic minority pupils, but for a recognition of the fact that we now live in a multiracial society and this should be reflected in the content of all the courses in colleges of education. There are only a few colleges where this issue is receiving any serious attention. Millins (1973) has remarked that:

The abiding impression is one of a growing divide, or rather of a dangerously yawning, and before long perhaps unbridgeable chasm between those administrators, tutors and teachers who are seeking to understand the needs of immigrant children and contribute to the evolution of a harmonious multi-cultural society, and those who are not.

It is reasonable to suggest here that those involved in teacher education are still in the early 1980s passing through a period of uncertainty and upheaval, and this places a great strain on teacher-training institutions. The future role, and even the existence, of many institutions has become uncertain as a result of the publication of the James Report (DES, 1972b). By 1981, very few colleges of education will retain their present organisation and curriculum. Most initial training courses will be in polytechnics or in institutions of higher education. These institutions have been created to provide a wide variety of general higher education. This reorganisation of teacher-training courses seems to provide an opportunity for these institutions to give serious consideration for preparing people to work in a multicultural, and multiracial society. At present there are no means of assessing the extent to which this strategy has been put into practice. However, these institutions should also be able to organise short courses related to the needs of children of immigrants for those student teachers who know what they would be teaching in multiracial schools.

TEACHERS AND MULTICULTURAL EDUCATION

If a policy of multicultural education is to be successful, it must be supported by properly trained and well-motivated teachers. This requires the restructuring of teacher education and in particular a greater emphasis on in-service training programmes. Teachers need, for example, to have considerable knowledge of language skills, curriculum development and race relations; they should also have knowledge of, and respect for, the cultural backgrounds of their pupils.

A number of special courses have been designed by institutes of higher education and departments of education in Britain which give orientation in multicultural education. Unfortunately, such courses are still rare (Shillan, 1975). For example, in 1971 Edge Hill College organised an introductory seminar on 'Education for a Multicultural Society' for its 400 first-year students (Millins, 1973). Obviously these kinds of courses require the support of local education authority administrators, Head Teachers and staffs. Perhaps the most ambitious course of this kind is one leading to the Bachelor of Education degree (B.Ed.) offered by the City of Birmingham Polytechnic. This course is designed for the training of teachers in multicultural education. The course content includes studies of the historical background and current situation of ethnic minorities in Britain, the concept of multicultural education, teachers and pupils in multicultural schools, language and minority groups in a multicultural society, and curriculum needs in a multicultural society.

In-service training programmes should be organised to help teachers to examine the curriculum of their subject areas in order to avoid cultural, religious or historical bias and stereotype in presentation, and to produce teaching materials relevant to the cultural and linguistic character of the school or college. The need for such training is well illustrated by work carried out on the evaluation of curriculum innovation in the field of multicultural education (Verma and Bagley, 1973, 1979a; Verma, 1977a). The findings of this evaluation showed that the use of materials aimed at increasing the pupils' understanding and tolerance of each others' cultures was only likely to be successful in the hands of those teachers who were themselves sympathetic to the concept of multicultural education. The evaluation indicated that only a minority of teachers hold liberal views in this field. Provision of in-service training for teachers, and the greater emphasis provided in this training on both attitudes and professional skills, is certainly an important area for development.

Another solution to the problem would be to employ more teachers from 'immigrant' and minority groups. Although the flow of teachers from the West Indies and the Indian sub-continent into Britain has been stopped because of immigration controls a substantial number of qualified immigrant teachers are not employed in schools, and appear to be suffering racial discrimination in their search for employment in schools. Many immigrants had their training and experience as teachers in the Asian sub-continent, the Caribbean or in Africa. Some of these teachers do not want to take on the arduous task of teaching the often rebellious indigenous pupils in inner-city schools, but many have been unable to obtain teaching jobs for inexplicable reasons; perhaps their experience is not acceptable to local education authorities! However, there is also evidence to show that those who have completed additional courses at British institutions have found considerable difficulty in obtaining employment.[9] One of the crucial factors in their unemployment seems to be the conservatism and indeed the prejudice of administrators and some headmasters in British schools (M. Jackson, 1974, 1975). Teacher-training institutes must give careful thought as to how they can improve their recruitment of students from ethnic minorities, and the career prospects of these teachers.

It seems pertinent to point out that students currently being trained to teach in multiracial schools will be teaching fewer and fewer 'immigrants'. Rather they will be teaching young black or brown Britons, born here, and who will be seeking the same educational and occupational chances as their white counterparts. If they are denied these chances they will suffer as individuals and British society as a whole will suffer from their deprivation and alienation (Bagley *et al.*, 1979c).

Programmes to promote equal opportunity for ethnic minorities in education and teacher training will have no significant effect if strategies are adopted in a diffused and uncoordinated way. The policy of multicultural education is one of great promise which has yet to be fully realised in Britain. In order to achieve this it requires much investment from the Department of Education and Science in terms of educational materials and training, and much open-mindedness and goodwill on the part of educational planners, teachers and public alike.

NOTES

1. Children of West Indian origin are generally considered as 'second dialect learner'; children of Asian origin are generally considered as 'non-English-speakers' who as a result of schooling become 'second-language learners'.
2. *Scope 1*: an introduction course for pupils 8–13 years (1969); *Scope Handbook 2*: pronunciation for English-speaking children from India, Pakistan, Cyprus and Italy (1971); *Scope Senior Course*: for Non-English Speaking Students 14 years and over (1972); *Scope Handbook 3*: language work with infant immigrant children (1973).
3. *The Times Educational Supplement* (London), 12 December 1975; 16 July 1976; and 22 October 1976.
4. On 23 May 1966, Roy Jenkins, the then Home Secretary, addressing a meeting of the Voluntary Liaison Committee, at the Commonwealth Institute, London, defined the concept of integration 'not as a flattening process of assimilation but as equal opportunity accompanied by cultural diversity, in an atmosphere of mutual tolerance'.
5. The Education of Immigrant Pupils in Special Schools for Educationally Subnormal children (ILEA 657), September 1968.
6. See Chapter 6 in this volume, 'The Problems of Vocational Adaptation of "Asian" Adolescents' by G. K. Verma, for a discussion of disadvantaged position for ethnic minority pupils.
7. *The Times Educational Supplement* (London), 9 December 1977–'More than two cultures'.
8. *The Times Educational Supplement* (London), 28 April 1972.
9. *The Guardian* (London), 8 September 1973; *The Times Educational Supplement* (London), 15 August 1975; 19 September 1975; 3 October 1975.

10 Language and Culture Maintenance Programmes in Canada

JOTI BHATNAGAR

Ever since General De Gaulle's declaration of 'Vive Québec libre', the problems of French minorities in Canada have received world-wide attention. Because of this preoccupation with French–English relations the extent of Canada's ethnic diversity as a nation is often forgotten. It is not generally recognised that Canada has always been, and continues to be, inhabited by ethnically heterogeneous groups. Before the 'discovery' of Canada by Europeans, the 250,000 to 300,000 people who lived in the territory that now constitutes Canada belonged to about 50 societies and dozens of linguistic groups, (Brunet, 1979). Massive immigration coupled with conquest and physical extermination turned the original inhabitants of Canada into politically and economically insignificant minorities in a land of minorities. Canada has no majority group. Of the total population of 22 million, 6 million are French–Canadians, 10 million British–Canadians and another 6 million belong to that bothersome category 'other'. Even this does not give a true picture of the Canadian demographic scene. The three big cities – Toronto, Montreal and Vancouver – absorb an overwhelming proportion of new immigrants to Canada, resulting in a large concentration of immigrants in these metropolitan areas. The 1971 census figures, our last official census, show that in Toronto, for example, close to half of the household heads were born outside Canada, another one-fifth had at least one foreign-born parent and only 29 per cent were born in Canada and had both Canadian-born parents. Figures published by Toronto Board of Education show that as of September 1976 more than 50 per cent of the 93,000 students served by the Board did not claim English as their mother-tongue (D. Green, 1977). A little over 10 per cent of the students reported Italian as their mother-tongue, about 5.6 per cent reported Portuguese, 6.1 per cent Chinese and another 14.1 per cent some other language. Of these over 5000 were born in Portugal, over 3000 in Italy, over 2500 in China or Hong Kong, over 4900 in the Caribbean, over 2000 in Greece, over 4000 in other European countries, over 2000 in parts of Asia and the Middle East, and 1100 in parts of Central or South America. Canada is indeed a land of immigrants.

What is the behaviour pattern expected from an immigrant before he will be considered assimilated and accepted as a full-fledged member of Canadian society? As a Toronto Board of Education (1976) document points out, these expectations appear to have undergone a change over time. Until the early 1960s Canada (including the Province of Quebec where more than 80 per cent of the population is French-speaking) was openly and abashedly British. Assimilation into the Canadian version of the British culture was the only hope offered to the immigrant. In order to get a fair deal many immigrants not only had to adopt British customs and mannerism but also had to change their names in order to conceal their ethnic identity. For some, especially the second-generation European immigrants, it was possible; for visible minorities it was not. And then came the turbulent 1960s; years of social upheaval in North America. In the United States there were campus riots, the destruction of the black ghettos, the opting-out of young people, the drugs, the rock music scene, the emergence of black power. In Canada things were less volatile and the change subtle but just as, if not more, far-reaching. The Province of Quebec underwent what has come to be known as the 'quiet revolution'. French–Canadians in that province increasingly began to identify themselves as Québecois. No longer satisfied with a role subservient to the British, they demanded a bigger role in business, government and industry.

English Canada faced another challenge from a different quarter. A 'third force' emerged on the Canadian social and political scene. Inspired by the black power movement in the United States, the fall of the British Empire and the rise of ethnics all over the world, people whose background was neither English nor French were getting tired of the 'founding races' philosophy. No longer willing to play second fiddle, they demanded recognition of their cultural heritage, of their contribution towards the emergence of Canada as a modern industrial state, and their rightful place in the Canadian mosaic. It was claimed that government policies failed to meet the real needs of immigrants (Ontario Economic Council, 1970) and that ethnic communities deserve much better status and role in policy-making bodies. The federal government's response was the setting up of the Royal Commission on Bilingualism and Biculturalism 'to enquire into and report upon the existing state of bilingualism and biculturalism in Canada and to recommend what steps should be taken to develop the Canadian confederation on the basis of an equal partnership between the two "founding races"'. The primary purpose of the Royal Commission was to inquire into the English– French relations and to look into other ethnic groups in so far as they affected the English–French relations. Many briefs submitted to the Commission soon made it clear that there were a host of ethnic groups who were interested in a multicultural and not a bicultural Canada. After several years of research and public hearings the Commission published a volume on *The Cultural Contribution of the Other Ethnic Groups* (Information Canada, 1970). This volume is a gold-mine of information on topics such as integration, assimilation, discrimination, cultural heritage and language. The role of education in responding to the needs of New Canadians is discussed. The recommendations made by the Commission in this volume were accepted in their entirety by the Government. As a response to the Commission's reports, the Government developed the policy of 'multiculturalism within a bilingual framework'. Prime Minister Trudeau put it in no uncertain terms:

> The policy of multiculturalism within a bilingual framework commends itself to the Government of Canada as the most suitable means of assuring the cultural freedom of Canadians. National unity, if it is to mean anything in the deeply personal sense, must be founded on confidence in one's own individual identity; out of this can grow respect for that of others and a willingness to share ideas, attitudes and assumptions. A vigorous policy of multiculturalism will help to create this initial confidence. It can form the base of a society which is based on fair play for all.

In order to achieve this goal Trudeau proposed:

> First, resources permitting, the government will seek to assist all Canadian cultural groups that have demonstrated a desire and effort to continue to develop a capacity to grow and contribute to Canada, and a clear need for assistance, the small and weak groups no less than the strong and highly organized.

> Second, the government will assist members of all cultural groups to overcome cultural barriers to full participation in Canadian society.

Third, the government will promote creative encounters and inter-change among all Canadian cultural groups in the interest of national unity.

Fourth, the government will continue to assist immigrants to acquire at least one of Canada's official languages in order to become full participants in Canadian society (Trudeau, 1971).

Thus the government clearly recognised that not only is a high level of self-esteem towards membership in one's cultural group necessary for healthy and wholesome development of the individual, it is also a prerequisite for harmonious and cooperative intergroup relations. The first practical steps taken to implement this newly conceived policy of multiculturalism included creation of a new cabinet post of Minister of State for Multiculturalism, establishment of two advisory bodies – the Canadian Council on Multiculturalism and the Ethnic Advisory Committee, and development of a programme of grants to support ethnic groups in their efforts to maintain their language and culture. Thus, federal government began a programme to support after-school ethnic language classes, cultural festivals, music and dance classes and so on. These activities were organised entirely within the various ethnic communities, so children generally perceived these as being removed from the mainstream Canadian culture. Participation in these activities was often viewed as an esoteric exercise rather than as a manifestation of multicultural Canada. Since the education system in general, and teachers in particular, represent the authority of mainstream Canadian culture, it soon became evident that multiculturalism could not be implemented without enthusiastic participation of the school system. Such involvement from the children's vantage point would represent an endorsement of the concept of multiculturalism by the society at large. The school system responded in three ways: by providing opportunities for cross-cultural contact, by introducing language classes in the schools, and by implementing bilingual and bicultural programmes.

In 1977 Harbourfront, an 86-acre tract of land in the central waterfront area of Toronto, was used to develop a series of activities to support the theme 'Growing Up with Dignity'. More than 2000 students from some 30 Metro–Toronto schools participated in the week-long programme. The activities allowed:

students to discover, appreciate, and enjoy the similarities and differences among the many cultures which make up the Canadian mosaic. Participation and involvement were stressed in the hope that children would not only see demonstrations but also participate in the activities which were many and varied (McQuillan, 1977).

Students from Arab, East Indian, Chinese, Greek, Italian, Jewish, Portuguese and several other ethnic groups presented folk heroes, history, dance, paintings, games, food and cultural traditions to other children. The programme proved to be an outstanding success and has since been run on an year-round basis.

A second thrust aimed at raising the self-esteem of immigrant children through preservation of their language and culture was provided through offering a number of languages as electives in the secondary school curriculum. Toronto, for example, offers German, Italian, Chinese, Hebrew, Polish, Portuguese, Russian, Ukrainian, Greek, Hungarian, Latvian, and Croatian in its schools. Though such programmes are now well-established at the high-school level, they have been difficult to establish at the elementary-school level. In 1977 Ontario, the most populous of the Canadian provinces, adopted a Language Heritage Programme. Through this scheme financial assistance would be made available to any school board that decided to respond to parent groups' demand for ethnic language classes in the elementary school as part of the regular curriculum. Premier Davis noted that 'this programme might help Ontario's many ethnic groups retain a knowledge of their mother-tongues and continuing appreciation of their cultural backgrounds. The Government accepts and values the multicultural nature of our Province. . . . (Davis, 1978). Many school boards have been quick to take advantage of the offer while others have been hesitant.

Supplementary language classes by themselves have been found to be insufficient. Children view these as extra work and are, on the whole, not very enthusiastic about them. If immigrant children are to develop pride in their cultural heritage more than language classes are needed. Several school boards across Canada recognise this and have begun to experiment with bilingual bicultural programmes.

The Toronto Board of Education started an experimental programme in the autumn of 1965 in the Main Street school. At first, 75 students over 12 years of age were enrolled. Many of the teachers involved in the programme were themselves bilingual or multilingual. But more importantly, all of them were very sympathetic to the concept of multiculturalism. The programme recognised that problems of immigrant children go beyond linguistic difficulties. It emphasised communication, committment and dialogue that would allow the student to be resocialised at his own pace. The school's philosophy is best summarised by Mr La Fountaine in an internal memo to the Board:

> The real fact of life in this question of the new immigrant population in our school system is that the problem it presents is not, never has been, and never will be, a language problem. It is a cultural problem. Furthermore, it insists that the new immigrants' culture and ours be integrated, made compatible, in the personality of the immigrant himself. This means that there is only one valid principle to which the Board can look for its solution. The new immigrant must be provided with the opportunity and the possibility to effect the integration of his own culture with the new culture – which the school represents – for himself, on his own terms and in his own time (La Fountaine, 1976).

The methodology employed by the school is described by the principal:

> At Main Street there is a great deal of sharing of experiences. Teachers and students do things together – they work out projects together, they visit the community library, stores, and shops together, they eat their lunch together, they go on field trips together. The students are encouraged to talk about the way of life in their native land and of the changes Canada had meant for them and their families. There is no attempt to influence the students into adopting the clothes, food, and responses of other young Canadians. The fact that a boy's lunch consists of a thick chunk of meat and a slab of bread instead of a ham or cheese sandwich and an apple should, not be a source of confusion and embarrassment, but an opportunity for an exchange of inform-ation and ideas – and perhaps an exchange of food. The round lunch tables provide a setting for developing dialogue as a pupil eats with teachers and classmates. Here, as elsewhere in the school, the aim is not to assimilate these young people into our culture, but to integrate them (Sterioff, 1976).

The school obviously had very commendable aims. But did it succeed in helping its pupils? Evaluation studies by the Research Department did not show any large differences in the academic achievement between the graduates of this school and those from other regular schools. The school, however, proved to be very popular with the immigrant population and its enrolment increased. It also served as the inspirational model to other schools interested in experimenting in this area.

In two mid-town Toronto schools, 90 per cent of the children were of Chinese origin. In the early 1970s parents of these children began speaking out on the communication gap widening between themselves and their children – the children were more and more talking in English and becoming part of a new culture that seemed to be rejecting the older culture of their parents. There were after-school Chinese classes in the community, but they required a great deal of extra work and were too expensive for most families. The parents appealed to the school Board, and after much discussion the programme began in 1974. The Board's document outlining the rationale of the bilingual bicultural programme states:

> The existence of such a program in the school would place a recognition of integrity and worth of the Chinese culture within the child's frame of reference. Secondly it would represent compatibility between the home and school rather than a cultural competition for the children's allegiance (Toronto Board of Education, 1976).

In the first year, 300 students, including a few not of Chinese background, enrolled in the programme, which consists of withdrawing the students from regular classes for half an hour a day for instructions in Chinese language and culture. The programme was evaluated a year after its inauguration. The researchers found that most students, parents and teachers agreed that the Chinese programme was successful in making students more aware of Chinese culture. Receiving half an hour a day less instruction did not result in any lowering of academic achievement, while a very noticeable change in the self-esteem was observed. The students were better-informed and placed greater value upon their cultural heritage. The programme became a prototype of the several bilingual and bicultural programmes to follow (Deosaran and Gershman, 1976). A similar Greek bilingual programme is now being run in two schools in East Toronto.

In 1973 an experimental Italian transition programme was started in a junior and senior kindergarten. In this programme the children are initially taught in their mother-tongue – Italian in this case. They are then gradually introduced to English and are expected to catch up with regular classes in oral and written English by grade three. But would not lack of early instruction in the English language make these Italian children deficient in English? The psychologists who evaluated this programme did not find this to be the case. The children did not suffer in English-language comprehension. Their self-esteem improved considerably (Toronto Board of Education, 1977).

In an attempt to raise the self-esteem of Indian children and to ease their adjustment problems the Vancouver School Board, the University of British Columbia and Khalsa–Diwan Society (an East Indian community organisation) got together to organise a programme in the summer of 1971. The schedule of activities included field trips, arts and crafts, story time and publication of a weekly newspaper. The programme was staffed by 23 university and high-school students, both East Indians and Europeans, all volunteers. Evaluation of the programme showed considerable differences in the pre- and post-test scores of children both on cognitive and self-esteem variables. Programmes of this nature appear to be very beneficial to immigrant children if they are run by organisers who are enthuasistic, competent and have an aptitude for cross-cultural work. (Moody, 1971).

The Government of Quebec initiated a project (Project d'Enseignment de Langues d'Origin) to offer children of linguistic minorities the possibility of maintaining and developing their knowledge of the language and culture of the family. Three programmes, Greek, Italian and Portuguese, were developed by three production committees. The members of these committees belonged to the ethnic group concerned, had a thorough competence in the language and culture, had experience in teaching ethnic languages and were thoroughly familiar with the French language and Quebec school system. The programmes were open to children who had knowledge of the language concerned, and whose parents recognised themselves as belonging to the particular ethnic group. The programme was offered on a trial basis in the 1978–79 school year in the first grade in seven Montreal Catholic School Commission schools, and consisted of teaching ethnic language and culture for half of the school time. Preliminary results indicate a general satisfaction on the part of children, parents, teachers and organisers of the programme. The programme was extended to the second grade in the 1979–80 school year when the results of the experiment will be published (Bosquet, personal correspondence).

Language and culture programmes make sense only if the various minority groups do indeed wish to retain their cultural identity. O'Bryan *et al.* (1978) attempted to examine whether there is a real desire to support language retention as a viable source of cultural identity and preservation among members of groups whose mother-tongue is other than English or French. The study found a great deal of ethnic language usage among first-generation immigrants but by the third generation ethnic language was a fond memory. For children of immigrants, therefore, it was not a question of language retention but of reacquisition. This language loss was viewed as unsatisfactory not only by immigrants themselves but also by their children and grandchildren. The study found a strongly felt need for cultural and language retention both by those who retained the ancestral language and those who did not. Most immigrants preferred schools and not part-time language classes as vehicles of instruction. Many parents reported that should such language classes be offered in the regular school system they would insist upon their children taking them, and almost all agreed that they would encourage the children to do so. But what about Canadians of British and French origins who form the bulk of the Canadian population. Do they approve of language and culture retention? Berry *et al.* (1978) designed a study to answer the question whether all Canadians regard cultural diversity as a valuable resource and whether confidence in one's own identity is a prerequisite for accepting others. A national sample of 1849 respondents was interviewed. The study found little factual knowledge about multiculturalism in the Canadian population. Despite this lack of knowledge, attitude towards multiculturalism were generally positive, although behavioural intentions were less so.

Language and culture retention programmes as tools for developing a sense of pride in ethnic group membership, and thus raising self-esteem of minority groups, faces two major obstacles in Canada. Firstly, for the most part teachers do not understand the meaning of multiculturalism. Language and culture retention programmes have touched very few children so far. In most regular schools teachers, though well-meaning and hard-working, nevertheless work hard towards assimilation. They convey that children come from a different culture, an inferior culture. Teachers see Anglo-conformity as the only way for these children to gain social mobility and move out of the immigrant ghetto. It is hardly surprising that many immigrant children have poor self-esteem and do not do well at school. Some immigrant children have inadequate command over the English language when they first enter school. On the whole, teachers insist upon starting from scratch, as if the child was a *tabula rasa*, and ignore the wealth of the child's linguistic and cultural experiences.

Secondly, self-esteem of minority group children is unlikely to be high in a cultural environment which places low value on their ethnic group.

Although Berry *et al.* (1978) found that, on the whole, Canadian society
is more tolerant than most other multiracial societies and is relatively
open to the concept of multiculturalism, we get a different picture from
studies done in high-immigrant areas where most of the immigrants live.
Richmond (1976) reported that blacks and Asians were four times more
likely than whites to report employment discrimination and eight times
more likely to report discrimination in housing. Ramcharan (1974)
reported that 58 per cent of the West Indians claimed to have
encountered employment discrimination; 37 per cent in housing and 16
per cent in other areas. These studies are older than Berry's work; is it
possible that the situation has changed over time? Unfortunately, data
do not support such optimistic assumptions. A recent study in Toronto
(Henry, 1978) found 16 per cent of the population to be extremely racist;
35 per cent inclined towards racism; 19 per cent extremely tolerant and
30 per cent inclined towards tolerance. People in the low SES group with
low level of education were found to be less tolerant than others. This
may also be a function of the low self-esteem of these groups. As
Montgomerie (1978) points out it is difficult for children from these
backgrounds to show respect, love and understanding, and warmth to
these people from strange lands because no-one ever showed children
from the lower socio-economic groups any respect, love and
understanding – and they are not even from a strange land! One learns
to tolerate others when one learns to tolerate oneself.

Social climate in the community is reflected in the social climate inside
the school. If the situation in high-immigrant areas such as Toronto is
indeed as bad as the studies would suggest, there is little chance of the
immigrant child developing positive self-concept of his ethnic group
membership. The school Boards have attempted to remedy this
situation through providing in-service training for teachers and information for students. Toronto Board of Education, for example, has
developed multi-media packages on Greece, Italy, the West Indies and
so on for use with teachers, parent–teacher associations, and students.
These packages provide information on the cultural background of the
various groups. At least four Canadian universities now offer programmes in Multicultural Studies and more are likely to follow suit.

So where do we stand? Are language and culture maintenance
programmes the answer for providing appropriate education for
immigrant and minority group children? While there is considerable
controversy about the cognitive consequences of using English (or
French) as the medium of instruction in schools when the home
language of the child is different, there is little doubt that the child's self-

esteem suffers. On the other hand, every study seems to points in the direction of a markedly improved self-esteem in language and culture maintenance programmes. However, these programmes have not been in existence long enough to measure the long-term impact on cognitive, social and affective development.

11 Tests and Testing in a Multiethnic Society

GAJENDRA K. VERMA and KANKA MALLICK

INTRODUCTION

Educational and psychological measurement, assessment or testing – whichever words we decide to use – has been the target of much criticism in the last two decades. There are many, both within and outside the social sciences, who often express their scepticism concerning the principles of test construction and interpretation of test results. Another issue debated in many parts of the world today is the impact of tests on educational programmes. These issues apply with particular force to the area of race relations research or measurement in a multiethnic society where testing is viewed by many critics (including teachers, parents and administrators) as a dubious activity. However, their concern is not altogether trivial and unjustified.

A great deal of confusion exists at present concerning the nature of mental ability, and particularly its relationship to heredity. Some psychologists (e.g. Burt, Jensen, and Eysenck) claim that genetic differences play a major role in determining the intellectual capacity of individuals. Many people believe that IQ tests accurately measure these capacities, and that certain types of IQ tests can be used to compare the over-all ability levels of different ethnic/racial groups (Jensen, 1972, 1980). The recent work of Hirsch (1975) and Kamin (1977) concerning the heritability of IQ scores showed that the case for genetic inheritance of ability was greatly exaggerated. These writers have even raised a question mark concerning the integrity of Burt and Jensen. However, the nature/nurture controversy in the field of intellectual development has raged for as long as mental testing has been practised on both sides of the Atlantic. In the United States the School of Psychology which emphasised the genetic inheritance of ability has found considerable support from the pioneers of early testing (e.g. Thorndike and Terman), through to the writings of Jensen and Hernstein in recent years. In Britain the argument that there are genetically determined differences in mental ability has been put forward by early theorists like Spearman and Burt through to the contributors (who included Cyril Burt) to the *Black Papers* (Cox and Dyson, 1969/70), and the work of Eysenck more recently.

It would seem relevant here to mention briefly the emergence of the *Black Papers*. The rapid growth of comprehensive education and the setting up of Educational Priority Areas (EPAs) signalled a new phase in the English educational system (Monks, 1970). It also marked the beginning of a serious attempt to achieve not only equality of educational opportunity but also, as Halsey (1972) called it, 'equality of outcomes'. This educational philosophy produced a strong reaction from those who felt that educational standards were at risk, that able children were being penalised, and innate potentialities were being ignored. The *Black Papers* (1969, I; 1969, II; 1970, III;) gave expression to these fears. There was a considerable body of opinion, reflected in the contributors to the *Black Papers*, who looked up to Burt as a protagonist of educational sanity and the maintenance of educational standards. In the last years of his life Burt restated his views in the *Black Papers* (III, 1970) affirming his dogmatic and unchanged belief in selective schooling. Burt totally denied that the limits set by natural endowment could ever be outgrown. As he put it, 'a definite limit to what children can achieve is inexorably set by the limitations of their innate capacity', and this implies that no improvements in the quality of children's education can ever make any difference.

The argument that nurture of environment is the crucial factor in determining an individual's intellectual ability was first asserted in America by Lippman in the 1920s.[1] This view was not made explicitly in Britain until after the Second World War (see Halsey *et al.*, 1961). More recent writers (e.g. Hirsch, 1975; Kamin, 1977; Halsey, 1977) have cast significant doubt on the empirical basis of the genetic inheritance of intelligence. Halsey's (1977) collection of papers on genetics, population, IQ, social class and race is an indication of the changes in thinking which have taken place in this field. Kamin's (1977) review of several studies of separated twins have shown that although twins were brought up in separate families, they were brought up by close relatives, and often attended the same school, and even lived in the same area or street. In this work he has also highlighted the history of the political uses of IQ tests, and the racist and national-chauvinist ideologies which accompanied their development and use in America.

However, whatever the arguments for and against mental testing, whatever the line of debate, evidence in the literature clearly shows that the development and practical use of tests in America and England were geared to protect and sustain class interests (Karier, 1973, 1976; Kamin, 1977).

In England tests were promoted as part of the educational selection procedures $(11 + \text{selection})^2$ on the assumption that there was cultural homogeneity in society. In Burt's biography Hearnshaw (1979) has quoted Burt's views who regarded the social background of English school children as 'comparatively uniform'. This view clearly shows that Burt has limited grasp both of the range and of the subtlety of environmental influences on intellectual development (Hearnshaw, 1979).

The Spens–Norwood plan of tripartite selective secondary education became incorporated into the English education system following the publication of the Education Act of 1944. The school-leaving age was raised to 15 to provide a minimum of 4 years' secondary education following the selection process at 11 +. In the words of the Board of Education White Paper (1943) the aim was to provide all children with 'efficient full-time education suitable to the child's age and aptitudes'. The 11 + selection system was official educational policy for nearly 20 years until in 1965 a Labour Government announced its intention to end selection at 11 +. The 11 + selection system was opposed by many educational thinkers and social reformers who believed that selective schooling was bound to perpetuate class divisions. Other criticisms were that results could be substantially influenced by coaching and that it imposed too great a nervous strain on many children. Burt dismissed as of little importance some of the criticisms made of the 11 + exam. The various criticisms have been discussed by Brian Simon (1953) in his book *Intelligence Testing and the Comprehensive School.* He argued in this book that 'the present selective and graded system of schools serves the need of a class-divided society'. He went further to assert that 'the theory that children can be divided into different groups, that they have fundamentally differing mental capacities which determine their whole future development, is derived from the theory and practice of intelligence testing'. He strongly advocated the comprehensive secondary schooling.

Psychological tests as 'objective' methods of measurements were also regarded as potentially a significant improvement on the previous mechanistic and unreliable approach to assessment. Valentine (1932), a leading supporter of testing wrote:

> The instability of the marking of examination papers has been thrown into relief by the remarkable constancy of the marking of mental tests [and further added]. On the whole it seems safe to say already that this combination of written examinations plus carefully selected intelligence tests is likely to supply a more reliable means of selecting pupils for secondary schools at 11 + than will the examinations alone.

Although far more sophistication has been introduced into the process of testing in the last few decades, some of the issues have remained unresolved. For example, the problem of ethnocentric bias in psychometric tests, the concern of this chapter, has received very little attention so far in Britain (Haynes, 1971). This situation is likely to change rapidly in the light of contemporary political and educational trends in British society. These trends need to be mentioned briefly before proceeding to an appraisal of the crucial issues in testing in a multiethnic society.

In spite of the countervailing indices it would be hard to resist the proposition that British social policy has become markedly racist over the past two decades (Bagley and Verma, 1979). This trend is reflected not only in a series of legislation governing 'New Commonwealth' immigration since 1964, but in the changing rhetoric of political party spokesmen (from both the main parties). In 1979, for example, in one of her pre-election speeches Mrs Thatcher remarked that people in Britain were afraid of being swamped by another culture. The extent to which the current political manoeuvring (such as the one adopted by Mrs Thatcher) represents an accurate reading of popular sentiment, or the extent to which it actually creates the sentiment it seeks to reflect, is a matter for conjecture.

The second trend is the more recent renaissance in large-scale educational measurement programme under government sponsorship. The creation in 1974 of an Assessment of Performance Unit (APU) within the control of the Department of Education and Science (DES) to mount a national testing programme on the school population, in most areas of the curriculum, has provided a fresh impetus to testing that was in a state of some decline. Although at this point in time no-one seems to be sure to what uses the many tests now under development will be put, it seems fairly certain that the role of testing in the educational field will be greatly enhanced in the near future. It will be most unfortunate, however, if test results are linked with salary, allowances, promotions and status which would throw us back to the 'payment by results' era. Most people would agree that testing for diagnostic purposes is useful and has a value. Alarm centres on the spurious attempt to use tests as instruments to maintain or improve 'standards' but ignoring the fallacies and inefficiencies of testing as a process. Let us hope that decision-makers in Britain have learned from the 11 + mistakes by now.

Friedenberg (1969) has stated succinctly the general problem in testing:

> Educational measurement is an inherently conservative function, since it depends on the application of established norms to the selection of candidates for position within the existing social structure on terms and for purposes set by that structure. It cannot usually muster either the imagination or the sponsorship needed to search out and legitimate new conceptions of excellence which might threaten the hegemony of existing elites.

If Friedenberg's analysis is correct, there is a very serious question to be raised about the extent to which the planned expansion of centrally developed, nationally applied tests is likely to discriminate against ethnic minority groups in Britain, or at least to provide misleading information for policy determination.

SOME ISSUES OF MULTIETHNIC TESTING

The early testing movement reflected the strong elitist and racist values of the testers, and the common elements of their culture. Thorndike, the founding father of the American testing movement, and a major proponent of this movement for 30 years remarked (in 1903), 'We conquer the facts of nature when we observe and experiment upon them. When we measure them we have made them our servants' (Quoted by Joncich, 1968). During the First World War Thorndike was called upon to give to the Government of the United States all possible assistance in connection with psychological problems arising in the military service (Joncich, 1968). He was one of the many psychologists working on the rapid classification of conscripts for types of duty. He was soon put in charge of the Statistical Unit which launched the main test – the Army Alpha Test (Joncich, 1968; Kamin, 1977).

Many recent writings on this subject (e.g. Karier, 1976; Kamin, 1977) show the cultural and ideological bias of the early testers by examining some of the psychological tests developed during the First World War. These writers indicate that to hold opinions synonymous with the values held dear by the white, Protestant, northern European section of the American population was regarded as a valid indicator in the assessment of intellectual ability. Questions included in the First World War US Army Alpha Tests (quoted by Karier, 1976) seem to confirm this:

Why should you not give money to beggars in the street? Because – it breaks up families – it makes it hard for the beggar to get work, – it takes away the work of organised charities – it encourages living off others.

and:

If a man knew he would die in two weeks, he should:

blow in all his money;
make his will and straighten out his accounts;
go dig his grave;
start out on a sight seeing tour?

The right answers to the questions were the fourth and second respectively. The so-called 'objective' method of establishing ability level was the perfect instrument for test constructors to develop in order to legitimate their views of the world, and not the world as it was. Thorndike's (1920) work, *The Psychology of the Half-Educated Man*, is a clear indication of how test-developers measured people against the test-constructor's subjective model of a successful individual. Karier (1976) refers to a statement which was made by Thorndike in 1920: 'To him that hath a superior intellect is given also on the average a superior character'. It is quite obvious from the statement that the reference point for the scale of superiority was highly culturally specific.

The work of Karier (1973, 1976) and Kamin (1977) in particular indicates that even today many widely used ability and achievement tests are thoroughly permeated by the cultural and ideological perspectives of their developers. It should not be thought that this cultural and ideological influence is 'contamination' in the sense that the tests were generally acceptable but blemished by the cultural perspectives of their developers; in fact the tests are the products of their culture and ideology. The tests themselves are cultural artefacts, not merely bent at the edges by cultural biases. Kamin's recent research relating to the heritability of IQ scores shows that the case for genetic inheritance of ability has been greatly exaggerated. The ideas are fundamentally erroneous, yet they are widely held.

This kind of critique has also been levelled at policy-oriented international research. The International Educational Assessment (IEA) study of comparative cognitive achievement in 20 countries drew the following comment from Platt (1975) of UNESCO:

> There is good reason for suspecting that tests inadvertently were not culturally fair, that they were overdependent upon reading ability, upon Western concepts and values, and upon experience with the multiple choice format.

In the field of education on both sides of the Atlantic the testing movement produced massive discrimination between various racial and social groups (Karier, 1973). The questions inherent in this issue are raised with reference to psychological as well as all forms of standard-ised tests. Tests were utilised not only to discriminate against children in their education but to restrict employment opportunities for minority groups (Irvine, 1973). Furthermore, the testing movement helped to develop and perpetuate the myth of 'scientific objectivity'. Even today, most intelligence tests utilised in schools and other walks of life in America and Britain clearly reflect the common elements of a particular culture that is West European culture.

The New British Intelligence Scale (published as the British Ability Scales) has been developed after many years of research, but has failed to tackle some of the crucial issues concerning the nature of intelligence and its measurement. In 1965 a research project was established with the support and advice of a specially formed committee of the British Psychological Society (BPS) with the aim of replacing such tests as the Stanford–Binet and the various Wechsler Scales which are widely used in clinical work with children in Britain. Both the Stanford–Binet and the Wechsler are of American origin, and have been adapted for British use. However, the project responsible for the production of the British Abilities Scales was financed by the Department of Education and Science (DES), and was based at the University of Manchester.

The test battery covering a very wide range of different abilities is called the 24 British Ability Scales and provides a new approach to the individual assessment of children's abilities. The scales have been standardised on about 3400 children drawn from various social classes, rural and urban communities, and the main geographical areas of Britain. Norms are provided for children aged between $2\frac{1}{2}$ and 17 years. It is obvious that psychologists responsible for the development of this scale turned a blind eye to the fact that Britain is a multiethnic, multicultural society; and they have deliberately left out immigrant and ethnic minority children in the development and validation of this scale. This omission obviously has serious implications in terms of social policy.

During the last 30 years some psychologists have attempted to introduce broad culturally based tests while others claim to have sought this impossible: culture-free or culture-fair intelligence tests. This has been based on their belief that such tests can provide trustworthy comparisons of the ability levels of different racial and ethnic groups. 'The reasoning which underlies this belief is clearly fallacious and easy to refute' (Blum, 1978). The question is why this belief has gained wide acceptance, which it has! Such attempts also indicate their failure to understand the meaning of culture.

Haynes (1971) rightly remarks that intelligence tests given to 'immigrant' children in Britain are not able to measure their present or future performances because of their tests' verbal bias and cultural assumptions which are not those of children's culture. According to her children's scores on such tests they are unfair and may be misleading. In an attempt to resolve some of the issues of testing in a multiracial context Haynes has developed new tests which, she claims, are less culturally and verbally biased. Her main objective in devising such tests was to assess the learning ability of children with lignuistic handicaps.

Hegarty and Lucas (1979) have argued for the replacement of the concept of IQ by that of learning ability. They have pointed out various advantages of a test of learning ability over conventional tests of IQ, particularly with regard to the problems of reliability and validity. The notion of learning ability implies that every child is capable of quite advanced learning and can be taught to manipulate symbols and concepts. The purpose of testing, particularly with minority groups, then becomes an assessment of the additional tuition needed to enable them to reach the levels of the majority of children.

Early test-designers themselves were white, middle-class academicians who had little, if any, familiarity with the cultures of ethnic minorities. This means that IQ tests have been culturally biased since their inception. It did not become a major controversial issue, however, until after the Second World War.

In 1969 the nature/nurture controversy was brought into the arena of public discussion by Jensen's widely published paper on the inheritance of intelligence, which appeared in the *Harvard Educational Review*. His findings showed differences in intellectual ability between blacks and whites as measured by conventional intelligence tests. As soon as the Jensen article appeared it became the object of vigorous criticism, both for its methodological shortcomings and for technical inadequacies in sampling procedures (Bagley, 1975a; Stones, 1979). Commenting on Jensen's understanding of genetics Vetta (1977) wrote: 'Unfortunately, the very small sections of his work that concern genetical concepts show some confusion and are, in places, totally inaccurate. It is, therefore, important that researchers in fields of genetics and IQ be aware of the deficiencies of his excursions into genetics.'

Most current criticisms of testing amount to statements that tests are invalid or biased, that the use of tests is a cold, machine-like process and that the results of the tests are often misused. There may be a case for saying that we tend to rush into testing populations with more enthusiasm than care. For example, tests of intelligence, aptitude, attitude and personality, are standardised on one particular ethnic group, but are used with other ethnic and racial groups (e.g. The British Ability Scales mentioned earlier). Generalisations from the results of these tests have often given rise to a wide variety of misleading interpretations, especially from those who have little understanding of the populations. Thus, in the absence of adequate validation, tests tend to develop into self-fulfilling prophecies.

The issues are no longer matters of mainly academic debate. The controversy about test bias, particularly in intelligence and attainment testing, has led to the suspension of testing in many parts of America. In 1969 the American Association of Black Psychologists expressed its concern about test bias by calling for a moratorium on all testing of black people 'until more equitable tests are available'. More recently, Chief US District Judge Robert Peckham abolished the use of racially unfair IQ tests on the grounds that the tests measured skills rather than intelligence, and were biased in favour of children from white, middle-class backgrounds.[3] The judge declared that: 'Educators have too often been able to rationalise inaction by blaming educational failure on an assumed intellectual inferiority of disproportionate number of black children.' Although the call for a moratorium by black psychologists for the abolition of testing has been contested by some educationalists on the grounds that the absence of normative checks would result in increased discrimination, it has had considerable success, and has influenced test-developers to shift their attention from intellectual and attainment testing to measures of inter-ethnic attitudes and perceptions.

But measuring inter-ethnic attitudes and perceptions has proved to be as problematic technically as measuring ability and attainment has become politically. In the British setting there are only a few attitude measures (Warr *et al.*, 1967; Hartman and Husband, 1972) which have been constructed on an ethnocentric basis. Such tests contain culturally embedded assumptions which unreliably estimate or discriminate against cultural/ethnic minorities. Furthermore, those tests are technically defective and are difficult to adapt for ethnically mixed populations such as obtained in the UK. Technical deficiencies are numerous: they include lack of standardisation, poor statistical precision and thin empirical grounding, crudity, lack of credibility and obsolescence. For example, the scale used by Abrams in the Survey of Race Relations in Britain (Rose *et al.*, 1969) may be criticised for arbitrary item selection and weighting. There is also a complete lack of reliability or other psychometric information about this instrument. In spite of the research interest this area has generated in recent years (see Verma and Bagley, 1975b, 1979b; Bagley and Verma, 1979) a great deal of work has been done with minimally standardised measures of ethnic attitude constructed, *ad hoc*, for the purpose of a particular study (C. S. Hill, 1967; Kawwa, 1968) and disused thereafter. Above all, the ethnocentrism of attitude instruments is a well-known and persistent problem that seems incapable of resolution if the conventional procedure of test construction is utilised. Problems of ethnocentric bias have been recognised by many researchers in the field of race relations research (Biesheuval, 1949; Anastasi, 1959; Schwartz, 1962), yet ethnically biased tests are often used in multiethnic contexts.

Given the various issues and shortcomings associated with existing tests, there is a strong case for saying that the instruments in use in multiethnic contexts are not finely calibrated tools but, at best, rough-and-ready devices in a primitive stage of development (Jowell, 1973). Most tests in the area of race relations ask for crude responses and embody simplistic assumptions about the relations of these responses to the social reality they are intended to represent. The operation of 'response sets' in measurement of inter-group or inter-ethnic relations is particularly common. Thus, testing in the area of race relations presents problems unlikely to be solved immediately and conclusively.

THE NEED FOR MEASURING INTER-ETHNIC RELATIONS

Current controversy about tests in the area of race, whether intellectual or attitudinal, is a political and ideological one. It is political in the sense that the use of tests can be perceived by those tested, and by some psychometricians, as discriminatory in so far as it can differentially affect the life-chances of members of certain ethnic groups. Still, there is a need for a simple, valid and flexible instrument for measuring inter-ethnic relations, which can meet the needs of practitioners in the field of multicultural education. In this area in particular, we should agree with those psychometricians who argue that tests must be used with far more care than they have been in the past. A major attraction of testing, however, is that it holds out the possibility of a more precise appraisal of human characteristics which can be used in a variety of decision-making activities. Churchman (1971) suggests that measurement should be a 'decision-making activity designed to accomplish an objective'. Surprisingly, one of the few test-designers to warn against the dangers of using tests in places and at times for which they were not intended was Burt (1969). He wrote that 'the chief purpose of the work is not to present the teacher with an automatic set of measuring scales suited to all localities and occasions, but to show by actual illustration how he can construct and standardize more appropriate versions for himself'. Many educators feel that test data are the only hard data, and the only hope we have for bringing an element of 'objectivity' into evaluation.

The central problem is that a society determined to improve race relations needs to be aware of the policies which best promote changes and those which are counterproductive. This implies repeated and systematic evaluation of these policies. In Britain, for example, efforts to improve race relations are increasing at social policy and educational policy levels. These efforts need to be evaluated in order to guide future policy (Jenkins *et al.*, 1979). Current policy is controversial, i.e. people of different ethnic minority groups disagree about its likely effects, and about the motives of those who advocate different courses of action. Given this situation, it is crucial that the means of assessing the effects of social action should not be vulnerable to criticism on the grounds of bias. Psychometric measures can contribute to the monitoring of the effectiveness of policy initiatives which will have a greater degree of political and social acceptability than alternative forms of assessment. The research by Landis and his colleagues (1979) offers important research strategies in this direction.

The characteristics of racial, ethnic and migrant groups differ widely within each society, between societies, and at different historical periods. In studying race relations it is therefore necessary to come to terms with the differences between sets of inter-ethnic relations. From the ethnic and cultural differences between groups it follows that inter-ethnic attitudes will vary depending upon the group perceiving and the group being perceived. To measure inter-ethnic attitude/perception, therefore, a set of measures rather than a single measure must be used. Such tools can make useful contributions in the analysis of certain types of social phenomenon if used cautiously, creatively and in an egalitarian way.

An alternative approach to testing – one of many, perhaps, and at best only a conjecture about possible future developments – has been discussed elsewhere (Verma, 1979):

> In a multi-cultural, multi-ethnic society, a reasonable way forward would thus be to adopt an ethnocentric basis for the development of a set of loosely parallel forms of instrument to serve as a measure of inter-ethnic relations. Each scale should be developed within the boundaries and under the control of the ethnic community concerned. In the development of such tests it would be essential to gain an understanding of the expectations, habits, norms and values of the groups for whom the test is being designed.
>
> Initially, a test development programme in the area of inter-ethnic attitudes might begin with a scale which was not ethnically based, but by involving members of different ethnic groups in the development of tests appropriate and acceptable to themselves, it would be possible to move towards the development of a set of ethnically based instruments. Once the ethnocentric base of each of the tests is established (both conceptually and psychometrically), it may be possible to move from monitoring inter-ethnic perception/reaction to a situation where such instruments could help in defining a language for negotiation between groups. That is, by using each group's own test of its perceptions of other groups as a basis, it may be possible to characterize the differences in criteria, priorities and attitudinal structures between groups in terms of the instruments themselves: the instruments will have become expressions of the ethnic and cultural perspectives of their owners.

This approach, we believe, merits attention in the light of the current controversy. Without new approaches the controversy will continue and ultimately lead to such a decline in confidence in testing as to place its future in serious doubt.

CONCLUSION

It would seem from the foregoing discussion that class and cultural bias both in the use of testing and in the tests themselves varied from the subtle and implicit to the obvious and explicit. However, we do not believe that testing in the area of race should be wholly abandoned. While no-one would deny that people differ; that they differ in school performance and ultimate capabilities because of innate intelligence is the concept with which we must take issue. Furthermore, in this area in particular, tests must be used with far more care than they have been. It is up to test designers to ensure that tests are used properly, that their framing assumptions are made explicit to users, and that sufficient information is given on the purposes and on the settings for which they were developed. Test developers have an increasing responsibility in a multicultural, multiethnic society to see that tests are used within their design limits and that lay use of test results is informed by specialist advice.

We have based our argument in this chapter on the view that tests in the area of race are notoriously defective, and on the conviction that without a dramatic change in approach to the development of these, the current controversy about their value and their political acceptability will continue. Testing may be less vulnerable to criticism on the grounds of bias than other methods of assessment, but only if an approach to testing can be developed that reflects rather than denies the legitimate diversity of social democratic pluralism.

NOTES

1. For a summary of the American debate see Block and Dworkin, 1976. .
2. See Vernon, 1957. The 11+ examination made use of intelligence tests, standardised papers in English and Arithmetic.
3. *The Guardian* (London), 18 October 1979.

Part IV
Comparative Studies

12 Identity, Self-Esteem and Evaluation of Colour and Ethnicity in Young Children in Jamaica and London[1]

LORETTA YOUNG and
CHRISTOPHER BAGLEY

The concept of identity is a crucial one, and is pivotal in education and the social sciences. How a person sees himself, how he incorporates and synthesises the various aspects of his social world, involves both a psychological and sociological phenomena, concerning both the individual psyche, and the position an individual holds in social structure (Bagley *et al.*, 1979c). In ethnic relations it is frequently possible that a minority group, dominated in racist fashion, reacts to that domination in ways which have particular implications for global and ethnic identity.

Self-concept and self-esteem (what the individual sees about himself or herself as salient and important, and how such characteristics are evaluated) are important constituents of identity. Most writing about the concept of self in minority groups has concentrated on the notion of self-esteem and self-concept, rather than on identity, with a few exceptions (Erikson, 1965; Hauser, 1971; Milner, 1975; Weinreich, 1979). The literature on self-esteem has produced controversial findings. Earlier American literature (reviewed by Pettigrew, 1964) tended to suggest that many black children had to a large degree internalised the negative stereotypes which the majority community held concerning them, and in consequence had poorer self-esteem than whites. More recent research with children and adolescents in America has challenged this view, however, indicating that blacks do not have significantly poorer self-concept than whites (Bagley *et al.*, 1979b). Various explanations have been put forward, including a major paradigm shift in the way in which studies are carried out and interpreted (Adam, 1978); the effects of the 'black pride' movement of the 1960s and 1970s (Goldman, 1974); and the effects of changing reference groups, in which black children evaluate themselves according to the standards of their black peers, and of black rather than white reference groups (Rosenberg and Simmons, 1972). Other literature, however, suggests that black adolescents in America still suffer from institutional racism in terms of identity formation, which may be qualitatively different from that in white adolescents (Hauser, 1971; Hunt and Hunt, 1977). Studies of black adults, who are more crucially exposed than children and adolescents to the forces of economic and social racism in America, suggest that such racism still takes a considerable psychological toll (Gordon, 1972; Crain and Weisman, 1972; Clements and Sauer, 1976).

Studies in Britain of self-concept and self-esteem amongst minority children and adolescents have produced findings which have been both diverse and contradictory, reflecting the contradictions of recent American work (see Bagley *et al.*, 1979b for a review of British studies). Studies of young black children (e.g. Milner, 1973) suggested that they have considerable difficulty with the formation of an adequate ethnic identity and self-esteem. It appears, however, that as black children grow older they develop protective sub-cultures and new reference groups which encapsulate their identities from the grosser forces of racism. Davey's study in this book can also be interpreted in this light (Chapter 4). Problems of identity formation remain, however (Weinreich, 1979). An important structural variable seems to be the degree to which a black adolescent does have a black peer group which can give an adequate sense of ethnic identity. In practical terms, it seems that black children who are isolated in nearly all-white schools especially in socially disadvantaged areas, are more likely to have poorer self-esteem (Bagley *et al.*, 1979b).

MEASURING ETHNIC AWARENESS AND IDENTIFICATION IN YOUNG CHILDREN

There is a long tradition of doll studies in America (Clark and Clark, 1950; Porter, 1972; Fox and Jordan, 1973) in which attitudes to self and others are inferred, in both black and white children, from the ways in which the children evaluate dolls and puppets of various kinds. The American studies carried out in the 1970s show considerably more acceptance and positive evaluation of models which looked like them, in black children. However, in all studies either a majority or a substantial minority of black children still devalued blackness and black people in favour of white. White children, in contrast, still evaluate their own colour overwhelmingly positively, and tended to see black figures in consistently negative terms.

An important British study in this field by Milner (1973) replicated and confirmed the gloomy American results of an earlier period. Milner studied 100 West Indian, 100 Indian and Pakistani, and 100 white English children aged between 5 and 8, attending infant and junior schools in Brixton and Southall, in London. All the children were attending multiracial schools. Milner used adaptations of the classic doll and picture techniques developed by Clark and Clark (1950) and Morland (1966). The main areas investigated were Identity (e.g. 'Which doll looks most like you?'), Preferences (e.g. 'Which one do you like the best?'), and Stereotypes (e.g. 'Which one of these two men is the bad man?').

All of the white children chose the white doll in response to the question 'Which doll looks most like you?', but only 52 per cent of the black children and 76 per cent of the Asian children made the correct choice, choosing the black or brown doll respectively. A similar pattern emerged in the family identification tests – 35 per cent of the black children, and 20 per cent of the Asian children, misidentified the black figures. All of the white children would 'rather be' the white figure; but so would 82 per cent of the black children, and 65 per cent of the Asians. In response to questions about preferences for different ethnic group figures, 6 per cent of English children made out-group choices, while 74 per cent of Asian, and 72 per cent of black children, made out-group choices. None of the white children had negative stereotypes of their own group; but 65 per cent of Asian children, and 72 per cent of black children, had negative stereotypes of their own group.

These results pose the problem of whether these young black and Asian children who failed to identify themselves properly gave such responses because they thought they were white: that is, whether the responses of the ethnic minority children were the basis of cognitive confusion which results from being a minority group, rather than resulting from group and self-devaluation as such. Milner discounts this possibility, however, since the children did not show cognitive confusion in other areas. He suggests that the pattern of cause is the other way round: because many ethnic minority children evaluate their group in negative terms, they will in turn *deny* that they are black or brown, but will say they are white. Thus group-evaluation and self-evaluation are intimately linked. Milner suggests that this identification of oneself as white is a measure of poor self-esteem in his black subjects, and is at the same time a measure of a confused identity.

A study using a different methodology but reaching largely similar conclusions was carried out with random samples of children aged 5–10 in East London (Bagley and Coard, 1975). The subjects were asked, in the context of a longer series of questions, 'If you could be born again (just imagine being born again) how tall would you like to be? . . . (and then after several questions about physical characteristics) . . . What colour hair would you choose to have? What colour skin? . . . ' Responses were tape-recorded, and race of tester was varied; in fact, no significant differences between black and white investigators emerged. Eighty-eight per cent of the white subjects did not want to change their skin colour, compared with 57 per cent of the 42 black subjects. Sixty per cent of the black children wanted to change their skin colour, their hair colour or texture, or their eye colour, or all three. The black children in the study were also questioned about their knowledge of Africa. The responses frequently reflected the cultural stereotypes of colonialism: 'They're diseased. They don't live good lives . . . the people don't wear clothes, they live in the jungle . . . sometimes they have to be servants . . . it's hot. The people are coloured, and they dance about . . . I don't like it. People will think that all coloured people are like that.' Other questions indicated that the West Indian children had little knowledge of their Caribbean heritage, or of West Indian heroes such as Marcus Garvey. Children rejecting their ethnic identity tended to have low scores on a test of cultural knowledge (concerning Africa and the Caribbean), and tended also to be seen as behaviour problems by their teachers. Bagley and Coard suggest that aggression in the classroom may result from a combination of the alienating influences of a white-oriented curriculum, and poor self-esteem and weak identity formation in some black children.

In a study of 10- and 11-year-old black West Indian children attending four schools in working-class areas in London, Bagley *et al.* (1979a) found that poor personal and ethnic self-esteem was related to educational underachievement, alienation from school, pessimism about the world of work, parental authoritarianism, and having parents of Jamaican origin. Conversely, black children whose parents came from Caribbean areas other than Jamaica tended to be better-educated, more economically successful, less authoritarian, and had children with higher levels of self-esteem. No direct comparison was made of levels of self-esteem between white and black children in these schools, but the results are interesting because they point to a complex of circumstances which may influence self-esteem and identity formation in black children. Children of Jamaican parents seem to be in the most depressed circumstances, have the poorest self-esteem, and are particularly likely to underachieve.

A study of a large population of 10-year-olds in London schools (Varlaam, 1974) has shown that West Indian children are particularly likely to be seen as being ill-behaved by their teachers; and they are also likely to be under-functioning on tests of reading. Varlaam suggests that failure in reading is likely to precede the manifest behaviour disorders which appear to be particularly common amongst black children in London schools. This higher proportion of 'behaviour disorders' in West Indian children can be interpreted in several ways: it can be seen, in clinical terms, as a reflection of a general pattern of psychological maladaptation which includes poor self-esteem and a poorly integrated global identity; or more realistically, it can be seen as a rebellious reaction against an alienating school system; or the 'behaviour disorders' may even be an artefact of the bias in teachers' perception (since the instruments used are usually completed by teachers). It is possible too that all three factors are at work. It could be that school itself is an alienating institution which contributes to the poor self-esteem of many black children, and that their incipient behaviour disorder of rebellion is a confirmation of the initial prejudices of teachers.

ETHNIC IDENTITY AND SELF-EVALUATION IN JAMAICA

No studies have been carried out in Jamaica (nor indeed in any British-speaking Caribbean country) which we can discover, on self-perception, self-regard, self-esteem, identity, or evaluation of personal ethnic characteristics which have used young children as subjects. A number of studies have, however, been carried out on older children, and in particular on adolescents and older students.

Vernon (1969) in his monograph *Intelligence and Cultural Environment*, which compared aspects of cognitive functioning in cultures in Africa, Europe, North America and the Caribbean, included in his test battery the Goodenough Draw a Man test, which has sometimes been used as a test of racial identification. Vernon's fieldwork was carried out in 1963, and included samples (boys aged $10\frac{1}{2}$–11 years) from both rural and urban areas. Vernon noticed considerable differences in the ability to draw a man between urban and rural samples in Jamaica. Urban children had a much more sophisticated drawing ability than rural children; but both urban and rural children were similar in that, 'not a single drawing attempted to portray skin colour or other local cultural features, apart from occasional palm trees' (Vernon, 1969, pp. 173–4). Vernon does not go into such detail about the Goodenough drawings of his Ugandan, Eskimo and American Indian subjects, but it is clear that the figures drawn by both Ugandan and Eskimo boys displayed considerably more sophistication than those drawn by Jamaican boys.

Phillips (1973) in his monograph *Adolescence in Jamaica* mentions a number of studies of self-concept in adolescents, including his own work, and unpublished thesis work. King (cited by Phillips, 1973) asked 200 12- to 15-year-old boys and girls at a junior secondary school in the urban areas of Kingston, Jamaica, to write freely on the topic, 'All the things I like about myself and all the things I dislike about myself'. Analysis of the responses showed that physical self was the most frequently mentioned of the categories used by these pupils. King observes that ' . . . this reflects the shade and race consciousness which is so pervasively a part of the Jamaican and West Indian psychological make-up'.

The most comprehensive studies of self-concept and self-esteem are those of E. Miller (1969 and 1972). Miller's subjects were 987 boys and girls aged 11–14 attending high schools and junior secondary schools in urban Kingston. The subjects completed an open-ended description of self-characteristics, with questions such as 'What do you like about yourself?' and 'What do you dislike about your body?' Subjects associated Caucasian characteristics as desirable, and Negroid characteristics (hair, skin, lips, nose, skin colour) as undesirable: 'The stereotype of the beautiful girl is almost identical to that of the handsome boy in terms of facial features and colour. The beautiful girl has Caucasian features and is Fair and Clear in colour, as in the case of the handsome boy . . . ' (E. Miller, 1969, pp. 86–7).

Tidrick (1973) has investigated aspects of evaluation of skin colour in 111 students attending the University of the West Indies and the College of Art, Science and Technology in Kingston. Subjects were shown a picture of either a white adult, or a brown Jamaican adult, and were asked to ascribe, by means of a thematic Apperception Test, need for achievement to the individual described in the picture. Higher need for achievement was attributed to the white rather than the brown figure; and light-coloured subjects attributed more need for achievement to the white figure than did dark-coloured subjects. At the College of Art, Science and Technology, where subjects tended to be both darker, and destined for lower-level technical qualifications, projected need for achievement was less. The least need for achievement was expressed by black students evaluating the dark-coloured subject. Moreover, black upper-class subjects projected significantly less need for achievement than did light upper-class subjects. Reviewing this and other evidence Tidrick concludes that 'It seems fair to say that a persistent white bias in Jamaican society contributed substantially to the results'.

It should be noted that all of these studies, with the exception of that of Vernon (1969) have investigated urban subjects in relatively advantaged settings. Yet there are considerable rural–urban differences in Jamaica; 77 per cent of the population are black people of largely African descent, and this ethnic group is both economically disadvantaged and disproportionately rural-dwelling. Many of the subjects studied by Phillips, Miller and Tidrick were not of pure African, but of mixed, ancestry; given the patterns of racial disadvantage endemic in Jamaican social structure, these subjects are likely also to come from relatively advantaged backgrounds.

Lowenthal (1967), comparing a number of West Indian societies, indicates that the rigidity of the class/colour system in Jamaica meant that virtually the only way to achieve occupational and educational advancement was to emigrate. In consequence many black, rural people have left Jamaica for Britain, Canada and America. Nancy Foner (1977) reporting the adaptation of young Jamaicans in Britain also found that the majority of migrants to Britain came from rural areas, and came from lower-status families.

Foner (1977) suggests that

> Black skin has long been devalued in Jamaica. This stems from Jamaica's history as a plantation colony based on African slavery. . . . White bias has permeated the entire society since the eighteenth century. . . . I would argue that it is mainly because being black stands for being poor in Jamaica that so many black Jamaicans place a negative value on black skin.

As she makes clear, this diagnosis held true until very recent times. What is important, we think, is that the parents of Jamaican children in British schools today grew up in a society which devalued blackness; that devaluation was accepted by the vast majority of blacks, who themselves formed the majority of the population. Unlike America, in Jamaica the mystifying ideology of the inferiority of blackness still has a powerful hold.

THE DEVELOPMENT OF A STANDARDISED MEASURE OF ETHNIC AND COLOUR EVALUATION

One problem in evaluating the doll preference studies that have been carried out in America and Britain in the last two decades has been that of a lack of standardisation of test material. Williams and Morland (1976) have developed two tests, the Colour Meaning Test (CMT) in which children aged 4–7 are required to evaluate black and white animals; and the Pre-School Racial Attitudes Measure (PRAM) in which children of a similar age are asked to evaluate pairs of pictures of black and white people of various ages and sexes. Twenty-four different pairs of individuals are presented; one pair in each picture. One of the figures is 'white' (i.e. has pinkish skin complexion) while the other is identical in every respect except that his or her skin is medium brown, and the figure has dark hair and brown eyes. Interspersed with these 24 pictures are 12 further pairs of pictures measuring sex-role identification, showing two similar figures, half of whom are black pairs, and the other white pairs, but in which a man is contrasted with a woman, or a male child with a female child. The purpose of this aspect of the test is to assess sex-role evaluation, cognitive evaluation, and also to act as a distractor from the racial evaluation items. Examples of stimulus items are: 'Here are two women. One of them is a nice woman. She does nice things for her husband and children. Which is the nice woman?'

The maximum score on the CMT and the PRAM is 24 in each case; the higher the score the more the positive evaluation of white and the negative evaluation of black. In an ideal world we would expect very young black children to have a significant pro-black bias, and white children to have a definite pro-white bias, indicating appropriate levels of ethnic pride and self-esteem in both groups. Children of mixed ancestry, or with one parent white and one black, might be expected to have scores in the middle range.

The studies by Williams and Morland (1976) with these instruments using white and black American children as subjects indicate significant departures from these ideal patterns. While white children showed the expected white bias, which would be expected in young children with a properly situated sense of ethnic awareness and pride, black children also showed considerable pro-white bias and anti-black bias, both on the CMT (measuring colour evaluation) and the PRAM (measuring ethnic evaluation). In both groups of children, white and black, the CMT and the PRAM had strong and significant correlations. One implication of this finding is that negative evaluation of colour, which is built into language as part of Western institutional racism (with the implicit ideologies of 'black looks', 'blackmail', 'black day' and so on) forms part of the cognitive and affective basis of negative evaluations of people of different colour, and is one of the ways in which white children learn to be prejudiced, and some black children acquire negative views of themselves.

Although the tests designed by Williams and his colleagues (the CMT and the PRAM) are not specifically designed to measure identity and self-esteem, there are nevertheless clear implications in this work for the study of identity development in young black children who hold negative views about their colour and their ethnic group.

We wished to test directly the hypothesis that negative colour evaluation in young black children in England and in Jamaica would be related to poor self-esteem. In reviewing the literature on self-esteem measurement it became clear that there are few valid and reliable methods for measuring self-esteem in young children. We attempted to construct a workable measure of self-esteem in children aged 4–7 by a slight adaptation of the Ziller technique (Ziller, 1972) which requires children to place models, figures or drawings of themselves spatially, in relation to other significant figures. The measure we used involved presenting the child with a series of circles in a horizontal line, in which the child had to place a very bad boy or girl, a very good boy or girl, and then himself or herself. The spatial proximity of the child to the good or bad figure was then measured, and a score obtained. The reliability of the measure has been established by its consistency over time when administered to the same subjects. Validity is more difficult to establish, but we have shown that children with high scores on this test (indicating the possibility of poor self-esteem) tend to be social isolates or to have few friends in the classroom (as measured by a standardised sociometric test).

SUBJECTS AND METHODS OF STUDY

Our research had several purposes. We wanted to establish the reliability and validity of the CMT and PRAM in Britain and Jamaica, and to examine these measures as bases of identity development in young children. In addition, we wanted to compare the responses of Jamaican children in Jamaica with children of Jamaican parents in London, and to examine the types of colour evaluation in various ethnic groups – English, West Indian, African, Cypriot and Asian – in the London schools in which we have worked. Further, we wished to examine various structural factors, such as school curriculum, ethnic mix in the classroom, and ethnicity of the teacher which might be related to colour evaluation.

In all, we tested 400 children attending nursery and infant schools in Clarendon, Jamaica, and in north London. All children were tested individually, and completed the CMT, the PRAM, and the Ziller self-esteem measure. In addition, children in the infant-school classes in north London completed the sociometric measure.

The tester in all cases was L.Y., a black Jamaican. The fact that the tester was black may have influenced the evaluations of colour produced by the young children, though in what direction we cannot be sure. There is no clear evidence in the literature what the effect of a black tester on black children's self-evaluation might be.

RESULTS

We found that in all groups of subjects the CMT and the PRAM had good internal reliability, as measured by split-half correlations, item-to-whole correlations, and principal components analysis. Calculation of mean scores on the CMT and PRAM (Table 12.1) gave some indication of validity, in that the range of scores was rather similar to that found in the American studies of different ethnic groups. As in Milner's (1972) study using different methods white subjects have the highest scores indicating the most pro-white bias, while black children also display a considerable residue of pro-white (or anti-black) colour and ethnic evaluation. A comparison of the proportions in various groups giving responses which fall into the 'bias' groups (pro-black or pro-white) according to the criteria established by Williams and Morland (1976) is presented in Table 12.2. It will be seen that although the large majority of responses of the white children fall in the pro-white range (consistent with adequate levels of self-esteem in this group) only a small proportion of the responses of the UK West Indian Group (which includes 69 children with Jamaican parents) fall in the pro-black range Similarly, only a small proportion of the responses of the children in rural Jamaica

TABLE 12.1 Mean scores of different subject groups on the CMT II and the
PRAM II

Subject group	CMT II		PRAM II		Correlation between CMT and PRAM
	Mean	SD	Mean	SD	
In London					
(A) Older English, (N = 73)	16.51	4.27	18.03	4.54	0.507**
(B) Younger English, (N = 27)	14.11	4.39	16.44	4.33	0.232
(C) Older West Indian, (N = 78)	16.19	4.34	13.24	5.84	0.260*
(D) Younger West Indian, (N = 35)	15.43	3.57	14.97	4.71	0.477**
(E) Jamaican, (N = 68)	15.91	3.97	13.74	5.75	0.326**
(F) African, (N = 23)	12.70	5.22	10.22	4.77	0.200
(G) Cypriot, (N = 30)	17.07	3.28	17.73	4.09	0.595**
(H) Asian, (N = 17)	15.29	4.57	17.18	4.97	0.749**
In Jamaica					
(I) Jamaican, (N = 117)	13.53	3.33	15.37	3.91	0.332**

* Correlation significant at the 5 per cent level.
** Correlation significant at the 1 per cent level.
NOTE: Subjects defined by the birthplace of both parents. Children of mixed marriages
have been excluded in the above analysis, and will be the subject of a separate
paper.

fall into this range. The only group to manifest more pro-black than pro-
white bias is the small group of African children; Cypriot children, by
contrast, are particularly likely to display pro-white bias.

Analysis of the CMT and PRAM scores by sex and age in the
British and rural Jamaican samples showed the tests to be largely
independent of sex (except that Cypriot boys were particularly likely to
have high scores on the PRAM, indicating much white bias). Age,
however, was significantly correlated with CMT and PRAM scores in
several groups. In the white English, West Indian, Asian, Cypriot and
rural Jamaican groups there was a significant tendency for pro-white
bias to increase with age. This could be related to the fact that as the
children in both cultures are progressively exposed to cultural norms

TABLE 12.2   Percentages in UK, Jamaican, American and European groups
with white and black 'biases' in the CMT II and PRAM II

	CMT			PRAM		
Group	'Black bias' 0–9	'No bias' 10–14	'White bias' 15–24	'Black bias' 0–9	'No bias' 10–14	'White bias' 15–24
White, English (N = 100)	6	34	60	5	21	74
UK West Indian (N = 113)	3.5	34.5	61.9	16.8	43.4	39.8
UK Jamaican (N = 69)	2.9	33.3	63.8	13.0	42.0	44.9
UK African (N = 23)	30.4	47.8	21.7	43.5	43.5	13.0
UK Cypriot (N = 30)	0	16.7	83.3	3.3	16.7	80
UK Asian (N = 17)	11.8	29.4	58.8	5.9	23.6	70.6
Rural Jamaican (N = 117)	7.7	59.8	32.5	3.4	42.7	53.0
White, American (N = 159)	1.2	24.5	74.2	10.1	28.9	61.0
Black, American (N = 176)	6.8	42.0	51.1	12.5	34.1	53.4
White, German (N = 56)	3.6	30.4	66.0	5.4	33.9	60.7
White, French (N = 65)	3.1	41.5	55.4	4.6	32.3	63.1
White, Italian (N = 24)	12.5	12.5	75	0	17	83
'Normal' distribution	15.4	69.2	15.4	15.4	69.2	15.4

NOTE: Figures for American, German, French and Italian children obtained from
Williams and Morland (1976), Best *et al.* (1976) and Best *et al.* (1975).

and pro-white curriculum methods as they get older, so they internalise
these societal norms to a greater extent with age: thus both black and
white groups show an increased degree of pro-white bias with age.

We have analysed the variation in CMT and PRAM scores across the
different ethnic groups in our study, using the technique of analysis of
variance and the derived measure of relationship Eta, which measures
both linear and non-linear trends. Sex and age were controlled in
these calculations (Table 12.3). The variation of both the CMT and the
PRAM across ethnic groups is clearly significant, and for both the CMT

TABLE 12.3 Analysis of the variance of CMT II and
PRAM II across selected ethnic groups

Group	CMT Deviation from overall mean	PRAM Deviation from overall mean
African	−1.47	−4.19
Rural Jamaican	−0.86	0.40
Asian	−0.27	0.11
UK West Indian	0.17	−1.55
Cypriot	0.68	0.42
English	0.83	2.04

CMT: F (d.f. 5,399) 4.86; $p < 0.001$.
  Eta, controlling for age and sex, 0.26; $p < 0.01$.
PRAM: F (d.f. 5,399) 7.47; $p < 0.001$.
  Eta, controlling for age and sex, 0.30; $p < 0.001$.

and the PRAM African children have the most variation below the grand mean (indicating less white bias) while English children have the most variation above the grand mean (indicating more white bias).

Analysis of variance of scores on the Ziller self-esteem measure are presented in Table 12.4. Again, there is significant variation across ethnic groups; English children have the highest levels of self-esteem, followed by African children. Rural Jamaican have the lowest level of self-evaluation, followed by the British West Indian group (which includes a number of children with Jamaican parents) and Cypriot children. Table 12.5 presents the correlations of the Ziller self-esteem measure with the CMT, the PRAM, sociometric measures and sex. For

TABLE 12.4 Analysis of the variance of the Ziller
measure of self-esteem across ethnic groups

Group	Deviation from grand mean (2.31)
English	0.47
UK West Indian	0.09
Asian	0.11
African	0.21
Cypriot	−0.11
Rural Jamaican	−0.36

F (d.f. 5,399), 7.93; $p < 0.01$.
Eta (controlling for age and sex) .24; $p < 0.01$.

TABLE 12.5 Correlations of the Ziller measure of self-esteem with CMT II, PRAM II and sociometric variables

	Older English (N = 73)	Younger English (N = 72)	All English (N = 100)	Cypriot (N = 30)
CMT II	0.287*	0.201	0.274**	0.068
PRAM II	0.322**	0.307	0.318**	0.207
Sociometric isolate	−0.037	−0.193	−0.162	−0.413*
Popularity rating	0.197	0.233	0.198*	0.312
Sex (female)	−0.123	−0.236	−0.138	0.158
SELF-ESTEEM SCORE	2.88 (SD 1.03)	2.07 (SD 1.14)	2.66 (SD 1.66)	2.18 (SD 1.09)

	Older West Indian (N = 78)	Younger West Indian (N = 35)	All West Indian (N = 113)	UK Jamaican (N = 68)
CMT II	−0.278**	−0.082	−0.237*	−0.240
PRAM II	−0.246*	−0.137	−0.202*	−0.170
Sociometric isolate	−0.188	−0.003	−0.147	−0.131
Popularity rating	0.203	0.292*	0.209*	0.174
Sex	−0.106	−0.240	−0.123	−0.061
SELF-ESTEEM SCORE	2.50 (SD 1.14)	2.05 (SD 1.12)	2.30 (SD 1.27)	2.48 (SD 1.13)

	African (N = 23)	Asian (N = 17)	Harmony (N = 14)	Rural Jamaican (N = 117)
CMT I	−0.196	−0.417	0.314	−0.131
PRAM II	−0.266	−0.278	0.042	−0.275**
Sociometric Isolate	−0.384	−0.235	–	–
Popularity rating	0.532*	0.317	–	–
Sex	−0.09	−0.353	0.326	−0.079
SELF-ESTEEM SCORE	2.62 (SD 1.76)	2.5 (SD 0.78)	2.33 (SD 1.23)	1.91 (SD 0.85)

* Significant at the 5 per cent level.
** Significant at the 1 per cent level or beyond.

some groups of children, lack of popularity in the classroom is related to poor self-esteem. The measure has no significant variation across sex groups, however. In white English children there is a significant tendency for better self-esteem to be correlated with more pro-white evaluation on the CMT and the PRAM. The opposite is true in the British West Indian and in the rural Jamaican children, in whom higher levels of self-esteem tend to be associated with more pro-black responses. What this in effect means is that white children who think well of themselves also evaluate their ethnicity in positive terms; and black children who think well of themselves also evaluate their ethnicity positively, and thus tend to evaluate the colour black and the black figures (rather than the white) in the CMT and PRAM favourably.

We have analysed the data for the 175 pupils attending the infant-school classes in North London according to the ethnic balance (proportion 'black' including West Indian, African and Asian pupils) and ethnicity of teacher (four of the ten classes which we studied had 'black' teachers, including West Indians and Asians). Four of the ten classes studied had more than 50 per cent 'black', while two classes had less than 25 per cent. Analysis of variance (Table 12.6) was used in order to identify the effect of proportion black and having a black or Asian teacher upon the responses of children in these ten classes to the CMT and PRAM.

These analyses show that the ethnicity of the teacher has no significant effect on responses to the CMT and PRAM. However, scores on the CMT and PRAM were influenced by the proportion of black and Asian children in the class. Asian and African children themselves were too few in number to be included in the analyses of variance, but the analysis of data for the West Indian pupils shows a clear trend – the classes with a higher proportion of black or Asian pupils contained West Indian pupils with significantly more pro-black evaluation on the CMT and the PRAM. In contrast, white pupils in these classes with over 50 per cent of black and Asian pupils also showed a significant tendency to evaluate white and white figures positively. In other words, being in a minority seemed to have made the white children more conscious of and more favourable towards their somatic identity, while the opposite was true for black children. Being in a minority was associated with an unfavourable view of their somatic identity in the black children, while being in a majority was associated with some reversal of this trend. We would draw the conclusion that being in a majority has favourable effects on the self-image of black pupils, and has no adverse effects on the self-image of white children whose identity is, of course, supported by the wider society. The same cannot be said for the black children. The trends we have uncovered in this study are congruent with those studies which have examined self-esteem in older West Indian pupils (Bagley *et al.*, 1979a) indicating that a higher proportion of black pupils in a classroom is protective of the self-esteem of black pupils who are, in the wider society, a small minority.

A particularly interesting effect was that of 'extreme switching' in the responses of some West Indian children in the London schools, who changed from a white bias on the CMT to a black bias on the PRAM. Thirteen per cent of the 113 black children tested in London made such switches, compared with 1 per cent of the white children, and only 3 per cent in the rural Jamaican sample.

DISCUSSION

One of the aims of this research was to establish the reliability and validity of the CMT and PRAM in use with English children, and with black children outside the United States. The results which we have cited indicate that the CMT and the PRAM do indeed have some usefulness in the study of colour and self-perception in young children in Jamaica and Britain. An interesting pattern of results has occurred: children of Jamaican parents in our London sample have less pro-white bias than the children in rural Jamaica, despite the fact that these children rarely meet white people. We have implied that the colour concepts of these rural Jamaican children are based on the peculiarities of social structure and socialisation in Jamaica, stemming from ethnic stratification with historical roots in the traditions of colonialism and slavery. It seems that the effects of migration and the exposure to the more explicit forces of racism and ethnic evaluation which exist in Britain have been to give some black children a more critical conception of black identity. It is significant that very few children in rural Jamaica switched from a pro-white bias to a pro-black bias, although a significant minority of the children of West Indian parents in the London sample made such a switch, indicating a heightened consciousness of black identity.

What is most interesting in these results is the colour perception of the African children. All but one of these children came from West Africa, and the trend of their responses was to show much less pro-white bias, and to have better self-esteem, than did the black West Indian children in the same classrooms. Since both the African and the West Indian children were exposed to largely the same curriculum, the same

TABLE 12.6   Analysis of the variance of CMT II and PRAM II across 10 school classes containing 175 pupils, with differing ethnic balance, and race of teacher

Group	West Indian		English	
	Deviation from CMT grand mean 15.79	Deviation from PRAM grand mean 13.82	Deviation from CMT grand mean 16.09	Deviation from PRAM grand mean 17.47
50% or more black or Asian in class	−0.38	−0.75	0.01	1.30
Less than 50% black or Asian in class	1.13	2.02	−0.12	−0.47
Black or Asian teacher	−0.07	−0.10	0.08	−0.17
English teacher	0.06	0.08	−0.05	0.06

Analysis Variance:
CMT
West Indian pupils compared across classes with differing proportion of black puils, F (d.f. 1,90) 4.81; $p < 0.05$, > 0.01.
  Eta (controlling for age, sex, and race of teacher) 0.28, $p < 0.05$, > 0.01.
English pupils compared across classes with differing proportion of black pupils, F (d.f. 1,83) 0.52, not significant.
  Eta (controlling for age, sex, and race of teacher) 0.05, not significant.
West Indian pupils compared across classes with English or Black/Asian teacher, F (d.f. 1,90) 0.54, not significant.
  Eta (controlling for age, sex and ethnic balance in classroom) 0.06, not significant.
English pupils compared across classes with English or Black/Asian teacher, F (d.f. 1,83) 0.42, not significant.
  Eta (controlling for age, sex and ethnic balance in classroom) 0.09, not significant.

PRAM

West Indian pupils compared across classes with differing proportion of black pupils, F (d.f. 1,90) 7.65; $p < 0.01$.
  Eta (controlling for age, sex and race of teacher) 0.39, $p < 0.001$.

English pupils compared across classes with differing proportion of black pupils, F (d.f. 1,83) 5.47; $p < 0.01$.
  Eta (controlling for age, sex and race of teacher) 0.32, $p < 0.01$.

West Indian pupils compared across classes with English or Black/Asian teacher, F (d.f. 1,90) 0.33, not significant.
  Eta (controlling for age, sex and ethnic balance in classroom) 0.11, not significant.

English pupils compared across classes with English or Black/Asian teacher, F (d.f. 1,83) 1.53, not significant.
  Eta (controlling for age, sex and ethnic balance in classroom) 0.16, not significant.

classroom balance in terms of ethnicity, and the same kinds of messages about ethnicity from the wider community, we would presume that socialisation within the family, explicit or implicit, is an important influence on the way in which these young African children see themselves. By contrast, many West Indian families, even after migration, may transmit to their children negative feelings about colour and ethnicity derived from island traditions which have been largely absent in Nigeria and Ghana, where the subjective ethnic status of black people has been only marginally affected by colonial enterprises. These are speculations only, and the matter needs further investigation with a larger sample of children of African parents, compared ideally with a sample of children in West Africa.

An important finding of this research has been that West Indian children in the London schools studied in which over half of the pupils are black or Asian have significantly better levels of self-esteem as indicated by the evaluation of personal ethnic characteristics. Such a balance did not have any adverse effect on the self-evaluation of the white children in these classrooms, and this finding, if replicated, has important implications for the concept of multicultural education. Ideally, the school should transmit to ethnic minority children affective and cultural skills which will enable them to cope successfully in the wider society. But at the same time, the school should transmit to all of the ethnic groups in the multicultural school, English, African, Asian, Cypriot, West Indian and others – an intimate knowledge of, and a magnanimous pride in, the language and culture of their traditional society. At the same time, children in all ethnic groups may be enabled through the medium of the school to understand and appreciate the ethnicity and cultural background of their peers.

This ideal model of multicultural education is far from implementation in British schools. The evidence, unfortunately, points to a progressive trend towards alienation from school in many black pupils as they react to the many discriminatory forces in British educational system and in the wider society (Bagley, 1979a). It appears too that in order to achieve an adequate sense of ethnic identity, many black adolescents have to consciously reject many English institutions which have provided fundamentally racist messages about the nature of blackness and black culture (Bagley, 1976).

How will the infant-school children in our London sample view themselves and their ethnicity in the years ahead? We already have a partial answer to this question, for we have carried out research with older children in schools in the same area, involving in some cases the older brothers and sisters of the children in the present sample (Bagley *et al.*, 1979a). The results are not encouraging. A majority of the 10-year-old black children studied were underachieving, had rather poor self-conceptions, were seen negatively by their teachers, and had a pessimistic orientation to the future.

As they grow older, these children will probably recover an adequate level of self-esteem, if they are able to seek fresh reference groups which insulate them from the negative messages of the wider society. At the same time, the bases of identity of black adolescents, retaining a consciousness of minority group status, and subordinating the previous negative views about colour and selfhood which they had partly internalised, are often different from those of white adolescents (Hunt and Hunt, 1977; Weinreich, 1979). The next decade is an extremely important one for the black community in Britain. There are some optimistic strands in research accounts – for example, the findings by Cochrane (1979) in Birmingham on achievement and adjustment in black children there. At the same time, the balance of studies in this field (reviewed by Purushothaman, 1978) do not give ground for optimism.

Finally, we must note that the situation in Jamaica is also in a state of flux. It is not too much to say that Jamaica herself is undergoing an identity crisis as the black population who form the large majority of the island's inhabitants try and mould for themselves forms of political and social organisation which are independent, both socially and psychologically, of the patterns of orientation and living which are residues of slavery and colonialism, in which white values have dominated the consciousness of the people. How soon such changes will be reflected in such things as basic colour and ethnic evaluation in young children is an important field for further research.

NOTE

1. Based on a paper presented at the Third Annual Conference of the Society for Caribbean Studies, April 1979; A version of this paper also appeared in *New Community* (1979), volume 7.

13 The Comparative Structure of Self-Esteem in British and Indian Adolescents[1]

CHRISTOPHER BAGLEY,
GAJENDRA K. VERMA and
KANKA MALLICK

A major purpose of school curriculum according to Jeffcoate's analysis (1976) is the achievement of two broad affective goals, respect for others and respect for self. How this is to be achieved, however, is a matter of controversy, and it is clear that the school both as it reflects the symbolic stereotyping and the stratification systems of the wider society, and as it imposes hierarchies and reference systems of its own, may have a significant negative effect on both pupil self-concept and respect for others (Bagley et al., 1979c).

A particular problem in many schools is that of differential levels of self-esteem and self-concept[2] in pupils from ethnic minority groups. Although the DES suggested in a Green Paper in 1977 that 'Our society is a multicultural, multiracial one and the curriculum should reflect a sympathetic understanding of the different cultures and races that make up our society', these curriculum aims have not been realised; nor do the self-conceptions of many black children reflect a curriculum which meets their congnitive and affective needs. Young black children in particular often have very negative feelings about their self-characteristics, including their ethnicity (Milner, 1975; Young and Bagley, 1979), feelings which may cause difficulty in identity as the child grows older and has to subordinate these negative feelings within a self-concept which attempts to evaluate being black and belonging to a cultural minority in a positive rather than a negative way (Weinreich, 1979).

We have recently reviewed the literature on this topic and the evidence seems to indicate, despite a number of divergent findings, that in the late 1960s and early 1970s black adolescents (particularly boys) had somewhat lower levels of self-esteem than their white peers (Bagley, Mallick and Verma 1979b).

An important exception to this generalisation is the case of class-rooms with a high proportion of ethnic minorities: here the support given by a black peer group seems to be particularly helpful in self-esteem formation. At the same time, however, it is probable that some black adolescents have problems in identity formation (Weinreich, 1979), a problem which has a parallel in the struggles of blacks in America (Hunt and Hunt, 1977).

A number of problems inhere in self-esteem research, both meth-odological and theoretical. First of all, if as we suspect the motive to be esteemed by our significant others is a major one for all human beings (Becker, 1971) then there may be a tendency not only for many individuals to falsely aggrandise their levels of self-esteem, but also for measures of self-esteem to be unstable over time, as individuals seek out new reference groups and new situations which give positive rather than negative feedback (Thompson, 1974). There are various solutions to these problems, including the examination of more complex aspects of identity structure, which are more likely to reveal how an individual thinks about himself than are simpler measures of personal evaluation (Hunt and Hunt, 1977; Weinreich, 1979). If in fact a particular measure of self-esteem has good over-time reliability, such a finding may be of particular significance.

A further problem concerns the validity of self-esteem measures. Many researchers (e.g. Rosenberg and Simmons, 1973) cite the corre-lation of the test with other conventional measures, such as those of anxiety, as evidence of validity. But the question then arises: since some self-esteem measures correlate so strongly with measures of anxiety, is not the dimension being measured that of anxiety about the self in particular social contexts; and why indeed not use the conventional measure of anxiety instead? A more satisfactory measure of validity is a behavioural one, a method employed by Coopersmith (1967) and to a lesser extent by Ziller (1972). Ultimately, however, tests of validity of self-esteem and self-concept measures have to be phenomenological: the only true indicator of how a person thinks about himself must come from the individual concerned (Labenne and Greene, 1969).

A further, related, problem concerns the relationship of measures of self characteristics to other measures of personality and personal functioning. There are a number of contending arguments in this field concerning the relationship of self-esteem measures to those of personality and the degree to which measures of personal worth are stable (like personality measures); or are responsive to social context in ways which personality measures are not (Webster and Sobieszek, 1974; Epstein, 1973). If indeed self-esteem measures reflect the social situation in which the individual finds himself at any particular time, rather than a more enduring aspect of personal organisation, then stability of self-esteem measures across different contexts and time-periods is unlikely to be found. In our view, (as we argue elsewhere in this book), the evidence indicates that self-esteem is not only a stable, but also a central, part of personal functioning, and is crucial and pivotal in identity formation, attitude development and attitude change, and behaviour in various settings.

DEVELOPMENT OF MEASURES OF SELF-ESTEEM IN A BRITISH SETTING

Self-esteem research is not a well-developed field in Britain, where personality theorists such as Eysenck and Cattell have dominated both theory and measurement of 'self-sentiment'. Research that has been carried out in Britain on self-esteem and self-concept (e.g. Zahran, 1966; Thompson, 1974; Louden, 1978) has been well conducted. Nevertheless, a question mark hangs over studies which have attempted to use American measures in British settings without establishing their validity, and sometimes even their reliability, in use with British populations.

We have been interested in the development of measures of self-esteem for use with British schoolchildren for some years, and first developed an adjective rating scale of self-characteristics originally used by Nichols and Berg (1970). This scale was found useful in predicting occupational orientation in adolescents (Bagley and Evan-Wong, 1974). Parallel to this work, we piloted studies of the self-esteem inventory developed by Coopersmith (1967). Principal components analysis indicated two major factors in this 58-item scale, one a general factor which we termed general self-esteem; and the other a sociability factor. Scores on these two scales which emerged in studies of British adolescents were found to correlate significantly with Eysenck's measures of neuroticism and extraversion respectively (Bagley and Evan-Wong, 1975). In further work it was found that the Coopersmith scale, either the full version or the 23-item general self-esteem version, had significant correlations in excess of 0.300 with the established personality measures of Eysenck and Cattell; with the adjective checklist of self-characteristics (average 0.510); with various cognitive measures; with alienation from school life; with various measures of authoritarianism; and with various measures of prejudiced attitudes. The strongest correlation was with Castaneda's manifest anxiety scale (average 0.690) (Bagley *et al.*, 1979c). Factorial studies showed that, in adolescent boys in particular, poor self-esteem was associated with academic failure in school, being in a low stream, being alienated from school and from society in general, and expressing extremely hostile attitudes to ethnic minorities (Bagley and Verma, 1978). The average test–retest correlation of the short version of the Coopersmith scale was 0.681 over a 6-month period. This is slightly poorer than the correlations reported by Coopersmith (1967) but does nevertheless point to the fact that the scale is part of an enduring self-system, as Ziller (1976) implies.

We found that the Coopersmith scale was somewhat unreliable with subjects of 10 or younger, both because of item content and item complexity. As an alternative measure of self-esteem we selected the Piers–Harris scale (Piers, 1969), which on face value seems ideal for children in the age-range 8–13. A factorial study established both the internal reliability of this scale with a British sample, and the basis for a short (39-item) version of the scale. One of the reasons for developing short versions of this and the Coopersmith scale is our desire to compare the face validity of a number of self-esteem scales (Bagley and Mallick, 1978). It is clear from American work that what comparisons have been carried out, of just a few of the score or more self-esteem measures available, have shown that in a number of cases these scales are not correlated with one another at a significant level, and are presumably measuring different constructs of personal orientation and self-evaluation (Wylie, 1974; Wells and Marwell, 1976). On the other hand, more recent American work does indicate the possibility through joint factor analysis of a number of self-concept measures that, '. . . self-concept seems a more unitary construct than one broken down into distinct sub-parts or facets in the nomological network . . . much of the construct is shared, but like a daisy, individual petals or facets are distinct' (Winn *et al.*, 1977).

Before setting out on further work, comparing the Coopersmith and

Piers—Harris short forms in children in the middle-school range (11–14), we further developed the adjective rating scale of self charactersitics. Previously subjects were asked to rate themselves on a 5-point scale spread between two opposing pairs of adjectives (e.g. weak–strong). In a new form of the scale the contrasting pairs of adjectives were distributed randomly through the scale, and each adjective or adjective phrase was rated separately on its own by 'very like me', 'a bit like me' and 'not like me'.[3] The three scales, Coopersmith short form, Piers—Harris short form and adjective rating scale were completed by some pupils attending multiracial middle-schools in West Yorkshire and Outer London.

The results of the comparisons of the three scales and the factor analysis of the scales with sex and ethnicity included, are presented in Table 13.1. There are strong grounds for concluding, from the results of the correlation and principal-components analysis, that the scales are measuring the same underlying construct, and are tapping not only self-evaluation, but important and salient dimensions of self-conception in children from different ethnic backgrounds. Ethnicity does not emerge as a significant factor in this analysis. Female sex has some tendency to load with self-esteem measures, indicating a tendency for girls to have poorer self-concept or self-esteem than boys, a finding in line with earlier British work (Zahran, 1966; Bagley *et al.*, 1979c).

It is interesting to note that the two halves of the adjective rating scale, positive and negative words, do not correlate perfectly. In fact, scores on the negative half of the scale (mean 6.10; SD 4.48) are significantly lower than scores on the positive half (mean 9.23; SD 4.71), suggesting that children are more likely to evaluate themselves negatively when faced with positive adjectives. Nevertheless, each of these halves of the adjective rating scale could serve as a proxy for the other measures of self-esteem, according to the factorial evidence.

THE STRUCTURE OF SELF-ESTEEM IN DIFFERENT ETHNIC GROUPS IN BRITISH SCHOOLS

In a comparison of data from the Coopersmith self-esteem scale (the 23-item version previously developed for use with British students), we found that in samples of students aged 14–16 drawn from 39 secondary schools in various urban centres in England that West Indian males had significantly poorer self-esteem than their English peers in the same classrooms; the same was not true for West Indian girls, however, who

TABLE 13.1 Correlation and principal components analysis of three measures of self-esteem in middle-school children aged 11–14

A. *Correlations between scales*	1	2	3	4
1. Coopersmith short form	–			
2. Piers–Harris short form	0.706	–		
3. Adjective rating scale	0.641	0.674	–	
4. Adjective rating scale: positive words	0.637	0.637	0.850	–
5. Adjective rating scale: negative words	0.595	0.562	0.565	0.515

NOTE: All correlations are significant at the 1 per cent level or beyond

N for Coopersmith	r Piers–Harris	310
N for Piers Harris	r adjective rating scale	381
N for Coopersmith	r adjective rating scale	310

B. *Unrotated principal-components analysis: general factor accounting for 21.5 per cent of variance*

Item	Loading
Coopersmith short form	0.887
Piers Harris short form	0.920
Adjective rating scale	0.918
Adjective rating scale–positive	0.873
Adjective rating scale–negative	0.830
Female sex	0.203
English ($N = 159$)	–0.025
West Indian ($N = 68$)	0.100
Cypriot ($N = 47$)	0.142
Asian ($N = 36$)	0.074

NOTE: High scores on the scales indicate poorer self-esteem

had levels of self-esteem as high as their English female peers (Bagley *et al.*, 1979b). In the present study we have combined the data from this 39-school sample with further data from four multiracial middle and secondary schools in the London area in an item analysis of the 58 questions which comprise the Coopersmith self-esteem scale (full version). Three ethnic groups have been compared: English; West Indian; and Asian (a miscellaneous group of pupils whose parents originate from Punjab, Gujerat (sometimes via East Africa), Pakistan and Bangladesh). A further comparison has been made with Coopersmith data collected in secondary schools in India.

As a first step in the analysis item means for the two ethnic minority groups, West Indian and Asian, and the English control subjects (two English pupils of the same sex, randomly selected from the same school class) were calculated.[4] It should be mentioned that the higher the score on a negatively phrased item (e.g. I spend a lot of time day-dreaming), the better the self-esteem, while the higher the the score on a positively worded item (e.g. I can usually take care of myself) the poorer the self-esteem.

An inspection of the results show that West Indian boys tend to have somewhat higher levels of self-esteem than their English peers with regard to school-related items, but statistically different scores on self-esteem items concerning relationships with parents. Although a number of significant differences emerged (which contributed to the significant difference on the 23-scale) the picture is generally one of similarity rather than of difference. The similarity of means on the item responses is also a feature of the comparisons between the Asian group and their English counterparts, and again, although some significant differences between items occurred, these differences largely balanced one another. The findings indicate that for West Indians and Asians some sources of self-esteem are different, the overall picture is one of similarity, with the possible exception of West Indian males.

A comparison of the first two principal components in the unrotated analysis of the 58 items in the Coopersmith scale again reveals a picture of similarity rather than difference.[5] The purpose of the unrotated, as opposed to a rotated, components analysis, is to identify either general factors or factors accounting for as much of the variance as possible.[6] Rotation throws certain items into high relief, but means that the number of significant loadings (conventionally accepted as 0.300 or above) become much fewer. The rationale for the use of unrotated components analysis is taken from previous work on attitude structures (Wilson and Bagley, 1973; Bagley *et al.*, 1974) which established the reliability of this method, and showed, among other things, remarkable similarities in factor structure across cultures, despite significant differences in the mean scores of the items analysed and basic differences in demographic characteristics of those sampled.

Inspection of the results shows that the first two unrotated components for West Indian girls are very similar to those of the English control group. The first, unrotated factor is of the nature of a general factor, measuring general aspects of self-esteem, and both in the West Indian girls and controls bears a strong resemblance to principal-components analyses with earlier subjects which formed the basis for establishing the short, 23-item scale.

THE STRUCTURE OF SELF-ESTEEM IN INDIAN SUBJECTS

In a study which has attempted to evaluate the progress of reforms aimed at the vocationalisation of Indian secondary education (Verma *et al.*, 1980) we collected a variety of data, including responses to Coopersmith's 58-item self-esteem inventory. Some 1100 subjects were included in this study, with sexes equally balanced. The adolescents, aged 14–16, were attending high schools in Bombay, New Delhi, Patna, Calcutta and Bangalore. In most of these schools the medium of instruction was English, and the pupils came from middle-class backgrounds, with a strong expectation of academic success. One of the findings of this study was the similarity of the responses of the pupils sampled in diverse urban centres on questionnaires concerning achievement motivation and occupational choice. Parallel to this finding, no between-school significance was found in responses to the Coopersmith inventory, and we felt justified therefore in pooling the data for a principal-components analysis. For this analysis 505 of the Indian pupils were randomly selected.

This analysis (Table 13.2)[7] has like the previous analyses emphasised the first two unrotated components in a search both for a general factor in the self-esteem inventory, and for comparability between cultural groups. On first inspection, the pattern of means and of factor loadings seems to bear only a small similarity to those of the Asian group we studied in British schools. It should be borne in mind that our Indian survey contains no pupils from Gujarat or Punjab, from which regions came many of the parents of the British Asians.

On many of the items the Indian pupils have strikingly better levels of self-esteem than the British group, including the Asian pupils whose levels of self-esteem are much closer to those of their British peers than those of the Indian pupils within India itself. These differences may be an example of the acculturation effect observed by Ghuman (1975); or it could be due to the high status of the Indian pupils in the social and educational hierarchy in India, or the differences could be artefacts of measurement; or the self-esteem items may have different cultural meaning for the pupils in India. It should also be noted that many of the high loading items on the first, unrotated component of Coopersmith items for the Indian pupils are positively worded items, indicating the possibility of some response-set effect.

What is more remarkable, however, is that the second unrotated component in the Indian analysis bears a significant relationship to the first unrotated component in the analysis of the data on the British Asian group. These and other results are discussed below.

TABLE 13.2   The first two Components in an unrotated principal-components analysis of the Coopersmith self-esteem items in 505 Indian adolescents sampled from secondary schools in Bombay, Delhi, Patna, Bangalore and Calcutta

Coopersmith item	Mean	SD	Loadings on component I	II
1. I day-dream a lot	1.168	0.97	124	224
2. I'm sure of myself	0.719	0.69	−571	−102
3. I wish I were someone else	0.745	0.89	−104	308
4. I'm easy to like	0.956	0.93	−294	−236
5. I enjoy activity with parents	0.437	0.69	−654	−117
6. I never worry	0.642	0.93	070	−107
7. Hard to talk before class	1.157	0.99	024	344
8. I wish I were younger	1.362	1.02	−007	376
9. I'd change myself	0.697	0.85	−088	070
10. I can make up my mind	0.719	0.86	−262	092
11. Others enjoy being with me	0.406	0.77	−603	−051
12. I'm easily upset at home	1.232	0.96	359	352
13. I do the right thing	0.899	0.97	−104	−292
14. Proud of my school work	0.500	0.81	290	−093
15. Told what to do	1.497	0.97	091	376
16. I don't adjust to new things	1.048	0.98	144	399
17. I'm sorry for the things I do	0.806	0.98	082	269
18. I'm popular	0.344	0.69	486	−190
19. Parents consider my feelings	0.313	0.72	465	015
20. I'm never unhappy	0.891	0.91	−094	092
21. I'm doing my best work	0.594	0.65	489	−051
22. I give in easily	1.019	1.00	−015	315
23. I can take care of myself	0.304	0.79	215	−122
24. I'm pretty happy	0.313	0.88	279	042
25. I'd mix with group	0.919	0.99	000	−435
26. Parents expect too much	0.871	0.91	−047	308
27. I like everyone I know	0.406	0.68	666	−138
28. I like being called on in class	0.940	1.04	052	043
29. I understand myself	0.469	0.78	134	−116
30. Pretty tough being me	1.244	1.05	083	298
31. My life is all mixed up	1.01	0.99	102	412
32. I influence school friends	0.894	0.54	068	−192
33. No attention at home	1.648	1.12	136	315
34. I'm never told off	1.160	0.99	115	−177
35. Not doing well in school	0.709	0.87	063	014
36. I can make up my mind	0.531	0.81	221	−160
37. I don't like being a boy/girl	1.337	1.03	020	362
38. I have a low opinion of myself	1.500	0.86	204	451
39. I don't like being with others	1.551	1.03	−017	250
40. I'd like to leave home	1.243	0.98	107	385

TABLE 13.2   (*Contd.*)

Coopersmith item	Mean	SD	Loadings on components I	II
41. I'm never shy	1.281	0.95	096	−092
42. I often feel upset in school	1.319	0.95	136	308
43. I often feel ashamed of myself	1.113	0.99	099	294
44. I'm not as nice looking as most people	0.999	1.00	023	358
45. If I have something to say I usually say it	0.625	0.34	−205	−139
46. Other pupils pick on me very often	0.921	1.00	074	351
47. My parents understand me	0.531	0.87	−532	−030
48. I always tell the truth	0.891	0.91	−154	001
49. My teacher makes me feel I'm not good enough	1.253	1.06	−004	318
50. I don't care what happens to me	1.419	1.01	048	226
51. I'm a failure	1.594	1.13	335	248
52. I get upset easily when I am told off	1.403	1.01	338	191
53. Most people are better liked than I am	1.019	0.99	157	470
54. My parents are too demanding	1.038	1.00	140	431
55. I always know what to say to people	0.953	0.98	−184	−389
56. I often get discouraged in school	1.369	1.03	268	345
57. Things usually don't bother me	0.937	0.97	−301	−221
58. I can't be depended upon	1.184	0.98	131	386

NOTE: All items scored 0 for 'like me', 1 for unsure and 2 for 'unlike me'.

A COMPARISON OF MEANS AND FACTOR LOADINGS BETWEEN GROUPS FOR THE COOPERSMITH DATA

The rank order correlations of the item means in the Coopersmith self-esteem inventory for the various ethnic and cultural groups have been calculated. The comparisons in the British groups indicate correlations which are *all* in excess of 0.80, and are highly significant. What this means is that the rank order of means is very similar for all groups considered, West Indians male and female, Asians male and female, and the various English control groups. What is most interesting is the similarity of the rank order of means in the Indian subjects to the rank orders in the British subjects. These are shown in Table 13.3. It will be seen that the correlation based on the rank order of the 58 Coopersmith

TABLE 13.3   Rank order of means of 58 Coopersmith items compared between Indian and British subjects

British group	Correlation with rank order in Indian subjects
West Indian females	0.652
English controls for West Indian females	0.624
West Indian males	0.639
English controls for West Indian males	0.730
Asian males	0.749
English controls for Asian males	0.775
West Indian males and females	0.673
English controls for West Indian males and females	0.700
Asian males plus females	0.764
English controls for Asian males plus females	0.769

All correlations significant at the 1 per cent level or beyond.

items yields values which in all cases are in excess of 0.60, in the comparisons with the various British groups.

A similar kind of comparison of the rank orders of the factor loadings for the first two unrotated components in the analysis of Coopersmith items in the various British groups yields a consistent picture. Component 1 is similar in all groups (average correlation 0.55) except in West Indian males.[8] The average correlation between component scores for component II is equally high, indicating that component II loadings are similar between ethnic groups, again with the exception of West Indian males. However, component I in West Indian males does bear a significant relationship to component II in the other groups, while component II in the West Indian males bears some relationship to the first component in the other groups.

The comparison of rank order of loadings for the first two unrotated components for the Indian group with the rank orders for the various British groups indicates a less clear-cut picture (Table 13.4). What is clear, however, is that component II in the Indian students does bear some resemblance to component I in some of the British groups. The correlation is strongest, as might be expected, for the Asian boys and girls in the British sample. However, the rank orders of loadings and of mean scores in these Asian adolescents bear a much stronger resemblance to those of their British peers than to those of the Indian group.

TABLE 13.4   Rank order of factor loadings (components I and II) compared between Indian and British subjects

	Correlation with rank order in Indian subjects	
British group	*Component I*	*Component II*
West Indian females I	0.057	0.374*
West Indian females II	0.323	−0.146
Controls for West Indian females I	−0.152	−0.038
Controls for West Indian females II	0.108	−0.236
West Indian males I	0.085	−0.103
West Indian males II	−0.023	−0.063
Controls for West Indian males I	−0.192	0.158
Controls for West Indian males II	0.105	0.189
Asian males I	−0.105	0.352*
Asian males II	0.379*	−0.141
Controls for Asian males I	−0.170	0.387*
Controls for Asian males II	0.283	−0.114
West Indian males and females I	−0.134	0.246
West Indian males and females II	0.085	−0.078
Controls for West Indians I	−0.224	0.325
Controls for West Indians II	0.125	−0.144
Asian males plus females I	−0.176	0.397*
Asian males plus females II	0.247	−0.078
Controls for Asians I	−0.088	−0.169
Controls for Asians II	0.346*	0.103

* Correlations of 0.33 and above are significant at the 1 per cent level or beyond.

DISCUSSION

An important purpose of multicultural education is to foster feelings of positive identity and self-concept in all ethnic groups, as necessary prerequisites for achievement and social competence in the wider society. Such a policy poses many problems for teachers, however, and the assessment of the success or failure of various multicultural policies presents problems too. Identity, within which self-concept and self-esteem are incorporated, is a necessarily complex phenomenon, since it represents for the individual a combination of all the roles he or she has to play, previous developmental experiences, and the kinds and quality of feedback received from a variety of social experiences, as well as an appraisal of self characteristics in various role performances. It is not surprising that the identity grounding of some ethnic groups may not resemble the complex identity structures and anchorages of other groups. Sources and levels of self-esteem within culturally rooted identities may show distinctive chracteristics which do not necessarily represent, in global terms, a poorer self-esteem. Thus although our older male West Indian subjects show, overall, somewhat poorer self-esteem as measured by the Coopersmith scale, we have to exercise care in interpreting this finding. What is perhaps of equal importance is that although the mean levels and intercorrelations of scale items (as reflected in a somewhat different factor structure from other groups) in the West Indian males differ from those in other groups, the overall rank ordering of the items is remarkably similar.

This similarity of rank ordering extends to the pupils we have studied in Indian high schools. In other words, there is some similarity across ethnic and cultural groups in the frequency with which certain items (which researchers have thought to be important in self-esteem formation) are rated 'like me' or 'unlike me'. It is interesting to note too, that items ranked with medium frequency (middle third) in *all* cultural and ethnic groups are much more likely to be those which contributed to the general factor from which the short Coopersmith scale was derived: 8 per cent of items endorsed with the most frequency as being like or unlike the subjects in a direction indicating poor self-esteem, are in the 23-item scale; 65 per cent of the items in the middle third are in the 23-item scale; and 36 per cent of items in the least frequently scored items in the direction of poor self-esteem are in the short scale. This finding has interesting psychometric implications which deserve exploration.

Previous studies comparing self-esteem in Indian subjects with other cultural groups have produced complex and sometimes contradictory results (Ziller *et al.*, 1968; E. Driver, 1972; Ghei, 1963; Agrawal, 1978). One problem is the lack of validation of instruments in the Indian context, a criticism which must apply to our own work. However, the cross-cultural similarities, both of ranking and to a lesser extent of factor structure, do point to some validity for the coopersmith scale in the Indian context. With regard to the British subjects, the strong intercorrelations of three different measures of self-esteem (Coopersmith, Piers—Harris and adjective rating scale) suggest that the same underlying construct is being measured. This evidence of face validity is a further encouragement for workers who wish to use these scales in this important area of self-concept research. One possibility for future research is the construction of relevant tests of self-esteem, self-concept and identity by the ethnic minorities themselves, in the move towards the 'democratisation of test construction' (Verma, 1977b, 1979).

CONCLUSION

We have developed three measures of self-esteem for use with British children aged from about 10 years to late adolescence – a short, factorially derived version of the Coopersmith Self-Esteem Inventory; a short, factorially derived version of the Piers–Harris Self-Concept scale; and an adjective rating list of self characteristics. These three scales correlate together strongly and load on the same general factor, suggesting that they are measuring the same underlying construct of self-esteem. The three scales correlate equally well in subjects drawn from a number of British ethnic groups, Asian, Cypriot, English and West Indian. They do not, however, differentiate between these groups at a significant level, indicating the possibility that in the late 1970s (in contrast to an earlier period) ethnic differences in self-esteem in older children in British schools are the exception rather than the rule. There is, however, a tendency in all groups, except the West Indian, for girls to have somewhat poorer self-esteem than boys.

In the second part of this research, the complex factor structure of Coopersmith's 58-item Self-Esteem Inventory (Coopersmith, 1975) has been compared between matched groups of English, West Indian and Asian subjects attending British secondary schools. Largely similar factor structures emerged (with the possible exception of the West Indian males) as well as similar rank orders for mean responses to the 58 items. Indian adolescents attending secondary schools in urban areas of India showed a somewhat different factor structure for self-esteem items. However, the rank ordering of items in terms of their importance in assessing self-esteem had clear similarities to those of British subjects in different ethnic groups.

We conclude that although there are cross-cultural and cross-ethnic similarities in the structure and meaning of self-esteem, it is unwise to conclude that one ethnic group has 'poorer' self-esteem than another ethnic group. Self-esteem, as part of a more complex identity structure, has different grounding and different meanings in different ethnic groups. In a pluralistic framework of society, different ethnic groups have different psychological orientations; these have to be mutually understood and tolerated for successful, plural multiculturalism (Triandis, 1976).

The consistent finding that girls have lower or different levels of self-esteem than boys (except in the West Indian group) within each ethnic group may be due to the different roles and interests which women have. However, before we interpret this difference in pluralistic terms, we should first investigate the relationship of self-esteem responses in girls to their lower status and lack of social power. Pluralism, true pluralism, must be based on equality of power between the groups involved.[9]

NOTES

1. Based on a paper presented to the Annual Conference of the British Psychological Society, Oxford, September 1979.
2. Self-esteem concerns the evaluation of characteristics which the individual believes himself to have, or thinks are important about himself. Self-concept involves both the evaluation of those characteristics, and their organisation and development in a more complex identity structure. 'Global self-concept' and 'identity' are probably equivalent concepts. See Young (1978) for a detailed review.
3. The adjectives, in the sequence in which they appear in the questionnaire are: strong; clumsy; weak; clever; good looking; horrible; ugly; nice; intelligent; dim; normal; backward; odd; good at learning; cheerful; pleased with myself; gloomy; friendly; not satisfied with myself; unfriendly; made fun of; interesting; boring; looked up to; a failure; shy; unpopular; successful; a good mixer; popular.
4. For the economy of the space the table has not been included here. Further information about the results may be obtained from the authors. See also Coopersmith (1967) for the test items which were used in the British studies.
5. The table has been excluded for the economy of space. Results of principal-components analysis may be obtained from the authors.
6. Principal-components analysis is a statistical technique for identifying groups of variables which are related to one another in a significant and sometimes complex way. See Hope (1968) for an account of this technique.
7. For the sake of brevity in presentation here, the Coopersmith items have been paraphrased and shortened.
8. Various calculations, using rho, phi, and Pearson's *r* all give a similar picture.
9. Cf. our distinction between racialism and pluralism in evaluating multiethnic societies. The essence of successful pluralism is equality of social power between groups (Bagley, 1972).

14 Identity and Adaptation of Migrants from the English-Speaking Caribbean in Britain and North America

ELIZABETH M. THOMAS-HOPE

Emigration from the former British Caribbean has dispersed West Indians[1] throughout the Caribbean coastlands of Central and South America, to the eastern cities of the United States and Canada and to most of the large urban centres of the United Kingdom. In the century which followed the abolition of apprenticeship laws in the British colonies, the immigration of foreigners and emigration of West Indian-born people proceeded simultaneously.[2] So dramatic was the increase in the numbers of those leaving the islands, that within 50 years they had superseded immigration both in volume and importance and institutionalised emigration had become an established aspect of Caribbean life (Thomas-Hope, 1978).

The first important migrations from the islands were to Central America, until increasingly stringent immigration regulations in the 1920s and 1930s eventually brought the movements to an end. By the early 1940s West Indians were being recruited to meet the manpower deficiencies of British and United States industry during the Second World War. The significance of this movement lay not in its volume, but in the fact that it signalled the shift from the former migration primarily focused upon the Caribbean basin, to one dominated by flows to North America and Britain.

By 1971 there were approximately a quarter of a million West Indian-born people in both Britain and the United States and 65,000 in

227

Canada.[3] Numerical estimates of total 'West Indian' populations are
unreliable because of ambiguities over the definition of those persons
born at the migration destinations of West Indian parentage. They are
variously included in official figures of total numbers of 'West Indians',
reflecting the variability of the extent to which the West Indian identity is
maintained among subsequent generations. Although the present
discussion concentrates upon the migrants themselves, the characteristics of their adaptation and identity are examined with respect to
their implications for the integration of future generations into the wider
society.

THE RESIDENTIAL DISTRIBUTION OF THE WEST INDIAN COMMUNITIES IN BRITAIN AND NORTH AMERICA

West Indians in Britain, the United States of America and Canada are
concentrated in a few major cities. Over 70 per cent in the United States
live in the New York City Metropolitan area, with lesser concentrations
in Miami and Los Angeles. More than half of those in Britain reside in
the Greater London region and the major proportion of the rest live in
the Midland cities of Birmingham, Wolverhampton, Manchester,
Nottingham and Leicester. Seventy-five per cent of the total in Canada
are in the three cities of Toronto, Montreal and Vancouver, the majority
being in Toronto.

   Secondary concentrations are to be found in towns and cities close to
the primary centres of settlement from which people have dispersed
outwards. These include the industrial zones of New Jersey and
Connecticut in close proximity to New York City, the industrial centres
of the counties of Berkshire and Hertfordshire adjacent to the London
metropolitan area, and the industrial towns of the province of Ontario,
close to Toronto. On a national scale, therefore, the pattern of West
Indian residential location is markedly similar for the United States,
Britain and Canada.

   Despite the national levels of urban concentration, in detail, the
characteristics of the distribution in the United States differs from that
of Britain and Canada in that, in the United States, West Indians live
chiefly in areas already identified with black residence. In New York
City the traditional areas of West Indian settlement are in Brooklyn and
central Manhattan (in Harlem), and for the middle class, the Jamaica
area in the borough of Queens and the north Bronx. In the United
States middle-class West Indians are no exception to those of lower

socio-economic status in that they reside in exclusively non-white neighbourhoods. By comparison, the concentrations of working-class West Indians in Canada and Britain create highly visible zones of minority residence in areas otherwise occupied by white residents. This is different in the case of the middle-class migrants who tend towards greater dispersal and have only limited contact with other West Indians.

The implications of residential location for the processes of adaptation and assimilation are not clear, though various associations have been made between these two factors. Nor is it clear how much residential choice really exists for the West Indian working class in Canada and Britain and for West Indian blacks, whatever their class, in the United States. If spatial relations are only the condition and the symbol of human relations, as reflected in Georg Simmel's analysis of the 'stranger', then in itself, it does not necessarily imply that the residential dispersal of a minority population leads to their assimilation, and concentration to social segregation (Wolff, 1950). Certainly, adaptation occurs more readily among those West Indians living in close proximity to centres of West Indian communities and activities than among those who are more remotely located. Extreme loneliness, and lack of adjustment in consequence, is not unusual in cases of isolation from other West Indians, however comfortable their material conditions might be and however congenial their working contacts.

The most important aspect of residential distribution of West Indians overseas is associated with the nature of the competition which develops between themselves and members of the wider society. In Canada, competition for housing and jobs occurs to some extent with other ethnic minorities, which are chiefly white; in the United States, with the local black population; and in Britain, primarily with members of the white, British population. Despite strong similarities in the spatial distribution of West Indian residence in all three countries, therefore, there is an important contrast in the implications of those locations with respect to West Indian adaptation.

THE SOCIAL STRUCTURE OF THE WEST INDIAN MIGRANT GROUPS

West Indians overseas represent nationals from virtually all the English-speaking Caribbean territories. In any one city or area of West Indian settlement, migrants from a range of islands are included. While the heterogeneity of these overseas communities is due partly to horizontal stratifications and cleavages based on island or country of origin, the most significant variation, in terms of the processes of adaptation, is that of socio-economic class.

West Indians in the United States, Britain and Canada fall into a wide range of occupational categories. Although as a migrant group they have no distinct niche in terms of work, there are certain occupations in which West Indians are characteristically found. Owing to the selectivity of immigration regulations, the occupation and class structures differ at their various destinations. Selectivity in the United States and Canada since 1965 has been primarily on the basis of specific occupational categories, or the fact that close family members have already been granted permanent visas. In Britain there was no selective process until 1962, after which permits for residence were based on criteria of descent rather than occupation.

In spite of the wide range of occupations represented among the migrants, including a variety of trades in Britain, the labour demand in the post-war period was in factories, as well as in transport, hospitals and other services. Regardless of previous occupation, therefore, it was these jobs that the West Indians largely filled. This was later to become a source of regret by former tradesmen who felt that they had short-sightedly 'sold out' by migrating and taking employment in an unskilled capacity, thus losing the potential benefits which their skill could ultimately have realised.

Craftsmen, foremen, factory and service workers also form the largest group of West Indians in Canada and the United States. Clerical workers are, as in the British case, a second important category. However, in sharp contrast is the fact that professionals and trained workers constitute a large proportion of the migrants in Canada and the United States, whereas this group forms only a small percentage of the West Indians in Britain.

The over-all pattern of the occupational distribution of West Indians in the United States and Canada is skewed towards the more highly educated white-collar or skilled worker category, whereas in Britain it is weighted towards the blue-collar skilled worker. Therefore, the larger proportion of West Indians in North America are middle class or have middle-class orientations, as compared with the situation in Britain. There, the majority of West Indians are working class, have working-class orientations but nonetheless, with respect to their envisaged return to the Caribbean, have middle-class aspirations.

Variations in class identity and class orientation of the migrants have several implications for their adaptation. Firstly, the higher level of skills possessed increases their freedom in the job market and, as a consequence, in the housing market as well. Secondly, on account of their generally higher levels of educational attainment, they are culturally more flexible and adaptable, requiring less contact with other West Indians in order to reinforce their identity. Lastly, and perhaps most important in the present context, the aspirations and migration ideologies of the West Indian middle classes are based on more accurate information and are less ambitious in relation to the real opportunities which exist at the migration destinations.

MIGRATION GOALS AND EXPECTATIONS

Closely associated with the goals to which migrants aspire are their reasons for migrating. These goals are powerful agents in determining the expectations held by migrants and thus their subconscious demands and adaptation at their destinations. The over-simplification of economic explanations of West Indian migration and migrant aspirations has been misleading in the attempt to understand their adaptation. If West Indian migrants to North America or Britain were simply 'economic refugees escaping from grinding poverty in their homelands', then presumably their expectations and demands would be low, therefore easily fulfilled at their destinations (C. Hill, 1970).[4] In reality, the vast majority expect more than the alleviation of poverty. Even the bulk of the migrants to Britain, who by contrast with those to North America fell into a less specialised occupational bracket, were employed prior to migrating, and the noticeable drain from the West Indies was of artisans. Of those who suffer conditions of extreme poverty, few have the opportunity of migrating, and the ones who succeed do so at a high cost to their families, inflated expectations and a heavy burden of financial obligations.

Migrant aspirations are usually positive and related to the return home. A mere increase in the wages earned overseas is not, therefore, necessarily regarded to be adequate. For the return, sufficient financial capital is required that independence from local employers and the security of home-ownership can be ensured. Despite the ambitious nature of the aspirations, they have been realised in many instances. In any society, and not least in West Indian migrant communities, aspirations remain highest in those circles where some members achieve, for they become the reference groups against which goals are set.

There have been some exceptions to the positively oriented

migrations, for among the upper middle class, many left Guyana in the 1960s and Jamaica in the 1970s (in both cases to North America) because of what they perceived to be deteriorating political and social conditions. But for the overwhelming majority of West Indians, emigration has traditionally been seen as the means of circumventing the obstacles to upward social mobility in Caribbean society. It has become the acknowledged avenue to improvement through the enhanced economic and social status attainable on the return as a result of a successful migration. The goals and expectations of migration are high, and the need to achieve is felt most keenly among the members of those social classes for whom much depends on the fulfilment of these goals.

COMPARATIVE ASPECTS OF WEST INDIAN ADAPTATION IN THE UNITED STATES, CANADA AND BRITAIN

Adjustment, rather than assimilation, is a relevant concept with respect to West Indian migrant adaptation in North America and Britain, since it is the shorter-term process whereby the migrants themselves, as opposed to their next generation, deal with and relate to the circumstances of their new environment. Assimilation, on the other hand, denotes a longer-term process. This may be effected by the merging of behaviour patterns of the two groups or the subsuming of those distinctions and role signs based on ethnic or racial identities which distinguish minority sectors of the population from society at large. Otherwise, assimilation may be effected by incorporating those differences into an all-embracing, pluralistic, or multicultural framework. This may be more precisely defined as integration or plural accommodation (Bagley, 1975a). Of necessity, either alternative would involve fundamental changes in group norms in terms of attitudes and values both of the minority group and of the dominant sector of the society.

In contrast to the socio-cultural changes of identity implicit in assimilation, the transformations for the adjustment phase of adaptation are psychological and social. For this reason, migrant adaptation at that level may be assessed in terms of the satisfaction which the migrants felt about the opportunities in the new environment and the roles they have been assigned by the host society. Further indication of adaptation is given by the level of determination with which migrants expressed their intention to return to their countries of origin in the near future. They tend to be preoccupied with their wish to return home or to migrate elsewhere. They are held back from returning to the Caribbean as much by their lack of goal achievement as by domestic and financial circumstances. A more positive phase in terms of adjustment is associated with the wish to return home at some more distant time in the future, typically at retirement. The stage at which the original goals and transient intentions are replaced by the disposition to focus upon goals and an identity within the adopted society is in most cases gradual, with the primary and secondary sets of orientations existing together for some time. The point at which the re-defined goals predominate over the initial ones may be regarded as a significant threshold in the process of migrant adaptation. With reference to these criteria, the adaptation of West Indian migrants in the United States, Canada and Britain was compared by means of a questionnaire survey.[5]

A marked contrast in the samples was the consistently higher percentage of West Indians in the British cities who were very dissatisfied and fairly dissatisfied, as compared with the North American groups. For example, while 41 per cent of the London sample indicated that they regretted their decision to migrate, only 12 per cent of the New York City sample and 20 per cent of the Toronto group felt that way. At the opposite end of the scale, only 53 per cent of the London group were very satisfied or fairly satisfied, as opposed to 85 per cent and 74 per cent of the New York and Toronto samples respectively. A comparison of the London results with those of Birmingham, and Nottingham and Leicester combined, showed no difference, nor did the Hartford or Boston groups depart from the New York trend (Table 14.1).

TABLE 14.1   Levels of satisfaction recorded for the population samples in Britain, the United States and Canada

	1	2	3	4	5
London	30	23	6	9	32
Nottingham/Leicester	31	13	2	13	41
Birmingham	35	24	0	2	39
New York	47	38	3	6	6
Hartford/Boston	62	23	0	10	5
Toronto	46	28	6	0	20

1–very satisfied
2–fairly satisfied
3–not sure or indifferent
4–fairly dissatisfied
5–very dissatisfied

Figures given are percentages of the total for each sample: levels of satisfaction were measured on a 5-point scale.

A number of variables pertaining to the migrants were examined, especially in their relationship to the level of satisfaction expressed. These were the length of time the migrants had spent in previous migration destinations, time spent in the present country of residence, age and sex, and their intentions for leaving their present country of residence in the near future.

The level of migrant satisfaction, according to occupation group, demonstrated that those with the greatest regrets at having migrated were predominantly in the category composed of semi-skilled workers, non-specialised clerks and technicians, transport workers and others in non-professional tertiary activities. However, while the London group of unskilled workers were the next most dissatisfied, in New York it was the professional and highly specialised white-collar workers who fell into the second category.

Adjustment was less evident among men than women in all the sample populations. Taking the sub-samples of men only, it is only in the London case that the proportion of men who were dissatisfied was greater than those who were satisfied. Among the women in the London sample, as also in the New York and Toronto samples, a larger proportion showed evidence of adjustment than of non-adjustment.[6] Since men held the greater aspirations in relation to their migration than did the women, their lower levels of adjustment in Britain, and higher levels of adjustment in the United States and Canada, could at least partly be interpreted in terms of their greater sensitivity to the opportunities for goal achievement at the respective destinations.

While many of the West Indians in New York had not lost sight of the projected return to their home country, this was most often postponed for the distant future, usually at retirement, and only 29 per cent of the sample were seriously considering their return at the time of the interview. Of the Toronto sample, 36 per cent indicated that they were planning to leave Canada in the near future, and 52 per cent of the London group spoke of seriously considering their departure. Of this 52 per cent who expressed their intention to leave Britain, half were from among those who were satisfied, and 40 per cent from those who were not. This was similar for the Toronto sample, suggesting that while some were leaving because they had succeeded in reaching some satisfactory level and were ready to go home, others had become resigned to their inability to achieve, and were giving up. The New York data showed, by contrast, that 75 per cent of those who planned to leave were those who were satisfied with their migration achievements.

It is significant that the length of time the migrants had spent in their present country of residence could not account for the variation in their levels of adjustment. Only 1 per cent of the variation in level of satisfaction was accounted for by the variable representing time spent at the destination, when the data were submitted to a regression analysis. The frequently made assumption that migrant adaptation is chiefly dependent upon the individuals becoming accustomed to such factors as the differences of the environment between source and destination, especially when a rural–urban transformation was involved, is refuted by this evidence. With the passage of time, adjustment based on this type of factor would be expected to improve. That adjustment is conditioned by more fundamental factors relating to self-image in terms of role and identity, is supported by a number of epidemiological studies which have been conducted in Britain (Kiev, 1964, 1965; Hemsi, 1967; Bagley, 1971).

Over-all comparisons between observed adaptation of West Indians in select cities of Britain and North America, suggest that most difficulties have been experienced among migrants in Britain. The type of rapid success sought was not easy to achieve. The Welfare State made provision for medical and educational necessities, but wages were rarely high enough to permit the quick accumulation of capital which had been envisaged. Besides, relative to real earnings, Britain was very much less accessible to the West Indies than North America, hence making return visits more difficult. In general, migration to Britain demanded greater modification of initial goals, or the extension of the time span over which these goals could be realised. Those who failed to come to terms with the necessity to alter the original perceptions of migration and the destinations, have been the least able to adapt to the circumstances of their new environment.

Orientation towards the return to the Caribbean after a successful migration is only altered significantly if there are accompanying changes in the person's attitudes and beliefs. Change in the cognitive structure of the individual's frame of reference tends to take place when perceptions and aspirations begin to change, or when the person effectively changes his or her group membership. When the group as a whole accepts a new set of values – that is, when both cognitive and emotive frames of reference change – then new aspirations emerge, followed by acceptance of the new point of view which then represents the norm. This is determined as much by the adaptive disposition and mechanisms employed by the ethnic minority as also by the wider society.

Two elements are evident in the characteristics of West Indian adaptation in North America and Britain: the re-defining of original migration goals to focus upon success in the adopted country rather than on the return home, and the reliance upon support groups and the reinforcement of group identity almost as a prerequisite of adaptation. At an increasing rate, such adaptation brought about a change in the roles that the migrants assumed. The once much-required West Indian contribution to the labour force ceased to be seen as transient or confined to their original occupational roles. Instead, the community began to be associated with permanent neighbours and property-owners, children, adolescents and potential kinsfolk, active participants and leaders in the society. Moreover, hostility shown towards West Indians precipitated group solidarity, even across island cleavages, and has generally encouraged reliance upon their own communities for recognition of status. In London alone there are some 30 formal West Indian associations listed, and many more exist in other cities. The overwhelming affiliation to all-West Indian Pentecostal churches to include some who previously belonged to other denominations, further testifies to the need for group support which is felt among West Indian migrants and the efforts made towards the reinforcement of their identity.

The ability and disposition of the wider society to absorb the West Indians, with their changing roles and strengthened identities, into the mainstream of society, determines the possibilities for the complete adaptation and the eventual integration of future generations. This is determined by the existing ethnic and racial characteristics of that society, its perceptions of its own identity and, most importantly, its capacity for change.

THE SOCIETAL FRAMEWORK OF WEST INDIAN ADAPTATION IN THE UNITED STATES, CANADA AND BRITAIN

Central to the process of adaptation is the concept of identity. How individuals and groups in a minority situation see themselves and their roles, and how they are perceived by the rest of the society, together have a fundamental effect upon the processes whereby adaptation and future assimilation take place. The societal framework within which West Indian adaptation occurs at the migration destinations is conditioned both by factors relating to their West Indian ethnicity and their non-white racial characteristics. It is inevitable that varied forms of stress will arise due to the basic differences in both the migrant and dominant groups and due to the differences in the implicit demands and expectations of each.

Where the role of the migrant conforms to pre-existing expectations and what are regarded as a presence tolerable to the dominant society, then no demands of adaptation are made upon those sectors of society. However, where the migrants' own ethnic identity is reinforced in the attempt to adapt, their goals are re-defined and roles in society altered. Demands are then imposed upon the wider society and decisions concerning the future presence of the West Indians have to be made for conflict to be avoided. If the process of adaptation is distorted or some sectors of society become embittered by it, not only will the adaptation of the original migrant community be hindered but the integration of future generations might well be jeopardised.

The heterogeneity of the United States in terms of race and ethnicity contrasts with the relative homogeneity of the British situation. Despite Canada's considerable ethnic diversity, it has traditionally been a predominantly white population and, until the 1960s, had made every effort to maintain that character. Subsequently, it has only permitted the entry of non-white migrants on a highly controlled and selective basis. In the British case, though West Indians had lived in port cities for generations, the growth of a distinct West Indian ethnic and racial minority came into existence within just a decade. Although in the first instance they were predominantly workers, there was, even then, no pre-existing category by which the social relations with others could be defined. The relationship between host and migrant rapidly became economically competitive, socially unpredictable and showed signs of becoming politically inflammatory.

In North America, by contrast, and especially in the United States, another ethnic minority in the post-war period made little impact upon the existing structure. Although migration policies were specifically designed in the 1950s to control the increase in the size of the country's black population, once the increase occurred there were already in existence those established modes of conduct whereby such a group would relate to the rest of the society. These modes of conduct were undoubtedly racially determined but did not isolate West Indians as a distinct group. Rather, West Indians made use of their slight advantage within this system, emphasising their West Indian identity to dissociate themselves from black Americans.

The friction which this generated was between West Indians and members of the black American community rather than with the dominant white sectors of society. However, antagonisms have not usually been perpetuated beyond the immediate generation of migrants, as the American-born children of West Indians have typically become 'American' in the image they project of themselves as also by citizenship. Whenever individuals of this generation have played a role in public life, they have done so as 'Americans', not as 'West Indians'.

In the United States, unlike the situation in Canada and Britain, it is the middle-class West Indians who feel most excluded by attitudes towards race and colour in the society. This undoubtedly helps to explain the lower level of adjustment demonstrated among the West Indian middle class in the United States sample of the survey discussed in this study. It contrasts greatly with the higher than average level of adjustment of comparable groups in Canada and Britain.

Between West Indians as a group and the rest of society, the chief determinant of social distance in both Canada and Britain is that of race.[7] Second and third generations of West Indian parentage are, despite their Canadian or British citizenship, still seen to be 'West Indian' both by themselves and others. The tendency to perceive non-white racial characteristics as fundamentally incompatible with the national identity underlines those obstacles to assimilation solely based on phenotype. Against this perceptual background, policies relating to the prevention of the alienation of future generations of the black population could be usefully examined.

CONCLUSION

West Indian migrant aspirations mirror the ideologies and values of the society from which the migrants came. There can be no other frame of reference whereby the migrants first evaluate their roles, identity and, in general, the success of their migration. The adjustment of migrants reflects the initial gap which exists between their expectations and the reality, while adaptation monitors the changes taking place as personal goals and achievement opportunities converge. Such convergence depends only partly upon economic conditions at the destinations. It is also largely determined by the socio-political environment within which social distance is defined and social relations are developed. In this respect, the experience of West Indians in Britain, the United States and Canada, highlights the variable implications of ethnicity and race for migrant adaptation. Moreover, it demonstrates the nature and significance of migrant aspirations, roles and identities. Variations in the process of adaptation of first-generation West Indian migrants in Britain and North America, therefore, provide important indicators of the issues likely to characterise individual and group relations of future generations of West Indian descent in these three different milieux.

NOTES

1. In this chapter, the term 'West Indians' is used to refer to people from the English-speaking Caribbean.
2. After slavery was abolished in 1833, it was replaced by a system of apprenticeship, which prevented freedom of movement of workers until it was terminated in 1838.
3. Estimates are made from the 1971 Census of England and Wales, the Statistical Abstract of the United States and the Canada Year Book for successive years.
4. This quotation is given as a widely held view of the background to West Indian migration.
5. Samples of 100 persons each for London, New York and Toronto were compared and a second set of comparisons carried out with smaller urban centres to examine any possible variations due to the size of the centre. These latter samples were taken in Birmingham, Nottingham and Leicester for comparison with London; and from Hartford, Connecticut and Boston for comparison with New York. The age groups represented were: 21–40 and 41–60. Separate samples of the 15–21 year olds were examined. The migrants were placed in two groups according to year of arrival. With the exception of those in Toronto, who had all arrived since 1961, 50 per cent of the samples were arrivals between 1951 and 1960, and 50 per cent between 1961 and 1970.
6. For London, New York and Toronto, 67, 91 and 82 per cent of the females in each sample were very or fairly well adjusted. This compares with 44, 76 and 70 per cent of the men in the sample. Of the men in the London group, 50 per cent were very or fairly dissatisfied, while only 23 per cent of the women fell into that category.
7. A similar situation has been shown to occur in relation to French West Indians in France. See F. H. M. Raveau and J. Galap, 'de Recherche et d'etude des dysfonctions de l'adaptation', mimeographed report. F. Raveau, *et al.*, 'Approche Psycho-Anthropologique de l'adaptation de Migrants Antillais', *Cahiers d'Anthropologie*, 3 (1976), 71–107.

Bibliography

Adam, B. (1978) 'Inferiorization and "Self-Esteem"', *Social Psychology*, **41,** 47–53.

Adorno, T. W. *et al.* (1950) *The Authoritarian Personality*. New York: Harper.

Agrawal, P. (1978) 'A cross-cultural study of self-image: Indian, American, Australian and Irish adolescents', *Journal of Youth and Adolescence*, **7,** 107–16.

Alavi, H. (1972) 'Kinship in West Punjab Villages', *Contributions to Indian Sociology*, **6.**

Allen, S. *et al.* (1977) *Work, Race and Immigration*. Bradford: University of Bradford.

—— and Smith, C. (eds) (1975) 'Minority group experience of the transition from education to work', in *Entering the World of Work – some sociological Perspectives*. London: HMSO.

Allport, G. (1968) *The Person in Psychology*. Boston: Beacon Press.

Anastasi, A. (1959) *Psychological Testing*. New York: Macmillan.

Andrews, R. J. (1970) 'The relationship among self-concepts, motivations and pupil achievements in school'. Unpublished Ph.D. dissertation, University of Queensland.

Anwar, M. (1977) 'A sociological study of Pakistanis in a northern town in England'. Unpublished Ph.D. thesis, University of Bradford.

Aurora, G. S. (1967) *The New Frontiersmen*. Bombay: Popular Prakashan.

Ausubel, D. and Ausubel, P. (1958) 'Ego development among segregated Negro children', *Mental Hygiene*, **42,** 362–9.

Ayres, M. (1973) 'Counteracting racial stereotypes in pre-school children', *Graduate Research in Education*, **6,** 55–74.

Bagley, C. (1971) 'The social aetiology of schizophrenia in immigrant groups', *International Journal of Social Psychiatry*, **17,** 292–304.

—— (1972) 'Pluralism, development and social conflict in Africa', *Plural Societies*, **2,** 13–32.

—— (1973a) 'The education of immigrant children – a review of policy and problems', *British Journal of Social Policy*, **2,** 303–15.

Bagley, C. (1973b) Correspondence, *Race*, **14**, 489.

—— (1973c) *The Dutch plural society: A comparative study in race relations*. London: Oxford University Press.

—— (1975a) 'On the intellectual equality of races', in G. Verma and C. Bagley (eds), *Race and Education Across Cultures*. London: Heinemann.

——(1975b) 'The background of deviance in black children in London', in G. Verma and C. Bagley (eds), *Race and Education Across Cultures*. London: Heinemann.

—— (1976) 'Sequels of alienation: a social psychological view of the adaptation of West Indian migrants in Britain', in K. Glaser (ed), *Case Studies in Human Rights and Fundamental Freedoms*, vol. II. The Hague: Nijhoff.

—— (1979b) 'A comparative perspective on the education of black children in Britain', *Comparative Education*, **15**, 63–81.

——, Bart, M. and Wong, J. (1979a) 'Antecedents of scholastic success in West Indian ten-year-olds in London', in G. K. Verma and C. Bagley (eds), *Race, Education and Identity*. London: Macmillan.

——, Boshier, R. and Nias, D. (1974) 'The orthogonality of religious and racialist–punitive attitudes in three societies', *Journal of Social Psychology*, **92**, 173–9.

—— and Coard, B. (1975) 'Cultural knowledge and rejection of ethnic identity in West Indian children in London', in G. Verma and C. Bagley (eds), *Race and Education Across Cultures*. London: Heinemann.

——and Evan-Wong L. (1975) 'Neuroticism and extraversion in responses to Coopersmith's self-esteem inventory', *Psychological Reports*, **36**, 253–4.

—— and Mallick, K. (1978) 'Development of a short version of the Piers–Harris self-concept scale', *Education Review*, **30**, 235–8.

——, —— and Verma, G. K. (1979b) 'Pupil self-esteem: a study of black and white teenagers in British schools', in G. Verma and C. Bagley (eds), *Race, Education and Identity*'. London: Macmillan.

—— and Verma, G. K. (1972) 'Some effects of teaching designed to promote understanding of racial issues in adolescence', *Journal of Moral Education*, **3**, 231–8.

—— —— (1975) 'Inter-ethnic attitudes and behaviour in British multi-racial schools', in G. Verma and C. Bagley (eds), *Race and Education Across Cultures*. London: Heinemann.

Bagley, C. and Verma, G. K. (1978) 'Development, norms and factorial validity of scales for measuring racial attitudes in adolescents in multi-ethnic settings', *Educational Studies*, **4**, 189–200.

—— —— (1979) *Racial Prejudice, the Individual and Society.* Farnborough: Saxon House.

——, ——, Mallick, K. and Young, L. (1979c) *Personality, Self-esteem and Prejudice.* Farnborough: Saxon House.

—— and Young, L. (1979) 'The identity, adjustment and achievement of transracially adopted children: a review and empirical report', in G. Verma and C. Bagley (eds), *Race, Education and Identity.* London: Macmillan.

Baker, A. (1978) 'Asians are not all alike', *New Society*, 2 November.

Ballard R. E. H. and Holden B. M. (1975) 'The employment of coloured graduates in Britain.' *New Community*, vol, IV, no. 3.

Bannister, D. and Fransella, F. (1971) *Inquiring Man: The Theory of Personal Constructs.* London: Penguin.

Banton, M. (1958) *White and Coloured.* London: Jonathan Cape.

—— (1967) *Race Relations.* London: Tavistock.

Barker-Lunn, J. (1970) *Streaming in the Primary School.* Windsor: National Foundation for Educational Research.

Becker, E. (1971) *The Birth and Death of Meaning.* London: Pelican.

Beetham, D. (1967) *Immigrant School-leavers and the Youth Employment Service in Birmingham.* London: Institute of Race Relations/Oxford University Press.

Berger, E. M. (1952) 'The relation between expressed acceptance of self and expressed acceptance of others', *Journal of Abnormal and Social Psychology*, **47**, 778–82.

Berger, J. and Mohr, J. (1975) *A Seventh Man.* Harmondsworth: Penguin.

Berry, J. W., Karlein, R. and Taylor, D. M. (1978) 'Multiculturalism and ethnic attitudes in Canada', in *Canadian Consultative Council on Multi-culturalism Conference Report.* Second Canadian Conference on Multiculturalism. Ottawa: Minister of Supplies and Services.

Best, D., Field, J. and Williams, J. (1976) 'Color bias in a sample of young German children', *Psychological Reports*, **38**, 1145–6.

——, Naylor, C. and Williams, J. (1975) 'Extension of color bias research to young French and Italian children', *Journal of Cross-Cultural Psychology*, **6**, 390–405.

Biesheuval, S. (1949) 'Psychological tests and their application to non-

European peoples', in G. B. Jeffrey (ed.), *The Yearbook of Education.* London: Evans.

Block, N. J. and Dworkin, G. (eds.). *The I. Q. Controversy.* New York: Pantheon.

Blum, J. M. (1978) *Pseudoscience and Mental Ability.* New York: Monthly Review Press.

Board of Education (1943) *White Paper on Educational Reconstruction.* London: HMSO.

Bogardus, E. S. (1925) 'Measuring social distance', *Journal of Applied Sociology,* **9,** 229–308.

—— (1928) *Immigration and Race Attitudes.* Boston: Heath.

Bourdieu, P. and Passeron, J. C. (1973) *Reproduction in Education, Society and Culture.* Beverly Hills: Sage.

Box, S. (1980) 'Where have all the naughty children gone?' in *Permissiveness and Control: The Fate of the Sixties Legislation.* London: Macmillan (Edited by the National Deviancy Symposium).

Bowles, S. and Gintis, H. (1976) *Schooling in Capitalist America.* London: Routledge & Kegan Paul.

Bradford Metropolitan District Council (1976) *District Trends.*

Bradford Metropolitan Council (1979) *District Trends.*

Brittan, E. (1976) 'Multi-racial education. 2. Teacher Opinion on Aspects of School Life – Pupils and Teachers', *Educational Research,* **18** (3), 182–99.

Brody, E. (1969) 'Migration and adaptation', in E. Brody (ed.), *Behaviour in New Environments.* Beverly Hills: Sage.

Bronfenbrenner, U. (1974) *The Two Worlds of Childhood: U.S. and U.S.S.R.* London: Penguin.

Brophy, J. and Good, T. (1972) 'Teacher expectations: beyond the pygmalion controversy', *Phi Delta Kappan,* pp. 276–7.

Brunet, J. (1979) 'Myths and multiculturalism', *Canadian Journal of Education,* **4,** 43–58.

Budner, S. (1962) 'Intolerance of ambiguity as a personality variable', *Journal of Personality,* **30,** 29–50.

Bullock, A. (1975) *A Language for Life.* London: HMSO.

Bulmer, J. (1977) *Guide to the Teaching of Anthropology in Schools and Colleges.* London: School of Oriental and African Studies.

Burke, P. (1980) 'The self-measurement requirements from an interactionist perspective', *Social Psychology Quarterly,* **43,** 18–29.

Burney, E. (1967) *Housing on Trial.* London: Institute of Race Relations for Oxford University Press.

Burns, R. (1976) 'Attitudes to self and attitudes to others', *British Journal of Social and Clinical Psychology*, **15**, 319–21.

Burt, C. (1969) 'Intelligence and heredity: some common misconceptions', *Irish Journal of Education*, **3**, 75–94.

Caliguri, J. (1966) 'Self concept of the poverty child', *Journal of Negro Education*, **25**, 280–2.

Candlin, C. and Derrick, J. (1972) *Language. Technical Monographs 2.* London: Community Relations Commission.

Caplin, M. D. (1966) 'Self-concept, level of aspiration and academic achievement', *Journal of Negro Education*, **25**, 435–9.

Carpenter, T. R. and Busse, T. B. (1969) 'Development of self concept in Negro and white children', *Child Development*, **40**, 935–9.

Casey, T. (1974) 'Shocks instead of cane', *The Times Educational Supplement* (London), 1 March, p. 20.

Cattell, R. (1965) *The Scientific Analysis of Personality*. London: Penguin.

Cawson, P. (1979) 'Deviance and labelling of black children'. Paper given to postgraduate seminar, University of Surrey, November 1979.

Chazan, M. (1968) 'Inconsequential behaviour in school children', *British Journal of Educational Psychology*, **38**, 5–7.

Churchman, C. W. (1971) 'Why measure?', in B. J. Franklin and M. W. Osborne (eds), *Research Methods and Insights*. Wadsworth.

Clark, K. and Clark, M. (1950) 'Emotional factors in racial identification and preference in Negro children', *Journal of Negro Education*, **19**, 341–50.

Clements, F. and Sauer, W. (1976) 'Racial differences in life satisfaction', *Social Forces*, **43**, 621.

Coard, B. (1971) *How the West Indian Child is made Educationally Sub-normal in the British School System*. London: New Beacon.

Cochrane, R. (1979) 'Psychological and behavioural disturbance in West Indians, Indians, and Pakistanis in Britain: a comparison of rates among children and adults', *British Journal of Psychiatry*, **134**, 201–10.

Cohen, L. (1971) 'Dogmatism and views of the "ideal pupil"', *Educational Review*, **24**, 3–10.

Coleman, J. S. (1966) *Equality of Educational Opportunity*. Washington DC: Government Printers.

Coleman, J., Harzberg, J. and Norris, M. (1977) 'Identity in adolescence: present and future self-concepts', *Journal of Youth and Adolescence*, **6,** 63–75.

Collman, R. D. (1956) 'Employment success of ESN pupils in England', *American Journal of Mental Deficiency*, **60.**

Colton, F. (1972) 'Cognitive and affective reactions of kindergarteners to video displays', *Child Study Journal*, **2,** 63–5.

Commission for Racial Equality (CRE) (1978a) *Looking for Work: Black and White School Leavers in Lewisham.* London: HMSO.

—— with Walsall and Leicester CRCs. (1978b) *Aspiration vs. Opportunities.* London: HMSO.

Community Relations Commission (CRC) (1974) *Teacher Education for a Multicultural Society* (the Report of a Joint Working Party of the Community Relations Commission and the Association of Teachers in Colleges and Departments of Education). London: CRC.

—— (1976) *Between Two Cultures: A Study of Relationships Between Generations in the Asian Community in Britain.* London: CRC Ref. Series, No. 12.

Coopersmith, S. (1967) *The Antecedents of Self-esteem.* San Francisco: Freeman.

—— (1975) 'Self-concept, race and education', in G. K. Verma and C. Bagley (eds), *Race and Education Across Cultures.* London: Heinemann.

Cottle, T. (1979) 'Immigration to England: a personal problem', *Urban Education*, **14,** 5–17.

Cox, C. B. and Dyson, A. E. (eds) (1969/70) *Black Papers I*, 1969; *Black Papers II*, 1969; *Black Papers III*, 1970. London: The Critical Quarterly Society.

Crain, R. and Weisman, C. (1972) *Discrimination, Personality and Achievement.* New York: Seminar Press.

Crissman, L. (1975) 'The individual nature of culture', Urbana: University of Illinois (mimeo).

Crick, B. and Porter, A. (eds) (1978) *Political Education and Political Literacy.* London: Longman.

Cross, M. (1977) 'Teaching race as social policy', *New Community*, **5,** 473–9.

Davie, R. (1968) 'The behaviour and adjustment of seven-year-old children: some results from the national child development study', *British Journal of Educational Psychology*, **38,** 1–2.

——, Butler, N. R. and Coldstein, H. (1972) *From Birth to Seven.* London: Longman.

Davis, B. (1978) quoted in Amphlett, M. 'The Ontario Heritage Language Program', *Multiculturalism*, **1,** 7–8.
Davison, R. (1966) *Black British*. London: Oxford University Press.
DeBlaissie, R. E. and Healy, D. W. (1970) *Self Concept: A Comparison of Spanish–American, Negro and Anglo Adolescents Across Ethnic, Sex and Socio-economic Variables*. Las Cruces, NM: ERIC Clearinghouse on Rural Education.
Deosaran, R. and Gershman, J. (1976) *An Evaluation of the 1975–76 Chinese–Canadian Bi-cultural Program*. Toronto: Research Department, Toronto Board of Education.
Department of Education and Science (DES) (1971) *The Education of Immigrants. Education Survey 13*. London: HMSO.
—— (1972a) *The Continuing Needs of Immigrants. Education Survey 14*. London: HMSO.
—— (1972b) *Teacher Education and Training: The James Report*. London: HMSO.
—— (1973) *A Report by the Select Committee on Race Relations and Immigration. Sessions 1972–73*. London: HMSO.
—— (1978) *Observations on the Report by the Select Committee on Race Relations and Immigration – the West Indian Community*. London: HMSO.
Deutsch, M. (1960) *Minority group and class status as related to social and personality factors in Scholastic achievement*. Ithaca: Cornell University Press.
Dove, L. (1974) 'Heads buried in the sand', *The Times Educational Supplement* (London), 9 August, p. 21.
Drake, St. C. (1965) 'The social and economic status of the Negro in the United States', *Daedalus*, **94,** 771–814.
Driver, E. (1972) 'Self-conceptions in India and the United States: a cross-cultural validation of the 20-statement test', in J. Manis and B. Meltzer (eds), *Symbolic Interaction*. Boston: Allyn & Bacon.
Driver, G. (1977a) 'Cultural competence, social power and school achievement', *New Community*, **5**(4), 353–9.
—— (1977b) 'Ethnicity, cultural competence and school achievement'. Unpublished Ph.D. dissertation, University of Illinois Urbana/Champaign.
—— (1979) *Beyond Underachievement*. London: Commission for Racial Equality.
Eaton, W. and Clore, G. (1975) 'Inter-racial imitation at a summer

camp', *Journal of Personality and Social Psychology*, **32,** 1091–1105.

Eisenstadt, (1954) *The Absorption of Immigrants*. London: Routledge & Kegan Paul.

Epstein, S. (1973) 'The self-concept revisited: or a theory of a theory', *American Psychologist*, **28,** 404–16.

Erikson, E. (1955) 'Ego identity and psychological moratorium', in H. Witmer (ed.), *New Perspectives for Research on Juvenile Delinquency*. Washington DC: US Government Printing Office.

—— (1959a) 'Growth and crises of the healthy personality', *Psychological Issues*, **1,** 53.

—— (1959b) 'Identity and the life cycle', *Psychological Issues*, **1,** 1.

—— (1965) 'The concept of identity in race relations: notes and queries', *Daedalus*, Winter, 56–8.

—— (1968) *Identity, Youth and Crisis*. London: Faber.

Essen, J. and Ghodsian, M. (1980) 'The children of immigrants: school performance', *New Community*, **7,** 422–9.

Eysenck, H. and Eysenck, S. (1969) *The Structure of Human Personality* London: Routledge.

Fiedler, F. E. (1958) *Leader Attitudes and Group Effectiveness*. Urbana: University of Illinois Press.

Foner, N. (1977) *Between Two Cultures*. Oxford: Blackwell.

—— (1978) *Jamaica Farewell: Jamaican Migrants in London*. London: Routledge.

Fowler, B., Madigan, R. and Littlewood, B. (1977) 'Immigrant school-leavers and the search for work', *Sociology*, January.

Fox, D. and Jordan, R. (1973) 'Racial preference and identification of black American, Chinese and white children', *Genetic Psychology Monographs*, **88,** 229–86.

Frenkel-Brunswik, E. (1948) 'A study of prejudice in children', *Human Relations*, **1,** 295–306.

Freud, A. (1937) *The Ego and the Mechanisms of Defence*. London: Institute of Psycho-Analysis.

Friedenberg, E. Z. (1969) 'Social Consequences of Educational Measurement', *Towards a Theory of Achievement Measurement* (Proceedings of the 1969 Invitational Conference on Testing Problems). New Jersey: Educational Testing Service.

Ghei, S. (1963) 'Female personality patterns in two cultures', *Psychological Reports*, **33,** 759–62.

Ghodsian, M. (1977) 'Children's behaviour and the Bristol Social Adjustment Guide: some theoretical and statistical

248   *Self-Concept, Achievement and Multicultural Education*

considerations', *British Journal of Social and Clinical Psychology*, **16**, 23–8.

Ghodsian, M. and Essen, J. (1980) 'Children of immigrants: social and home circumstances', *New Community* (in press).

Ghuman, P. (1975) *The Cultural Context of Thinking*. Windsor: National Foundation for Educational Research.

Gibby, R. C. and Gabler, R. (1967) 'The self concept of Negro and white children', *Journal of Clinical Psychology*, **23**, 144–8.

Giles, R. (1977) *The West Indian Experience in British Schools*. London: Heinemann.

Goffman, E. (1959) *The Presentation of Self in Everyday Life*. New York: Doubleday Anchor.

Goldman, P. (1974) *The Death and Life of Malcolm X*. London: Gollancz.

Goldman, R. J. and Taylor, F. M. (1966) 'Coloured immigrant children: a survey of research studies, and literature on their educational problems and potential – in Britain', *Educational Research*, VIII (3), 163–83.

Goodenough, W. H. (1963) *Co-operation in Change*. New York: Russell Page.

—— (1970) *Culture, Language and Society*. Reading, Massachusetts: Addison Wesley.

Goodman, M. E. (1964) *Race Awareness in Young Children*. New York: Collier.

Gordon, C. (1972) *Looking Ahead: Self Conceptions, Race and Family as Determinants of Adolescent Orientation to Achievement*. Washington: American Sociological Association.

Gorsuch, R. and Cattell, R. (1977) 'Personality and socio-ethical values: the structure of self and superego', in R. Cattell and R. Dreger (eds), *Handbook of Modern Personality Theory*. New York: Wiley.

Green, D. (1977) 'Practical multiculturalism', in S. Dubois (ed), *Multiculturalism in Education*. Toronto: Ontario Association for Curriculum Development.

Greenwald, A. (1969) 'The open-mindedness of counterattitudinal role player', *Journal of Experimental Social Psychology*, **5**, 375–88.

Griffiths, E. (1977) Paper given to a seminar on the National Child Development Survey, University of Essex.

Gupta, Y. P. (1977) 'The educational and vocational aspirations of Asian Immigrant and English school-leavers', *British Journal of Sociology*, XXVIII, 185–98.

Hale, R. (1978) 'A factor analytic study of the Bristol Social Adjustment Guides in a rural school population', *Psychological Reports*, **42,** 215–18.

Hall J. and Jones D. C. (1950) 'Social grading of occupations' *British Journal of Sociology*, **1,** 31–55.

Halsey, A. H. (1972) *Educational Priority*. London: HMSO.

—— (ed.) (1977) *Heredity and Environment*. London: Methuen.

—— Floud, J. and Anderson, C. A. (1961) (eds), *Education, Economy and Society*. New York: Free Press.

—— and Goldthorpe, D. (1980) *Origins and Destinations: Family, Class and Education in Modern Britain*. Oxford University Press.

Hartley, E. (1948) *Problems in Prejudice*. New York: Kings Crown Press.

Hartley, J. and Holt, J. (1971) 'A note on the validity of the Wilson– Patterson measure of conservatism', *British Journal of Social and Clinical Psychology*, **10,** 81–3.

Hartman, P. and Husband, C. (1972) 'A British scale for measuring white attitudes to coloured people', *Race*, **14,** 2.

Hauser, S. (1971) *Black and White Identity Formation*. London: Wiley.

Hayakawa, S. (1963) *Symbol, Status and Personality*. New York: Harcourt, Brace & World.

Haynes, J. M. (1971) *Educational Assessment of Immigrant Pupils*. Slough: NFER.

Hearnshaw, L. S. (1979) *Cyril Burt: Psychologist*. London: Hodder & Stoughton.

Hegarty, S. and Lucas, D. (1979) *Able to Learn? The Pursuit of Culture – Fair Assessment* Slough: National Foundation for Educational Research.

Hemsi, L. (1967) 'Psychiatric morbidity of West Indian immigrants', *Social Psychiatry*, **2,** 95–100.

Henry, F. (1978) *The Dynamics of Racism in Toronto*. Toronto: York University.

Henton, C. L. (1964) *The relationship between the self concepts of Negro elementary school children and their academic achievement, intelligence, interests and manifest anxiety*. Urbana: ERIC (document ED 003 288).

Her Majesty's Stationery Office (1970) *Census of England and Wales*. London: HMSO.

—— (1979) *Aspects of Secondary Education in England*. London: HMSO.

Hewitt, J. (1976) *Self and Society*. London: Allyn & Bacon.

Hill, C. (1967) *How Colour Prejudiced is Britain?* London: Panther.

—— (1970) *Immigration and Integration.* Oxford: Pergamon Press.

—— (1974) 'Pentecostalist growth – result of racialism?' *Race Today.*

Hill, M. (1953) 'Some problems of social distance in intergroup relations', in M. Sherif and M. Wilson, (eds), *Group Relations at the Cross Roads.* New York: Harper.

Hiro, D. (1968) 'Unrealistic aspirations', *New Society*, 2 July.

Hirsch, J. (1975) *Educational Theory*, **25**, 3–27.

Hitchfield, E. (1973) *In Search of Promise.* London: Longman.

Hohn, R. (1973) 'Perceptual training and its effects on racial preference of kindergarten children', *Psychological Reports*, **32**, 435–41.

Hope, K. (1968) *Methods of Multivariate Analysis.* London: University of London Press.

Hraba, J. and Grant, G. (1970) 'Black is beautiful: a re-examination of racial preference and identification', *Journal of Personality and Social Psychology*, **16**, 398–402.

Hunt, J. and Hunt, L. (1977) 'Racial inequality and self-image: identity maintenance and identity diffusion', *Sociology and Social Research*, **61**, 539–59.

Humanities Curriculum Project (1970) The Humanities Project: An Introduction, London: Heinemann.

Hutchison, D., Prosser, H. and Wedge, P. (1979) 'Prediction of educational failure', *Educational Studies*, **5**, 1.

Hyman, H. and Wright, C. (1979) *Education's Lasting Influence on Values.* Chicago: University of Chicago Press.

Information Canada (1970) Report of the Royal Commission on Bilingualism and Biculturalism. Book IV. *The Cultural Contribution of the Other Ethnic Groups.* Ottawa: Information Canada.

Irvine, S. (1973) 'Tests as inadvertent sources of discrimination in personnel decisions', in P. Watson (ed.), *Psychology and Race.* Harmondsworth: Penguin.

Jackson, B. (1979) *Starting School.* London: Croom Helm.

Jackson, M. (1974) 'Recruiting minority group teachers', *Teacher Education and Community Relations*, **11**, 1.

—— (1975) 'The D. E. S. didn't seem to know much about us', *The Times Educational Supplement*, 18 July, pp. 8–9.

Jackson, P. (1970) 'Against protest', *New Society* (London), 29 January, pp. 171–2.

James, H. (1920) *The Letters of William James*, vol. 1. Boston: Houghton.

Jeffcoate, R. (1974) 'Schools Council project – education for a multi-racial society', *Multi-Racial School*, **3,** 7–12.

—— (1976) 'Curriculum planning in multiracial education', *Educational Research*, **18,** 192–200.

—— (1979) *Positive Image towards a Multi-cultural Curriculum.* London: Chameleon.

Jelinek, M. and Brittan, E. (1975) 'Multi-racial education I. Inter-ethnic friendship patterns', *Educational Research*, **18,** 44–53.

Jenkins, D. and Shipman, M. (1976) *Curriculum: An Introduction.* London: Open Books.

——, Kemmis, S., Macdonald, B. and Verma, G. K. (1979) 'Racism and educational evaluation', in G. K. Verma and C. Bagley (eds), *Race, Education and Identity.* London: Macmillan.

Jenks, C. (1973) *Inequality.* London: Allen Lane.

Jensen, A. R. (1969) 'How much can we boost I. Q. and scholastic achievement?', *Harvard Educational Review*, **39,** 1–123.

—— (1972) *Genetics and Education.* London: Methuen.

—— (1973) *Educability and Group Differences.* London: Methuen.

—— (1980) *Bias in Mental Testing.* London: Methuen.

John, G. (1972) *Race and the Inner City.* London: Runnymede Trust.

Joncich, G. (1968) *The Sane Positivist: a Biography of Edward L. Thorndike.* Middletown Weslyan University Press.

Jones, P. (1977) 'An evaluation of the effect of sport on the integration of West Indian schoolchildren'. Ph.D. thesis, University of Surrey.

Jowell, R. (1973) 'The measurement of prejudice', in P. Watson (ed.), *Psychology and Race.* Harmondsworth: Penguin.

Kamin, L. J. (1977) *The Science and Politics of I. Q.* Harmondsworth: Penguin.

Kanitkar, H. (1979) 'A School for Hindus?', *New Community*, **7,** 178–82.

Kaplan, H. (1975) *Self-Attitudes and Deviant Behaviour.* California: Goodyear.

Kardiner, A. and Ovesey, L. (1951) *The Mark of Oppression: Explorations in the Personality of the American Negro.* New York: Norton.

Karier, C. (1973) 'Ideology and evaluation: in quest of meritocracy'. Paper presented to the Wisconsin Conference on Education and Evaluation. School of Education: University of Wisconsin, 26–27 April.

—— (1976) 'Testing for order in the corporate liberal state', in R. Dale, G. Esland and M. MacDonald (eds), *Schooling and Capitalism.* London: Routledge & Kegan Paul.

Kawwa, T. (1968) 'A survey of ethnic attitudes of some British secondary school pupils', *British Journal of Social and Clinical Psychology*, **7**, 161–8.

Kelly, G. (1955) *The Theory of Personal Constructs*. New York: Norton.

—— (1963) *A Theory of Personality*. New York: Norton.

Kemper, L. (1977) *Migration and Adaptation*. Beverly Hills: Sage.

Kiev, A. (1964) 'Psychiatric illness among West Indians in London', *Race*, **5**(3), 356–63.

—— (1965) 'Psychiatric morbidity of West Indian immigrants in an urban group practice', *British Journal of Psychiatry*, III (460), 51–6.

Kimmel, D. (1974) *Adulthood and Aging*. New York: Wiley.

Kitzinger, S. (1972) 'West Indian children with problems', *Therapeutic Education*, Spring.

Kozol, J. (1967) *Death at an Early Age*. Boston: Houghton Mifflin.

Kuhn, T. S. (1962) *The Structure of Scientific Revolutions*. Chicago: University of Chicago Press.

La Fountaine, M. (1976) Quoted in Toronto Board of Education – *We are All Immigrants to This Place*. Toronto: Board of Education.

Labenne, W. and Greene, B. (1969) *Educational Implications of Self-Concept Theory*. California: Goodyear.

Landis, D., Day, H., McGrew, P., Thomas, J. and Miller, A. (1976) 'Can a black "culture assimilator" increase racial understanding?', *Journal of Social Issues*, **32**, 169–83.

—— and McGrew, P. (1979) 'Subjective culture and the perceptions of black and white urban school teachers', in G. Verma and C. Bagley (eds), *Race, Education and Identity*. London: Macmillan.

——, —— and Triandis, H. (1975) 'Behavioural intentions and norms of urban school teachers', in G. Verma and C. Bagley (eds), *Race and Education Across Cultures*. London: Heinemann.

Lea, J. (1980) 'The contradictions of the sixties race relations legislation', in *Permissiveness and Control: The Fate of the Sixties Legislation*. London: Macmillan (Edited by the National Deviancy Symposium).

Leach, D. and Raybould, E. (1977) *Learning and Behaviour Difficulties in School*. London: Open Books.

Lessing, E. and Clarke, C. (1976) 'An attempt to reduce ethnic prejudice and assess its correlates in a junior high school sample', *Educational Research Quarterly*, **1**, 3–15.

Lewin, K. (1936) 'Social psychological differences between the United

States and Germany', *Character and Personality*, **4**, 265–93.

Lijphart, A. (1978) *Democracy in Plural Societies.* New Haven: Yale University Press.

Linn, R. and Slinde, J. (1977) 'The determination of the significance of change between pre- and post-testing periods', *Review of Educational Research*, **47**, 121–50.

Little, A. (1975) 'The educational achievement of ethnic minority children in London Schools', in G. Verma and C. Bagley (eds), *Race and Education Across Cultures.* London: Heinemann.

Little, K. (1947) *Negroes in Britain.* London: Routledge & Kegan Paul.

Lomax, P. (1977) 'The self-concepts of girls in the context of a disadvantaging environment', *Educational Review*, **29**, 107–19.

Long, B. H. (1969) Critique of 'Self-perceptions of culturally-disadvantaged Children', by Soares and Soares. *American Educational Research Journal*, **6**, 710–74.

Louden, D. (1978) 'Self-esteem and locus of control: some findings in immigrant adolescents in Britain', *New Community*, **6**, 218–34.

Lowenthal, D. (1967) 'Race and Color in the West Indies', *Daedalus*, Spring, 580–626.

McCarthy, D. (1971) 'The organisation of a multi-racial primary school', in J. McNeal and M. Rogers (eds), *The Multi-Racial School.* London: Penguin.

McDaniel, E. L. (1967) *Relationships between self concepts and specific variables in a low-income culturally-different population.* Final Report of the Head Start Programme: Institute of Education Development. Washington, DC.

McIntosh, N. and Smith, D. (1974) *The Extent of Racial Discrimination.* London: Political and Economic Planning (vol. XL, Broadsheet No. 547).

McMichael, P. (1979) 'The hen or the egg? Which comes first – antisocial emotional disorders or reading disability?', *British Journal of Educational Psychology*, **49**, 22–38.

McNair Report (1944) *Teachers and Youth Leaders*, London: HMSO.

MacNamara, J. (1979) 'What happens to children whose home language is not that of the school?', in G. K. Verma and C. Bagley (eds), *Race, Education and Identity.* London: Macmillan.

McNeal, J. and Rogers, M. (1971) *The Multiracial School.* London: Penguin.

McQuillan, B. (1977) 'A cross-section of cultures: Education Week at Harbourfront', *Multiculturalism*, **1**, 13–15.

Marcia, J. (1966) 'Development and validation of ego identity status',

Journal of Personality and Social Psychology, **3**, 551–8.

Martin, J. G. and Westie, F. (1959) 'The tolerant personality', *American Sociological Review*, **24**, 521–8.

Maslow, A. (1954) *Motivation and Personality*. New York: Harper & Row.

Maxwell, M. (1969) 'Violence in the toilets: the experiences of a black teacher in Brent schools', *Race Today* (London), **1**, 135–9.

Mead, G. (1934) 'Mind, self and society', in A. Strauss (ed.), *George Herbert Mead: On Social Psychology*. Chicago: University of Chicago Press.

Miller, E. (1969) 'Body, image, physical beauty and colour among Jamaican adolescents', *Social and Economic Studies*, **18**, 72–89.

—— (1972) 'Experimenter effects and the reports of Jamaican adolescents on beauty and body image', *Social and Economic Studies*, **22**, 353–90.

Miller, H. (1969) 'The effectiveness of teaching techniques for reducing colour prejudice', *Liberal Education*, **16**, 25–31.

Miller, H. L. and Woock, R. R. (1970) *Social Foundations of Urban Education*. Hinsdale, Illinois: Dryden Press.

Millins, K. (1973) 'The preparation of teachers to educate minority groups', *London Educational Review*, **2**(1).

Milner, D. (1973) 'Racial identification and preference in black British children', *European Journal of Social Psychology*, **3**, 281–95.

—— (1975) *Children and Race*. Harmondsworth: Penguin.

Ministry of Education (1946) Pamphlet No. 5. *Special Educational Treatment*. London: HMSO.

Montgomerie, J. (1978) 'A person of worth', *Educational Leadership*, **15**, 12–18.

Monks, T. (1970) (ed.), *Comprehensive Education in Action*. Slough: National Foundation for Educational Research.

Moody, J. L. (1971) *An Evaluation of the Khalsa–Diwan Moberly Program* (Under the Mango Tree). Vancouver, Şummer 1971. Vancouver School Board, Department of Planning and Evaluation.

Moore, T. and Baltes, P. (1975) 'Training of white adolescents to accurately simulate black adolescent personality', *Adolescence*, **38**, 231–9.

Morland, K. (1966) 'A comparison of race awareness in northern and southern children', *American Journal of Orthopsychiatry*, **36**, 22–31.

Multi-Ethnic Education (1977) London: Joint Report of the Schools Sub-Committee of the Inner London Education Committee, November.

Mungo, C. (1980) 'Are ethnic minority children made to feel part of British Society?' Paper given to CRE Conference on Multi-cultural Education, University of Nottingham, April 1980.

Myrdal, G. (1944) *An American Dilemma: The Negro Problem and Modern Democracy*, New York: Harper.

Nash, R. (1973) *Classrooms Observed*. London: Routledge & Kegan Paul.

—— (1976) *Teacher Expectations and Pupil Learning*. London: Routledge & Kegan Paul.

NATFHE (1980) *Evidence for the Committee of Inquiry into the Education of Children from Minority Groups*. London: National Association of Teachers in Further and Higher Education.

National Committee for Commonwealth Immigrants (1966) Report prepared by the Sub-committee on Teacher Training of the Education Panel. London: Community Relations Commission.

Nichols, K. and Berg, I. (1970) 'Schools phobia and self-evaluation', *Journal of Child Psychology and Psychiatry*, **11,** 133–41.

Nicol, D. (1971) 'Psychiatric disorders in the children of Caribbean immigrants', *Journal of Child Psychology and Psychiatry*, **12,** 273–88.

Noble, G. (1973) *Children in Front of the Small Screen*. London: Constable.

North Lewisham Project (NLP) (1977) *Report on the Supplementary School*. London: North Lewisham Project (206 Evelyn Street, London, SE8).

Ntuk-Idem, M. (1978) *Compensatory Education*. Farnborough: Saxon House.

O'Bryan, O., Kuplovista, O. and Reitz, J. A. (1978) 'A review of the principle results', in *Canadian Consultative Council on Multiculturalism Conference Report*. Second Canadian Conference on Multi-culturalism. Ottawa: Ministry of Supplies and Services.

Ontario Economic Council (1970) *Immigrant Integration: Our Obligations – Political, Social and Economic – to the 1,700,000 People who have come to Ontario in the Past Quarter Century.* Toronto: Ontario Economic Council.

Park, R. E. (1921) *Introduction to the Science of Sociology*. Chicago: University of Chicago Press.

Patterson, S. (1968) *Immigrants in Industry*. London: Oxford University Press.

Peak, H., Muney, B. and Clay, M. (1960) 'Opposite structures, defences and attitudes', *Psychological Monographs*, **74** (whole number 495).

Pettigrew, T. (1964) *A Profile of the Negro American*. New York: Van Nostrand.

Phillips, A. (1973) *Adolescence in Jamaica*. Kingston and London: Jamaica Publishing House and Macmillan.

Phillips, C. (1979) 'Educational under-achievement in different ethnic groups', *Educational Research*, **21**, 116–30.

Pidgeon, D. A. (1970) *Expectation and Pupil Performance*. Slough: National Foundation for Educational Research.

Pierce, C., Carew, J., Pierce-Gonzales, D. and Wills, D. (1977) 'An experiment in racism: T. V. commercials', *Education and Urban Society*, **10**, 61–87.

Piers, E. (1969) *Manual for the Piers–Harris Children's Self-Concept Scale*. Nashville: Counselor Recordings and Tests.

Platt, W. (1975) 'Policy-making and international studies in educational evaluation', in A. C. Purves and D. U. LeVine (eds), *Educational Policy and International Assessment: Implications of I. E. A. Surveys of Achievement*. California: McCutchan.

Porter, J. (1972) *Black Child, White Child*. Cambridge, Mass.: Harvard University Press.

Price, E. (1978) *Bilingual Education in Wales, 5–11*. London: Methuen/Evans Educational.

Proshansky, H. and Newton, P. (1973) 'Colour: the nature and meaning of Negro self identity', in P. Watson (ed.), *Psychology and Race*. Harmondsworth: Penguin Education.

Proudfoot, M. (1950) *Population Movements in the Caribbean* Port of Spain, Trinidad, Caribbean Commission Central Secretariat.

Pullum, G. (1980) 'Mother tongue, bilingualism, and British education'. Paper given to CRE Conference on Multicultural Education, University of Nottingham, April.

Purushothaman, M. (1978) *The Education of Children of Caribbean Origin: Select Research Bibliography*. Manchester: Centre for Information and Advice on Educational Disadvantage.

Radke, M., Sutherland, J. and Rosenberg, P. (1950) 'Racial attitudes of children', *Sociometry*, **13**, 154–71.

Raimy, V. C. (1948) 'Self reference in counselling interviews', *Journal of Consulting Psychology*, **12**, 153–64.

Rainwater, L. (1966) 'Crucible of identity: the Negro lower-class family', *Daedalus*, Winter.

Ramcharan, S. (1974) 'Adaptations of West Indians in Canada'. Unpublished Ph.D. dissertation, York University, Toronto, Canada.

Redbridge Community Relations Council (1978) 'Cause for Concern. West Indian pupils in Redbridge'. Black People's Progressive Association and Redbridge Community Relations Council.

Rees, O. and Fitzpatrick, F. (1980) *The Origin and Development of the Mother Tongue and English Teaching Project*. University of Bradford, MOTET Working Paper No. 1.

Remmers, H. (1931) 'Propaganda in the schools – do the effects last?', *Public Opinion Quarterly*, **2**, 197–210.

Rex, J. and Moore, R. (1967) *Race, Community and Conflict*. London: Oxford University Press.

Richmond, A. H. (1955) *The Colour Problem*. London: Penguin.

—— (1976) 'Black and Asian immigrants in Britain and Canada: some comparisons', *Journal of Community Relations Commission*, **4**, 501–23.

Rist, R. (1970) 'Student social class and teacher expectations: the self-fulfilling prophecy in ghetto schools', *Harvard Educational Review*, **40**, 3–39.

Rist, R. (1975) *The Urban School: A Factory of Failure*. Massachusetts: M. I. T. Press.

Roberts, K. (1977) 'The social condition, consequences and limitations of careers education programmes', *British Journal of Guidance and Counselling*, **5**(1).

Robins, L. (1978) 'Sturdy childhood predictors of adult antisocial behaviour; replications from longitudinal studies', *Psychological Medicine*, **8**, 611–22.

Rogers, C. R. (1951) *Client Centered Therapy*. Boston: Houghton Mifflin.

Rokeach, M. (1948) 'Prejudice and rigidity in children', *American Psychologist*, **3**, 362.

—— (1960) *The Open and Closed Mind*. New York: Basic Books.

Rose, E. J. B. *et al.* (1969) *Colour Citizenship: A Report on British Race Relations*. London: Oxford University Press.

Rosenberg, M. J. (1965) *Society and the Adolescent Self Image*. Princetown: University of Princeton Press.

—— and Simmons, G. (1973) *Black and White Self-Esteem: The Urban*

258   *Self-Concept, Achievement and Multicultural Education*

School Child. Washington, DC: American Sociological Association.

Rosenthal, R. (1973) 'The Pygmalion effect lives', *Psychology Today*, **7**, 56–63.

—— and Jacobson, L. (1968) *Pygmalion in the Classroom*. New York: Holt, Rinehart & Winston.

Rubovits, P. C. and Maehr, M. L. (1973) 'Pygmalion black and white', *Journal of Personality and Social Psychology*, **25**, 210–18.

Rutter, M. and Madge, N. (1976) *Cycles of Disadvantage*. London: Heinemann.

Rutter, M. *et al.* (1979) *Fifteen Thousand Hours*. London: Open Books.

——, Tizard, J. and Whitmore, K. (1969) *Education, Health and Behaviour*. London: Longman.

Saifullah Khan V. (1975) 'Pakistani Villagers in a British City'. Unpublished Ph.D. thesis, University of Bradford.

Samuels, S. (1973) 'An investigation into the self-concepts of lower- and middle-class black and white kindergarten children', *Journal of Negro Education*, **42**, 467–72.

Saunders, C. (1973) 'Assessing race relations research', in J. Ladner (ed.), *The Death of White Sociology*. New York: Random House.

Sawdon, A., Tucker, S. and Pelican, J. (1979) *Study of the Transition from School to Working Life*. London: Youthaid.

Schwartz, P. (1962) 'The AID/AIR test development project', *Inter-African Labour Institute Bulletin*, **9**, 70–7.

Schools Council (1973) *Multiracial Education: Need and Innovation*. London: Evans/Methuen Educational.

Senior, C. and Manley, D. (1955) *A Report on Jamaican Migration to Great Britain*. Kingston, Jamaica: Government Printing Office.

Sennett, R. (1970) *The Uses of Disorder*. New York: Knopf.

Shaw, H. E. and Wright, J. M. (1968) *Scales for the Measurement of Attitudes*. New York: McGraw-Hill.

Sheerer, E. T. (1949) 'An analysis of the relationship between acceptance of and respect for self and acceptance of and respect for others', *Journal of Consulting Psychology*, **13**, 169–75.

Shillan, D. (1975) 'A Diploma in Education for a multicultural society', *New Community*, **4**, 345–8.

Simon, B. (1953) *Intelligence Testing and the Comprehensive School*. London: Lawrence & Wishart.

Smith, D. (1976) *The Facts of Racial Disadvantage*. Harmondsworth: Penguin.

Spradley, J. P. (1970) *You Owe Yourself a Drunk: an Ethnography of Urban Nomads*. Boston: Little Brown.

Stanton, M. (1970) 'Teachers' views on racial prejudice', *English for Immigrants* (London), **4**, 15–19.

Stenhouse, L. (1971) The Humanities Curriculam Project: the Rationale. *Theory into Practice*, **10**, 3, 154–162.

—— (1975) 'Problems of research in teaching about race relations', in G. K. Verma and C. Bagley (eds), *Race and Education Across Cultures*. London: Heinemann.

—— (1980) *Curriculum Research and Development in Action*. London: Heinemann.

Sterioff, J. L. (1976) 'Experiments on the Main Street', *Toronto Education Quarterly*, 1965–66, pp. 2–3. Quoted in Toronto Board of Education, *We Are All Immigrants to This Place*.

Stock, D. (1949) 'An investigation into the interrelations between the self, concept and feeling directed toward other persons and groups', *Journal of Consulting Psychology*, **13**, 176–80.

Stone, M. (1980) *The Education of the Black Child in Britain: The Myth of Multiracial Education*. London: Fontana.

Stones, E. (1979) 'The colour of conceptual learning', in G. Verma and C. Bagley (eds), *Race, Education and Identity*. London: Macmillan.

Stott, D. (1966) *The Social Adjustment Guide: Manual to the Bristol Social Adjustment Guides* (3rd edn.). London: University of London Press (see, too, 5th edn.,1974, and 6th edn. 1976).

—— (1978) *Helping Children with Learning Difficulties*. London: Ward Lock.

——, Marston, N. and Neill, S. (1975) *Taxonomy of Behaviour Disturbance*. London: University of London Press.

Taylor, J. A. (1953) 'A personality scale of manifest anxiety', *Journal of Abnormal and Social Psychology*, **48**, 285–90.

Teplin, L. A. (1977) 'Preferences versus prejudice: a multi-method analysis of children's discrepant racial choices', *Social Science Quarterly*, **58**, 390–406.

Thomas-Hope, E. M. (1978) 'The establishment of a migration tradition: British West Indian movements to the Hispanic Caribbean in the century after emancipation', in C. G. Clarke, *Caribbean Social Relations*. Liverpool: Centre for Latin American Studies, the University of Liverpool, Monograph Series, No. 8, pp. 66–81.

Thompson, B. (1974) 'Self-concepts among secondary school pupils', *Educational Research*, **17**, 41–7.

Thomson, D. (1978) 'A Scottish study', in D. Stott (ed.), *Helping Children with Learning Difficulties*. London: Ward Lock.

Thorndike, E. L. (1920) *The Psychology of the Half-Educated Man.*
    New York: Harper.
Thurstone, L. L. and Chave, E. J. (1929) *The Measurements of Attitude.*
    Chicago: University of Chicago Press.
Tidrick, K. (1973) 'Skin shade and need for achievement in a multi-
    racial society: Jamaica, West Indies', *Journal of Social
    Psychology*, **89**, 25–34.
Tomlinson, S. (1979) Ph.D. thesis, University of Warwick.
—— (1980) *Educational Sub-Normality – a study in Decision-Making.*
    London: Routledge and Kegan Paul.
Toms, K. (1979) 'The function of special units for pupils with special
    difficulties'. Paper given to the British Educational Research
    Association annual conference, September.
Toronto Board of Education (1976) *We are All Immigrants to This
    Place.*
—— (1977) *Transition from Italian.*
Townsend, H. E. R. (1971) *Immigrant Pupils in England: The L.E.A.
    Response.* Slough: National Foundation for Educational
    Research.
—— and Brittan, E. M. (1972) *Organisation in Multiracial Schools.*
    Slough: National Foundation for Educational Research.
Trager, H. and Yarrow, M. (1952) *They Learn What They Live.* New
    York: Harper.
Triandis, H. (1975) 'Social psychology and cultural analysis', *Journal for
    the Theory of Social Behaviour*, **5**, 80–106.
—— (1976) 'The future of pluralism', *Journal of Social Issues*, **32**, 179–
    208.
—— and Triandis, L. M. (1960) 'Race, social class, religion and
    nationality as determinants of social distance', *Journal of
    Abnormal and Social Psychology*, **61**, 110–18.
—— —— (1962) 'A cross-cultural study of social distance', *Psycho-
    logical Monographs*, **76** (whole number 21).
——, Davis, E. E. and Takezawa, S. I. (1965) 'Some determinants of
    social distance among American, German and Japanese
    students', *Journal of Personality and Social Psychology*, **2**,
    540–1.
Trudeau, P. (1971) 'Canadian culture: announcement of implemen-
    tation policy of multi-culturalism with bilingual framework'.
    Debates 8, Canadian Parliament, 28th Parliament, 3rd Session,
    8 October.
United States Department of Commerce (1974) *Statistical Abstract of*

the United States. Washington DC: Bureau of the Census.

United States Department of Justice *Immigration and Naturalization Services*, Annual Report 1974.

Valentine, C. W. (1932) *The Reliability of Examinations.* London: University of London Press.

Varlaam, A. (1974) 'Educational attainment and behaviours at school', *Greater London Intelligence Quarterly*, **29**, 29–37.

Veness, T. (1962) *School Leavers: Their Aspirations and Expectations*, London: Methuen.

Verma, G. K. (1977a) 'Some effects of curriculum innovation on the racial attitudes of adolescents', *International Journal of Intercultural Relations*, **1**(3).

—— (1977b) 'The democratisation of test construction: a response to the problems of educational measurement in a multi-ethnic society'. Paper presented to the Third International Symposium on Educational Testing, University of Leyden, The Netherlands, 27–30 June.

—— (1979) 'Attitude measurement in a multi-ethnic society', *Bulletin of the British Psychological Society*, **32**, 460–2.

—— (1980) *A Feasibility Study of Books and Ethnic Minorities.* Sponsored by the British National Bibliographical Research Fund, London: The British Library.

—— and Bagley, C. (1973) 'Changing racial attitudes in adolescents: an experimental English study', *International Journal of Psychology*, **8**, 55–8.

—— —— (1975a) 'Introduction: curriculum studies', in G. K. Verma and C. Bagley (eds), *Race and Education Across Cultures.* London: Heinemann.

—— —— (1975b) (eds), *Race and Education Across Cultures.* London: Heinemann.

—— —— (1978) 'Teaching styles and race relations: some effects on white teenagers', *The New Era*, **59**, 53–7.

—— —— (1979a) 'Measured changes in racial attitudes following the use of three teaching methods', in G. K. Verma and C. Bagley (eds), *Race, Education and Identity*. London: Macmillan.

—— —— (1979b) *Race, Education and Identity.* London: Macmillan.

——, —— and Mallick, K. (1980) *Illusion and Reality in Indian Secondary Education.* Farnborough: Saxon House.

—— and Beard, R. (1979) 'Evaluation of the Bradford College Occupational Selection Course', *CORE: An International Journal of Educational Research* (published in microfilm), **3**(1).

Verma, G. K. and MacDonald, B. (1971) 'Teaching race in schools: some effects on the attitudinal and sociometric patterns of adolescents', *Race*, XIII (2), October.

—— and Mallick, K. (1978) 'The growth and nature of self-esteem – attitudes and feelings in multi-ethnic schools', *The New Era*, **59**(4), July/August.

—— —— (1980) 'Social, personal and academic adjustment of ethnic minority pupils in British schools', in J. Bhatnager (ed.), *Educating Immigrants*. London: Croom Helm.

—— —— (1981) 'Hinduism and multicultural education', in J. Lynch (ed.), *Teaching in the Multi-cultural School*. London: Ward Lock Educational.

Vernon, P. E. (1969) *Intelligence and Cultural Environment*. London: Methuen.

—— (1957) (ed.) *Secondary School Selection*. London: Methuen.

Vetta, A. (1977) 'Genetical concepts and I.Q', *Social Biology*, **24**, 166–9.

Wallace, A. F. C. (1961) *Culture and Personality*. New York: Random House.

Ward, J. (1963) 'Hierarchical grouping to optimize and objective function', *Journal of the American Statistical Association*, **58**, 236–44.

Warnock Report (1978) *Special Educational Needs* – report of the Committee of Enquiry into the Education of Handicapped Children and Young People. London: HMSO, p. 47; and forthcoming White Paper, 1980.

Warr, P. B. *et al.* (1967) 'A British ethnocentrism scale', *British Journal of Social and Clinical Psychology*, **6**, 267–77.

Webster, M. and Sobieszek, B. (1974) *Sources of Self-Evaluation*. New York: Wiley.

Wedge, P. and Prosser, H. (1973) *Born to Fail?* London: Arrow.

Weinreich, P. (1979) 'Cross-ethnic identification and self-rejection in a black adolescent', in G. K. Verma and C. Bagley (eds), *Race, Education and Identity*. London: Macmillan.

Wells, L. and Marwell, G. (1976) *Self-Esteem: Its Conceptualization and Measurement*. London: Sage.

West, C. and Fish, (1974) 'Relationships between self concept and school achievement: a survey of empirical investigations'. Urbana, Illinois: ERIC Clearinghouse.

Widlake, P. and Bell, L. (1973) *The Education of the Socially Handicapped Child*. London: Nelson.

Wight, J. and Norris, R. (1970) *Teaching English to West Indian Children* London: Evans/Methuen.

Williams, J. and Morland, K. (1976) *Race, Color and the Young Child*. University of North Carolina Press.

——, Best, D., Boswell, D., Mattson, L. and Greaves, D. (1975) 'Pre-school racial attitudes measure II', *Educational and Psychological Measurement*, **35**, 3–18.

——, Boswell, D. and Best, D. (1975) 'Evaluative responses of pre-school children to the colours black and white', *Child Development*, **46**, 501–8.

Willis, P. (1977) *Learning to Labour*. Farnborough: Saxon House.

Wilson, G. (1973) *The Psychology of Conservatism*. London: Academic Press.

—— and Bagley, C. (1973) 'Religion, racialism and conservatism', in G. Wilson (ed.), *The Psychology of Conservatism*. New York: Academic Press.

Wilson, J. (1973) 'Adjustment in the classroom – I. Teachers' ratings of deviant behaviour', *Research in Education*, **10**, 26–34.

Winer, B. J. (1962) *Statistical Principles in Experimental Design*. New York: McGraw Hill.

Winn, P., Marx, R. and Taylor, T. (1977) 'A multitrait–multidimensional study of three self-concept inventories', *Child Development*, **48**, 893–901.

Wolff, K. H. (1950) (ed.), *The Sociology of Georg Simmel*. Glencoe, Illinois: The Free Press.

Wylie, R. (1974) *The Self Concept: A review of Methodological Considerations and Measuring Instruments*. Lincoln: University of Nebraska Press.

Young, J. (1978) *Programmes of the Brain*. London: Oxford University Press.

Young, L. (1978) 'A Comparative Study of the Evaluative Meaning of Colour; Implications for Identity and the Development of Self-Esteem in Young Children'. M. Phil. thesis, University of Surrey.

—— and Bagley, C. (1979) 'Identity, self-esteem and evaluation of colour and ethnicity in young children in Jamaica and London', *New Community*, **7**, 154–69.

Yule, W. (1968) 'Identifying maladjusted children', in *The Child and the Outside World*. Report of the 29th Conference of the Association for Special Education, pp. 73–81.

——, Berger, M. and Rutter, M. (1975) 'Children of West Indian Immigrants, 2. Intellectual Performance and Reading

Attainment', *Journal of Child Psychology and Psychiatry*, **16,** 1–17.

Zahran, H. (1966) 'The self-concept in relation to the psychological guidance of adolescents. Ph.D. thesis, University of London.

Ziller, R. (1972) *The Social Self.* Oxford: Pergamon.

—— (1976) 'A helical theory of personality change', in R. Harré (ed.), *Personality*. Oxford: Blackwell.

——, Long, B., Remana, K. and Reddy, V. (1968) 'Self–other orientations of Indian and American Adolescents', *Journal of Personality*, **24,** 251–6.

Zirkel, P. A. and Moses, H. E. (1971) 'Self concept and ethnic group membership among public school students', *American Educational Research Journal*, **8,** 253–65.

Index

Abrams, 185
Acceptance of Self scale, 25
  higher scores for men, 26
  use of, 26
achievement
  accounting for different West Indian and white, 142–5
  data behind study of, 107–8
  data on ethnic minority groups', 109–42
  definition of ethnic minorities in study of, 109–10
  differential health and behaviour variables per group affecting, 130–5
  differential social and demographic variables per group affecting, 136–40
  differential variables in ethnic groups affecting, 110, 111–14
  effects of disadvantage on West Indian behaviour and, 145–7
  health and behaviour variables affecting, 116, 117–21
  results of Draw-a-Man test, 140–1
  social and demographic factors affecting, 121–9
  types of data available for analysis, 108–9
Adam, B., 192
Adorno, T. W. et al., F scale, 20
Agrawal, P., 224
Alavi, H., 92
alienation
  from school, 10, 12, 141, 147, 153, 195, 210
  resistance to, shown in behaviour disorders, xiii–xv, 195
  Sumner scale of, 12
  Verma scale of, 12

Allport, G., on personality, 57
Allen, S.
  and Smith, C., 90
  et al., 86
Anastasi, A., 185
Andrews, R. J., 72
Anwar, M., 92, 94
Asians
  British areas of settlement, 86
  deprivation among, 94
  difficulties of, 153
  in Britain, 85–6
  private education for, xx
  'professional' view of children's problems, 102, 106
  self-esteem in schools, xiii, 94
  special help with languages, 135
  vocational adaptation, see separate entry
Association of Black Psychologists, US, 184
Association of Teachers in Colleges and Departments of Education, 160
  'Teacher Education for a Multi-Cultural Society', 161
Aurora, G. S., 92
Ausubel, D. and Ausubel, P., 54
Ayres, M., 5

Bagley, Christopher, ix, xii, xiii, xiv, xvi, 3, 16, 41, 92, 93, 107, 141, 147, 154, 184, 191, 210, 212, 232, 235
  and Evan-Wong, J., 9, 214, 215
  and Mallick, K., 215
  and Verma, Gajendra K., ix, xv, 5, 6, 7, 41, 84, 145, 155, 179, 185, 215
  and Young, L., xii

265